Northern Paiutes of the Malheur

HIGH DESERT RECKONING IN OREGON COUNTRY

David H. Wilson Jr.

UNIVERSITY OF NEBRASKA PRESS

LINCOLN

The University of Nebraska Press is part of a land-grant institution with campuses and programs on the past, present, and future homelands of the Pawnee, Ponca, Otoe-Missouria, Omaha, Dakota, Lakota, Kaw, Cheyenne, and Arapaho Peoples, as well as those of the relocated Ho-Chunk, Sac and Fox, and Iowa Peoples.

Library of Congress Cataloging-in-Publication Data
Names: Wilson, David H., Jr., author.
Title: Northern Paiutes of the Malheur : high desert reckoning in Oregon Country / David H. Wilson Jr.
Description: Lincoln : University of Nebraska Press, [2022] | Includes bibliographical references and index.
Identifiers: LCCN 2021037028
ISBN 9781496230454 (hardback)
ISBN 9781496231222 (epub)
ISBN 9781496231239 (pdf)
Subjects: LCSH: Paiute Indians—Oregon—Malheur County—History—19th century. | Paiute Indians—Oregon—Malheur County—History—20th century. | Paiute Indians—Wars—1866–1895. | Indians of North America—Wars—Oregon—Malheur County. | Malheur County (Or.)—History—19th century. | Malheur County (Or.)—History—20th century. | BISAC: SOCIAL SCIENCE / Ethnic Studies / American / Native American Studies | HISTORY / United States / State & Local / Pacific Northwest (OR, WA)
Classification: LCC E99.P2 W55 2022 | DDC 979.004/9745769—dc23
LC record available at https://lccn.loc.gov/2021037028

Set in Janson by Laura Buis.
Designed by N. Putens.

To Nancy Egan,
great-great-great-granddaughter of
Paiute chief Egan

In truth, the tragedies of the wars are our national joint property, and how we handle that property is one test of our unity or disunity, maturity or immaturity, as a people wearing the label "American."
—PATRICIA NELSON LIMERICK, *Something in the Soil*

Oh! that the desert were my dwelling place
—LORD BYRON

CONTENTS

ILLUSTRATIONS

ACKNOWLEDGMENTS

Paiute historian, author, and direct descendant of Chief Weyouwewa, Wilson Wewa, met with me and then answered my emails and phone calls, bringing me facts and insights available from no other source. His guidance was indispensable. Fred Townsend could not have been more generous with his time and family history. He told me about his grandmother Annie Adams, who was four during the Bannock War, and his mother, Rena Beers, who had recently died just shy of her one-hundredth birthday. He took me to the Burns Paiute graveyard to visit the grave of his mother and to see as well the memorial for Chief Egan and his brother-in-law Charlie.

The writing of this book took on a new character after Nancy Egan met with my wife and me. Nancy is a direct descendant of Chief Egan and custodian of the Egan family records. From her candor and trust I came away humbled and burdened by an appreciation that the narrative that I was in the process of unearthing was likely to touch her, her family, and her people, more profoundly than I could know.

I'm indebted to Matthew Bokovoy, Nebraska Press senior acquisitions editor, and his assistant, Heather Stauffer, for their commitment to this project and their expertise, guidance, and support in bringing it to completion.

Also patient with my questions and generous with her time was Carol Smyth Sawyer, who took me to the Smyth family graveyard, guided me through the complex Smyth family tree, and took my many phone calls with good cheer.

Nothing contributed more to the life of this book than its enthusiastic adoption by Ian Frazier, a prolific and acclaimed author and two-time winner of the Thurber Prize. He was ready with guidance and support at every turn.

Karen Nitz, archivist of the Claire McGill Luce Western History Room of the Harney County Library, seemed to welcome every opportunity to introduce me to more of southeast Oregon—to people, documents, collections, and ideas. Many of them found their way into vital roles in the narrative. She brought a deep knowledge of southeast Oregon to the multiple tasks she undertook for me, including review of two drafts. All of her contributions came with unfailing enthusiasm and good cheer.

Closer to home, the work of the endlessly resourceful librarians of the Oregon Historical Society and the Multnomah County Library, both in Portland, enriches every chapter of this book.

In addition to reading multiple drafts, providing regular counsel and support, and keeping up with every development for eight years, Steve Rose also recruited Richard Meeker, author and publisher of several newspapers. Richard met with me regularly as creative thinker, editor, cheerleader, and therapist. Richard also recruited Brent Walth, of the University of Oregon School of Journalism and Communication. I'm still unpacking the wisdom Brent imparted in half a day.

Buck Parker accompanied me to the North Fork of the John Day River, where we were guided by Christine Helberg of the Forest Service. Buck was also with me on an attempt to locate the Indians' camp on Steens Mountain. Rich Jenkins, whose family was one of the earliest on the mountain, was leading us in his horse trailer, ten miles in, when I cracked my oil pan on a rock, ending the endeavor. Buck's edits and comments are models of clear thought and good sense, and were always there when I was most in need.

Kerry Tymchuk, executive director of the Oregon Historical Society, knows his way around a book and Oregon's past (and a tennis court and golf course). His insights, both microscopic and macroscopic, are my global positioning satellites.

As chair of the Columbia Gorge Commission, Jill Arens Jernstedt earned an extraordinary level of respect from Native Americans. From her I have begun to learn the humility that one of European descent owes to the original inhabitants of this land.

No one has been called upon to read more drafts or listen to more ideas than my wife, Nely Johnson. Through it all not a word that could be mistaken for praise has passed her lips. Yet the wisdom keeps me coming back.

I am indebted to many whose works are the foundation of this book, in particular Sally Zanjani, author of *Sarah Winnemucca*, and Susan Stowell, for her exhaustive PhD dissertation on the Burns Paiutes.

I had invaluable guidance from many readers, including my brother and sister, Robert and Jenny Wilson, Maryann Keddington-Lang, John Stevason, Ken Jernstedt, Tom Stacy, Mark Knudsen, Tom Barkin, and Dan Prock. Others whose support and expertise have been important include Fred Peterson, Ray Stangeland, Gary Stein, Joyce White, and Mike Baker.

AUTHOR'S NOTE

Royalties

All royalties have been donated to the American Indian College Fund.

Historians and Race

Having shared their continent with Euro-Americans for centuries, Native Americans have learned to be wary of the word of their white neighbors. That suspicion lives on in the twenty-first century, and extends not only to land ownership, treaty compliance, and reservation management, but also to proclamations of the histories of aboriginal Americans. White Americans have not distinguished themselves in their portrayals of Indians, Indian history, and Indian leaders. These efforts have ranged from distorted, romanticized stereotypes to diatribes, such as that of one frontiersman who condemned Indians as "a set of miserable, dirty, lousy, blanketed, thieving, lying, sneaking, murdering, graceless, faithless, gut-eating skunks as the Lord ever permitted to infect the earth."[1] It is hardly surprising, then, that Tribesmen look on with skepticism when yet another white writer attempts to narrate the story of a people to which he does not belong.

Northern Paiutes of the Malheur, however, is not the story of one people. It is as much about white intruders as it is about the victims of that intrusion. Most of the harm suffered by Paiutes, as related in this tale, was inflicted by words spoken and written by and between whites. The wrongdoing revealed by this book is for the most part evidenced by white documentation of white actions arising from the white culture.

During this era Euro-Americans generated copious records in the Office of Indian Affairs and the Interior Department, as well as military reports and news accounts. While the written documents give full voice to the

whites' propaganda, they also record mundane functions and communications, day in and day out, that collectively tell a different story, one that
sweeps aside the pretense.

The wrongs unveiled by this book have remained hidden for almost 150
years and remain hidden as I write these words. Allowing misinformation
to continue to pass for history would be a disservice to both Natives and
whites. Indeed, Nancy Egan, spokesperson for the Egan family, welcomes
this book as "the true story of the Paiutes, hidden for almost a century
and a half."

DRAMATIS PERSONAE

NORTHERN PAIUTES

Chief Weyouwewa: head Paiute chief until his death in 1873

Chief Paulina: half-brother of Weyouwewa

Chief Oits: cousin of Weyouwewa

Chief Truckee: Nevada chief committed to friendship with whites; father of Winnemucca

Chief Winnemucca: Nevada chief who came to the Malheur Reservation in Oregon in 1875 with his daughter Sarah

Chief Natchez Winnemucca: Winnemucca's son

Sarah Winnemucca: Winnemucca's daughter

Lee Winnemucca: Winnemucca's son

Chief Leggins: subchief of Winnemucca

Chief Egan: a Cayuse who became a Paiute chief; arrived at Malheur Reservation in 1873

Chief Ochoho: peaceful chief who avoided reservations after starving at Yainax

Jerry Long: Sarah's cousin, Egan's son-in-law, and Rinehart's translator

Mattie: Lee Winnemucca's wife; Egan's niece and adopted daughter

INDIANS OF OTHER TRIBES

Buffalo Horn: Bannock leader in Bannock War

Kamiakin: chief of Yakamas

Joseph: chief of a nontreaty Nez Perce people

Toohoolhoolzote: Nez Perce chief who feuded with General Howard

Alexsee: Tenino chief

OFFICIALS OF THE INTERIOR DEPARTMENT
AND OF THE OFFICE OF INDIAN AFFAIRS

Joe Lane: first Oregon territorial governor (1848) and Oregon territorial Indian superintendent

Anson Dart: Oregon territorial superintendent of Indian affairs (1850–53)

Joel Palmer: Oregon territorial superintendent of Indian affairs (1853–56)

Isaac Stevens: Washington territorial governor and superintendent of Indian affairs, 1853–57

Robert Thompson: eastern Oregon Indian agent under Palmer, 1854–56; steamboat magnate

Samuel Ball Parrish: special commissary for Malheur Reservation, 1873; agent for Malheur Reservation, 1874–76

Edward Geary: Oregon Indian superintendent, 1859–61

William Rector: Oregon Indian superintendent, 1861–63

John Webster Perit Huntington: Oregon Indian superintendent, 1863–68

Alfred B. Meacham: Oregon Indian superintendent, 1869–72; peace commissioner in Modoc War

T. B. Odeneal: Oregon Indian superintendent, 1872–73

Carl Schurz: secretary of the interior, 1877–81

Ezra Hayt: commissioner of Indian affairs, 1877–80

E. M. Marble: acting commissioner of Indian affairs, 1880–81

Hiram Price: commissioner of Indian affairs, 1881–84

William V. Rinehart: Indian agent for Malheur Reservation, 1876–78

James H. Wilbur: Indian agent for Yakama Reservation until 1882

Robert H. Milroy: Wilbur's successor

MILITARY PERSONNEL

William Tecumseh Sherman: commander in chief, U.S. Army

General Oliver Otis Howard: commander of U.S. forces in Nez Perce War (1877) and Bannock War (1878)

Charles Erskine Scott Wood: Howard's aide-de-camp and confidant

General Irvin McDowell: commander, Division of the Pacific, and Howard's superior

Major Elmer Otis: commanding officer, District of the Lakes

Captain Ruben Bernard: cavalry captain under General Howard

Dr. John Fitzgerald: army surgeon who traveled with Bernard and Howard during Bannock War

Jack Scott: contractor who hauled lumber for Fort Harney and conspired with Agent Rinehart

THE CONFUSION OF OITS AND MULTIPLE OTISES

Oits: Paiute chief

Major Elmer Otis: sympathetic to the Paiutes, he set the boundaries of the Malheur Reservation

General Oliver Otis Howard: commander of U.S. forces in Bannock War

Dr. George Alexander Otis: curator of United States Army Medical Museum and assistant surgeon general of the United States Army

PREAMBLE

There are two similar memorials in Harney Valley, Oregon, fifty
   miles apart,
One of cement blocks, one of flat rocks cemented into a cairn.
Each is about four feet high and four feet wide.
Neither is positioned or marked to draw attention.
Each appears to be intended for quiet reflection.
Each marks remains of two related men.
All four were good men, family men.
All came to Harney Valley in 1872–73.
All died in 1878.
Each pair died together.
Their deaths were violent,
   undeserved.
Bone alone remained.
Two were white.
Two were Paiute.

NORTHERN PAIUTES OF THE MALHEUR

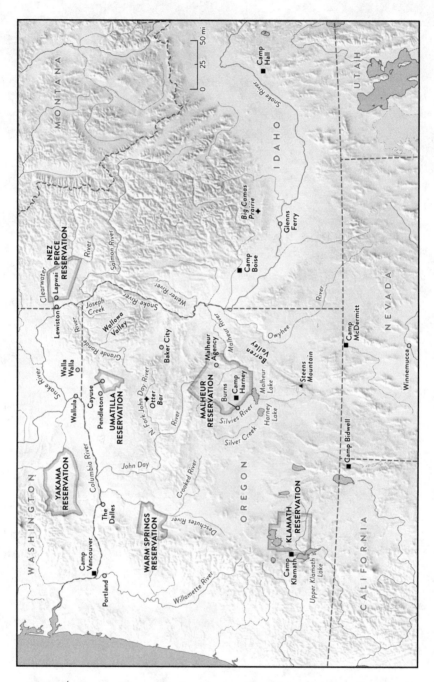

MAP 1. The Oregon Country before the treaties of the mid-1850s. Cartography by Erin Greb.

Introduction

The choice lands in the Willamette Valley of western Oregon lured about sixty-five thousand settlers across the continent in the 1840s and 1850s. By the end of that period, as good land west of the Cascade Mountains became scarce, immigrants were increasingly drawn to the dry lands east of the mountains. As these newcomers settled along lakes and rivers and in prime grasslands that were sources of the plants and creatures that nourished the Northern Paiutes, frictions developed, escalated into shooting, and finally into the Snake War. Federal troops charged with keeping the peace in eastern Oregon were gone by the fall of 1861, called away to Civil War duty. They were replaced by inexperienced, untrained volunteers. Throughout the early 1860s volunteers, trailing wagon upon wagon of supplies, lumbered about in futile pursuit of the nimble Paiutes. The Paiutes' knowledge of "the landscape, terrain, food supply and water resources put the whites at a considerable disadvantage." The quoted language, by Patricia Nelson Limerick, a scholar of the American West, is not a description of the Snake War or of any particular war. Rather, it is one of a dozen patterns that typify white-Indian wars generally. The patterns are not universal laws, but "are true more often than they are not."

Another of Limerick's patterns is that whites "were often quite disorganized themselves," "so disunited that white Americans sometimes looked as if they might kill each other before the Indians got a chance at them." This pattern also holds true for the Snake War. In the early phases of that war the officer in charge of the Boise district allowed discipline to lapse and became so ineffective against the Indians that citizens became incensed.

Vigilantes hung sixty horse thieves, murderers, and highwaymen, including the sheriff of Boise. Once the Civil War ended, General George Crook was freed from fighting rebels, took command, and brought discipline to the federal forces in the Snake War.[1]

Most white-Indian wars did not pit whites against Indians, Limerick asserted in describing another pattern, because "Indians were usually on both sides," as indeed they were in the Snake War. The volunteers had rarely succeeded in engaging the Paiutes in pitched battle, but Crook believed in using Indians to fight Indians. He enlisted Warm Springs and Paiute scouts to find Indian winter camps, on which he mounted surprise dawn attacks from which escape was next to impossible.

This tactic brought into play another pattern—the difficulty of keeping "a clear line between combatants and noncombatants." Surprise dawn attacks on a sleeping Indian camp invariably produced a fight ensnaring as many women and children as warriors in "the darkest and grimmest dimensions of human nature."

While the Snake War conformed neatly to the patterns that white-Indian conflicts formed over the decades, the Paiutes' next and only other war did not. The Bannock War lies at the heart of this narrative. In typical white-Indian conflicts the Natives' knowledge of their land, of sources of food and water, of arroyos and caverns, gave them a significant advantage, but this was not so in the Bannock War because most of the fighting was on lands foreign to the Paiutes. The Bannock War defied other patterns as well—the whites did not lack unity; noncombatant involvement in battles was uncommon; and there was little in the way of "torture, maiming, rape, mutilation, murder." According to Sarah Winnemucca, daughter of Chief Winnemucca and a central figure in the Bannock War, Paiutes never even took a scalp.[2]

Yet this war that bucks many conventions of white-Indian conflict and that took fewer than one hundred lives of white and Native combatants combined was calamitous to these Paiutes.[3] Long after the shooting stopped, the war served as a vehicle for oppression of these Natives. A war that, as wars go, was relatively tame, and virtually free of the brutalities and atrocities that were so common in white-Indian conflicts, was in the long run at least as devastating to the Paiutes as any war was to any tribe.

The devastation was not inflicted by bullets or bayonets or torture. But "words are loaded pistols,"[4] and were the Paiutes' undoing. In the run-up to the war, during the war, and in its aftermath, a white war narrative evolved from dissembling government officials and from undiscerning press reports and histories. Nearly every history that discusses this war declares that the hostile Indian forces were led by the primary Paiute chief, Egan. None disagrees. For almost a century and a half Paiutes have lived under the dark shadow of this myth of the Bannock War.

The fate of these Paiutes was forged from a chorus of voices, from the Machiavellian Indian agent at Malheur, William Rinehart, across the continent to William Tecumseh Sherman, commander in chief, U.S. Army. The Paiutes had a remarkably able, if mercurial, advocate in Sarah Winnemucca, who was ideally matched with her steady and unflappable colleague, Paiute chief Egan. Yet the Paiutes' relationship with Sarah Winnemucca was complicated, for she had sided with the bluecoats in the Bannock War, she seemed to be in the company of whites as much as Paiutes, each of her three husbands was white and two of them deadbeats, and it was not uncommon to find her name in news accounts of bar fights and drunkenness.[5]

She gave speeches to white audiences explaining the wrongs that her people had suffered. "We want you to try us for four years," she told one audience, "and if at the end of that time we don't learn, or don't work, or don't become good citizens, then you can do what you please."[6] Her condemnation of the treatment of the Paiutes, and the enthusiastic response of her listeners and the press, reached three thousand miles from San Francisco to Washington DC and the office of Carl Schurz, secretary of the interior. He invited Chief Winnemucca, his daughter Sarah, and son Natchez to the capital. After hearing Sarah's account, Schurz declared that the Paiutes would be freed from their confinement, touching off a storm of opposition from government officials. "I protest," erupted James Wilbur, whom Schurz considered the best Indian agent in the nation.[7] Others were no less vocal.

From the conflicting voices and actions of these characters emerge the machinations by which the truth was concealed for 140 years. In the midst of that period Henry Roe Cloud, a Native investigator with two degrees from Yale and nationwide experience, studied the circumstances of these Paiutes. This account unearths the disinformation, traces it back to its origins, and follows it forward to its impact, revealing how, as found by Roe Cloud, such a gentle war reduced this Native people to the most destitute in the nation.

CHAPTER I

Paiute-White Encounters, 1826 and 1862

1826: Paiutes and Peter Skene Ogden's Fur Trapping Brigade

In 1826 the Oregon Country was in political and diplomatic limbo. The treaty of 1818 with the United Kingdom settled the northern boundary of the United States at the forty-ninth parallel between Minnesota and the Rocky Mountains. West of the Rockies no boundary was set. Both countries remained free to occupy, settle, and harvest furs in the Oregon Country.

In 1825 the British Hudson Bay Company built Fort Vancouver north of the Columbia River, across from present-day Portland, as the center for its fur trade in the Northwest. Peter Skene Ogden arrived at Fort Vancouver that year. He was the son of one judge, grandson of another, and brother of an attorney general, but he had different ambitions. By the time he arrived at Fort Vancouver at age thirty, he had married a Spokane and been promoted beyond his contemporaries in the British Hudson Bay Company.

Of short stature, muscular torso, sweeping shoulders, and agile step, Ogden was among the youngest in the Hudson Bay Company brigade of about one hundred that he led that winter. By early January, in the drainage of the John Day River in eastern Oregon, Ogden's party was struggling with hunger. His worries were shifting from profits to survival as New Year's Day brought their third consecutive day without food. Only later did Ogden learn that his daughter was born that day. Outwardly unflappable, he shared his fears with his diary: "God preserve us," and "What will become of us?" Dissatisfied with his Nez Perce guides, Ogden encouraged his party to make contact with Paiutes, then called "Snakes."

According to Ogden's diary, a young Paiute was captured, brought to the trappers' camp, given food, beads, and other gifts, and invited to return with furs to trade. The encounter may have been the first between a Paiute and Euro-Americans. The next day the young man came back with friends and relatives, all bearing beaver and otter skins.

The visitors were "fine, tall men, well dressed, and for so barren a country, in good condition," Ogden noted in his diary. One of the Paiutes became his guide and endeared himself to the entire brigade by shooting an antelope and four sheep and leading Ogden out of the John Day Basin to the Snake River.[1]

1861–62: Paiutes and Otter Bar Miners

Thirty-five years later, Paiutes had an encounter of a different kind with Europeans. Among the whites in that encounter were two young men from Watertown, New York, Cortez Eddy and William Failing. Weary of his duties at his father's "Failing's Hotel," William had announced to his family that he was going to California. His perpetually imminent departure had become a source of amusement to some of his eight siblings. The courage to leave his hometown finally seized William when his older brother and favorite sibling, Oliver, announced in the fall of 1860 that he was leaving for Memphis to start a lumber business. William then told his friend Eddy that he was ready to go, but the secession of South Carolina in December clinched his decision.

On the morning of January 1, 1861, Failing and Eddy departed Watertown for New York City and then for San Francisco via Panama. Failing would never see his family or Watertown again.[2]

After a brief stay in San Francisco the pair continued north to Portland, a primitive town of under three thousand in the midst of a gold excitement that swept up these two youths. They picked their way through muddy streets littered with stumps and debris, reading postings and newspaper ads. By early November they were on the roster of an expedition to the Otter Bar on the North Fork of the John Day River in eastern Oregon, led by Buell Woodward of Michigan and Elisha Lewis of Claylick, Pennsylvania. On November 18 Failing and Eddy joined Woodward, Lewis, and nineteen others aboard the Oregon Steam Navigation Company steamboat *Julia*, eastbound up the Columbia River.

At dusk the miners arrived at The Dalles and disembarked along with fifty horses, ten mules, two dogs, and provisions for four months, in a town of one street along the Columbia River. "Architecturally, the Dalles cannot be said to lean very heavily on the side of beauty," a traveler from the East Coast wrote in 1863.[3] Between the river on the north and a vertical bluff to the south lay the bulk of the town, including eight saloons, three hotels, three harness-makers, three wagon-makers, four blacksmiths, two gunsmiths, a free public school, a Methodist church, and a Catholic church.[4] The Dalles' notorious winds, which "possessed the novel faculty of blowing simultaneously from all points of the compass," capitalized on the treeless landscape and the arid, gritty soil to penetrate even microscopic breaches in the defenses of stagecoaches, boats, houses, clothing, and living bodies.[5] To the north the barren Columbia Hills helped funnel Arctic winds through the town.

Camp Dalles looked over the river from a bluff south of town. It was probably here that the miners inquired about Indians along their intended route. According to Failing's diary, excerpts of which were published afterward, the response was that "there were no Indians in this section."[6] Yet a Paiute raid on nearby Warm Springs had been reported to Captain Whittlesey at Camp Dalles just six weeks earlier.[7] Had the miners consulted Oregon Indian Superintendent William Rector before they left Portland, they would have learned that he considered the Paiutes a "much dreaded and powerful foe."[8] Instead the miners rode out of The Dalles unaware that they were entering the land of another people, that their horses and mules were treasured by that people above all other possessions, and that this was the season of that people's greatest need.

A few months after the shots on Fort Sumter that launched the Civil War, an explosion of a different sort rocked East Africa, showering the Red Sea with pumice and darkening the skies. The eruption of Mount Dubbi was the largest known in Africa.[9] The winter that followed the eruption—the most severe known in the Pacific Northwest of the United States—has led to speculation that the eruption had a role in the unprecedented weather.[10]

The winter began with the greatest known flood of the Willamette River.[11] By December 11 the Columbia River had risen fourteen feet at what is now Cascade Locks. On the east side of the Cascade Mountains, The Dalles, which has an average annual rainfall of about fifteen inches, was pummeled by four inches on December 8 alone.

Then the cold weather began. By January 3 the Columbia River was closed by ice at and above Vancouver (105 miles from the mouth). Deliveries across the Columbia between Portland and Vancouver were by sleigh. From late December through March there were repeated spells of cold, as low as minus twenty-nine degrees in Walla Walla and minus thirty-four degrees in The Dalles and Florence, Idaho. Snow in The Dalles reached fifty-four inches in depth.[12] By mid-February over eighty percent of the cattle in the Walla Walla vicinity had succumbed to the cold.[13] That winter was "without doubt the most severe ever experienced in the Northwest by white men up to that date."[14]

Regular U.S. troops had provided protection to miners and settlers in eastern Oregon, but as these miners were entering Paiute country, the last of the regulars were leaving for Civil War duty. The result, according to Captain George Currey, was "an extended border without military protection from [Indians]."[15] The *Oregon Statesman* demanded that United States troops "continue to occupy the military posts, and those withdrawn should be replaced without delay."[16]

Efforts to replace the regulars with volunteers ran afoul of Oregon's secessionist governor, John Whiteaker, who did his best to sabotage the plan. The *Oregon Statesman* accused Whiteaker of "fiddling for Jeff. Davis," and inquired whether the governor thought that Oregonians "should be massacred rather than seek the polluting protection of 'Lincoln's black republican army.'"[17] In addition the unexpected winter weather interfered with troop movements and training, and U.S. Senator Baker of Oregon, who had charge of the program, was killed at the Battle of Ball's Bluff.

The most daunting challenge, however, was making soldiers out of the untamed youths who answered the call for volunteers. They were typically unmarried and from the border states. A prominent early Oregon settler, Jesse Applegate, remarked that they "were probably brave enough, but would never submit to discipline as soldiers. If the President himself had started across the Plains to command a company, the first time he would choose a bad camp or in any way offend them, they would turn him out and elect someone among themselves."[18] The quality of the recruits could not have been improved much by the marginal training that followed. One officer recruit recalled that the officers with whom he trained had a combined military experience of one year that one man served as a volunteer. Despite their inexperience the only training that these officer recruits received was self-administered, from an infantry manual, even though they were cavalry.[19] The training of the troops was no better. A sergeant's diary described legitimate exercises that were regularly inter-rupted by idleness ("Sat in cabin all day. Got tired." "Still in camp doing nothing with a vengeance."), inebriation ("Two thirds of the men are funny and the rest are in the same fix, all on cider. Even the preacher."), and frivolity ("Boys bleat like sheep, men crow like chickens, bray like mules and bark like dogs. Funny people these.").[20]

In the end the plan for a regiment of ten companies was replaced with a plan for six. Anxious to deploy the new troops, Colonel George Wright, officer in charge at Camp Dalles, decided to proceed despite the sketchy training.[21] With all regular troops called away to Civil War duty; with the volunteer replacements virtually untrained; with most major tribes under treaty and on reservations; the Lewis-Woodward expedition launched into the most severe winter known in the Northwest, unaware that they were entering the lands of the most feared Natives in Oregon.

From The Dalles the miners rode south to Tygh Valley, crossed the Deschutes River on a newly erected bridge, and continued southeast to the John Day River. During the first three weeks they endured snow and cold, followed by a four-inch rainfall and then a squalid struggle prying horses out of a muddy bog. For Failing's friend Cortez Eddy, the bog ended his indecision. He and W. G. Wood turned back.[22]

The rest decided to continue—a decision that each came to regret. Another portentous event occurred the same morning that Wood and Eddy began their return. Seven horses were missing. Unaware that they were among Paiutes, the miners believed that the animals had somehow escaped their ties to the hitch rail. Lewis selected a search party of four to stay behind with him, but the horses were never found.

Paiute preparations for the winter of 1861–62, which brought conditions that they had rarely, if ever, experienced, were surely inadequate. Every task of subsistence living was more challenging this winter: chasing down a mule deer through four feet of snow, extracting cattails from ice and snow to fortify a shelter weakened by heavy snow and to make clothing and blankets, breaking frozen limbs from trees for fuel, pulling fallen limbs from beneath frozen snow, and keeping food storage pits from freezing. In the midst of this time of need for Paiutes, the miners' fifty horses and mules were among the greatest concentrations of wealth ever seen in these lands.

On the last leg of their journey, which was along the North Fork of the John Day River, a Paiute scout clandestinely watching them would have known landmarks along the way that the miners were blind to—the spot where the scout's son shot his first elk; then, the marsh that was a dependable source of goose feathers for the fletching of the arrows in his quiver; a scree field used for burial, where his grandparents lay; a dead-end dry tributary where deer and elk could be trapped and where he found the obsidian piece that became his knife; a pool with the best washing stones at low water; a camas meadow; a pool where in high water a channel could be dug to divert and trap fish; a stand of alders where a hunter could conceal himself when stalking game at the favorite watering hole.[23] As the lead miners rounded a bend and disappeared from view, the Paiute scout knew that they would next pass through a meadow where women gathered bitterroot, Lomatium, camas, balsam root, and yampah, and around the next bend the shaded spot next to the river where the women peeled and washed the roots; then a slope of diatomaceous earth for war paint; a corral with walls of sagebrush, rocks, and tree limbs; and a patch of milkweed used to make the twine for the net for the annual mud hen (coot) hunt. The miners might ride the same stretch another day without realizing it. The Paiute could close his eyes any day and picture every turn and feature.

The journey to Otter Bar took the miners forty-nine days, through mud that imprisoned horses, down icy slopes at electrifying speeds, across vertical cliffs with hundred-pound packs, and, occasionally, into freezing waters. They completed the ordeal without losing a man and with only two defections. At once they began building cabins.[24]

On the day of their arrival Quimby and his horse took a terrifying slide, in unison, down an icy slope. The next day he and Hightower packed their gear and started for home. About a week later Stephens and the four Frenchmen said their good-byes.

While the men were building cabins for their own comfort, their animals deteriorated dangerously, as temperatures slid to twenty-four below zero and then thirty below zero.[25] To save the animals and replenish supplies, they selected one man from each of the seven messes to take the animals back to The Dalles to recuperate and then return in better weather. To purchase supplies at The Dalles, they took all the money remaining, about $650, and all rings and watches. Five of the seven, Holdrich, Nutter, Hanly, Shaffer, and White, set out with twenty-one horses on January 19. The last two, Jo Seror and Buell Woodward, left with the remaining horses a week later.

On January 7 the miners were a single group of thirty.[26] By January 26 the single group had splintered into five widely dispersed groups of two, two, five, five, and sixteen. Almost all the animals were with the small, most vulnerable groups.

The last two to leave Otter Bar, Seror and Woodward, were on the thirteenth day of their return to The Dalles on the morning of February 7. First out of the tent, Woodward started a fire and went to check on the horses. From the tent Seror heard Woodward's excited voice in the distance, "The horses are gone!" A shot rang out, then an echo. In his moccasins Seror ran to Woodward. He thrust his hands under Woodward's shoulders. More gunshots and echoes. Clumps of snow jumped. He dragged Woodward to the tent. There were figures on the cliffs overhead. He tried to fire Woodward's gun, but the percussion caps fizzled. Cordite fumes filled the tent.

A bullet grazed his coat. Another his hat. He dashed out of the tent leaving behind shoes, food, water, Woodward. In tattered buffalo moccasins he ran toward the trail and turned upstream, toward Otter Bar and the sixteen men he had left two weeks earlier. After about seventeen miles, daylight faded. He sat on a hollow log to inspect the blisters where his moccasins had worn through. He crawled in the log.

The Otter Bar miners were raised thousands of miles away, in Pennsylvania, Ohio, New York, Iowa, Vermont, Canada, and France among other places. Other than Woodward and Lewis, few had experience east of the Cascade Mountains.

They had purchased and brought with them their food, shelter, clothing, tools, and weapons. They came to the North Fork valley to extract something that would not nourish, shelter, warm, defend, or have any practical use. One of the very few substances in the John Day drainage for which the Paiutes had no use was the only substance sought by the miners.

The miners believed that they were traveling through untrammeled wilderness. To the Paiutes, however, these strangers were intruding in the land where Paiutes originated, land that was partially composed of Paiute ancestors, whose blood and sacrifice had secured and protected it for generations.[27]

There is archaeological evidence that the Great Basin had been the home of Northern Paiute since about 1000 AD.[28] Linguistic studies point to a more recent date. The dialects of Numic speakers throughout the Great Basin show "very slight differences" from one another. The near-uniformity of the language over such great distances suggests that the Numic people had not been there long enough for the names of local plants, animals, birds, or geological formations to become engrained in the language or for local dialects to form. According to these studies the arrival of Numic speakers in eastern Oregon and other parts of the Great Basin was after 1492, and not "more than a very few centuries" ago.[29]

Northern Paiutes have occupied lands as far north as the upper valley of the John Day River in central Oregon, but not as far north as the Columbia River, which had long been occupied by Sahaptin-speaking tribes—Tenino and Umatilla. The markedly distinct Sahaptin dialects within a relatively small region and the detailed, elaborate Sahaptin vocabulary for local features and for animal and plant life in those places are among the clues that the Tenino and Umatilla tribes settled this region centuries before the arrival of Northern Paiutes.[30]

At the Otter Bar camp a day and a half later appeared a bedraggled, hollow-eyed shell of the Jo Seror who had left just two weeks before. Patchy remains of moccasins barely clung to his feet, which left a trail of blood in the snow.

Seror's tale ended the mining enterprise. Instead of building cabins, they built boats to carry them back down the North Fork, the first stage of their journey back to The Dalles. After fifty miles of collisions and capsizes, they loaded what they could in packs and continued on foot. Fresh Indian signs were at every turn. First Burnham and then Starr contracted scurvy. On February 24 they came upon a deserted camp. A search turned up burned ropes, straw from packsaddles, fragments of saddles spotted with blood, and a bloody fingerprint on a tree. These were the only clues ever found to the fates of Holdrich, Shaffer, White, Nutter, and Hanly.

There was no fire that night. They posted a double guard. The next morning began with their ration for the day, a mouthful of ham. Soon they came to another deserted camp. Pages torn from a French grammar, three pick handles, burned saddles, and burned rope told the broad outlines of the story, allowing their imaginations to fill in the details. The four French and Stevens brought the death count to eleven. A few hours later Hightower's bay appeared, as energetic and edgy as ever. No one could catch him. There was no other sign of Hightower or Quimby.

Of the three groups attacked by Paiutes, the first to leave Otter Bar—the four French and Stevens—were the first to die, at the camp furthest from Otter Bar. The second group to leave Otter Bar—the Holdrich five—was attacked before it reached the French camp. The last to leave Otter Bar, Woodward and Seror, were attacked before they reached either of the other two sites. The Paiutes deployed their forces to intercept each party before it reached a bloody camp that would alert it to the danger.

In the Tygh Valley fields were littered with the carcasses of cows, horses, and mules. They were forced to walk over the dead animals, sometimes piled as high as twenty feet. That winter got the name "the Old Cowcatcher" because it left the ground so soggy that much of the stock became mired in mud and then, perhaps attracted by the warmth of decomposition, in the corpses of their fellows.[31]

On March 8 the seventeen survivors limped in to The Dalles, half propping up and half-dragging Burnham. Failing's footwear was shreds of a blanket. Stevens's dog greeted them. All the other animals were gone. When an American flag came into view, however, they erupted in a spontaneous cheer, taking the flag to mean that the Union had not yet been defeated.

Wood and Eddy (the first to turn back) had returned safely. In April Quimby's body was discovered on a bank of the Deschutes, presumably the east bank. Hightower might well have drowned trying to cross the Deschutes.

Their pitiable condition brought out the best of The Dalles, where the survivors were compelled to stay for several days until the Columbia

River thawed enough to allow steamboat travel again. George knew the clerk at the Umatilla Hotel, owned by a pair of Irishmen, N. B. Sinnott, a "black republican," and big (over three hundred pounds) Dan Handley, a fervent Democrat. Both were known for their hospitality. They provided beds and food for a number of the miners. Individual citizens looked after the rest. A shoemaker fitted Failing with stockings and boots. Family after family donated clothing.

CHAPTER 2

Before Whites

The Sierra Nevada Mountains form the western edge of the Great Basin, a land of high desert covering Nevada and a slice of every neighboring state. Prevailing west winds striking the mountains are forced upward, where the air cools and drops its moisture on the western slope. Dry air descends the eastern slope, accelerating evaporation as it passes over the few tarns, meadows, and ponds in its path. Scores of short mountain ranges run north and south, forming small basins with no outlet. The northern valley floors reach four thousand to five thousand feet in elevation, surrounded by peaks up to ten thousand feet.

For centuries the Great Basin had been the home of three Numic-speaking nations, Northern Paiute, Shoshone, and Ute. Northern Paiute lived in what is now southeast Oregon, southwest Idaho, western Nevada, and a sliver of northeast California. Shoshone were east of the Northern Paiute; Ute were east of Shoshone. Among the features of southeast Oregon important to Northern Paiutes was a river that Peter Skene Ogden named "Malheur," French for misfortune, after furs he had cached on the river disappeared. The name caught on. It soon attached to a lake and to the local Northern Paiutes as well.

One source of the waters of Malheur Lake is runoff from the northwest flank of Steens Mountain (formerly Stein's Mountain). Over 9,700 feet, the summit of Steens is about 5,500 feet above everything in sight. Only forty-five miles to the north of Steens, Malheur Lake is immense, with fifty-eight miles of shoreline and over twenty miles across its long dimension. Yet a stranger passing anywhere between Steens Mountain and Malheur Lake might miss both. From the northwest, Steens looks less

FIG. 1. View to the south over Mann Lake; summit of Steens Mountain is directly above the two small "rabbit ears" peninsulas. Author photo.

like a mountain than a long, dreary rise past occasional stands of aspen trees to a nondescript plateau. The waters of Malheur Lake cover only the lower branches of most of the sagebrush that is rooted in its bottom and that, from many vantage points, disguises the lake as just another expanse of desert, dry as salt.

The waters of Malheur Lake are in plain view, however, to one of its most numerous visitors, migratory waterfowl on their way to or from California's Central Valley. The summer habitat of much of that population lies in far northern Canada, Alaska, and Siberia. The migration path between the

Central Valley and the northern breeding grounds is known as the Pacific Flyway, the westernmost of four flyways over North America. The other three have far more wetland staging areas. Although the Pacific Flyway passes over the Great Basin, which has many catch-basins, most have no outlet other than evaporation. Continued evaporation leaves hypersaline waters that support only limited species of waterfowl. In contrast, the Malheur Basin has sufficient drainage to keep salinity within the limits tolerated by ducks, geese, and swans. It therefore attracts these species in "greater numbers than any other part of the United States."[1]

Among the first arrivals in the spring are snow geese, soon followed by Canada geese, mallards, pintails, stilts, and avocets, to name a few. Paiutes attracted birds with decoys made by stuffing a duck skin or by knotting tule into a duck shape and covering it with feathers. Immersed in frigid waters, Indians herded the birds attracted by the decoys to the chosen spot, then shouted, frightening the birds into entrapping nets.[2]

During the spring migration, Ogden's choice of the name "Malheur" ill suits the land and its waters, which are alive with the gracefully curved beaks of curlews and ibis, the disembodied whistle of snipe wings plunging through desert air, the guttural cacophony of courting sandhill cranes, the base "thunking" of bitterns concealed in tule marshes, the freight-train scream of tens of thousands of snow geese in simultaneous song, as their chevron formations stratify a dawn sky. But the land is also harsh, unrelenting, unforgiving. Rare is the tree that provides relief from sun or wind. Desert air leaches the life from feathers, leaves, limbs, flesh.

Before whites began to affect their way of life, Paiutes (which always means Northern Paiute in this study) made a living on these stingy lands through ingenuity, steady labor, and logistics refined over generations. Wildfowl, game, and fish were part of their diet, but plants were the most dependable source of sustenance—roots, seeds, fruits, and nuts. Some yielded foods readily. In the spring women waded into marshes and reached deep below the surface to find new cattail shoots. Mothers peeled off the soggy leaves to expose the white spears for their young children.[3]

Other plants required more work and inventiveness. Women carried armloads of rice grass, for example, to a hard earth surface, where they moistened a handful of grass to place on a small fire. The moisture kept the grass from flashing while the small black seeds roasted, broke free of the stem, and dropped into the ash. Women then used a winnowing basket to separate the seeds, which they husked on a flat stone to make meal for a gruel.[4]

Oregon Paiutes made their homes up to five thousand feet above sea level. There was sufficient moisture and warmth for a reasonable growing season, but the timing was cursed. When there was moisture there was little heat and when there was heat there was little moisture, bookending the growing season between cold and drought.[5]

For Oregon Paiutes the first foods in spring included groundhogs, salmon from the Malheur River, and seeds and roots. Among the staples were a variety of roots and seeds, crickets, and huckleberries in summer and ponderosa pine nuts, chokecherries, elk, pronghorn, and rabbit in the fall.[6]

Once winter set in, the nourishment yielded by these lands dropped from a trickle to an occasional drip. Marshes froze, sealing away cattail roots and fish. Seeds from the last growing season had fallen and scattered. Rodents were in hibernation. Most birdlife had migrated south. Coyotes competed with the Paiutes for jackrabbits and other small prey. Whether supplies would last until spring was often in doubt. The first few months of each year represented "the hungry time, between the last of the stored food and the appearance of the earliest plant shoots."[7] Hunger was a regular companion. Starvation was no stranger.[8]

Before the changes that were brought on by the arrival of whites in the Northwest, the only Paiute group of importance was the family unit, sometimes called kin-clique. At the center of a typical family unit was a married couple and their children. Also included were widowed parents of either spouse and divorced and widowed siblings of either spouse.[9] Before whites, Northwest Paiutes had no bands and no chiefs. Decisions of any importance to a family were made by the family elders. There was no higher authority; "the principal social as well as political units within Northern Paiute society were the independent families."[10]

Each family acquired its own supply of food, which, except in unusual circumstances, was just for the family. Its members typically gathered food together, although it was common for men to hunt while women gathered roots or seeds.

The Paiute families did not coalesce into multi-family entities with central leadership because the relentless demands of food-gathering scattered and isolated them for the better part of each year. From early spring until late summer root and seed gathering were the Paiutes' principal activities. Although a family unit might join with one or two others, in general enlarging the group only reduced the yield per individual.[11]

There were other Paiute groups, but none diminished the ultimate authority of the family. In winter, groups of families, *nogadi*, camped together at a home tract, *tibiwa*. Groups of *nogadi* shared a *tibiwa*, which had multiple camping and foraging locations. There was, however, no chief of a *nogadi* or a *tibiwa*. There were headmen who helped facilitate group decisions on such matters as moving a camp, treatment of witches, and difficulties with neighbors. But these were temporary leaders only; their authority, minimal as it was, did not extend beyond the fifty or so individuals in their *nogadi*.[12]

Occasionally families joined for collective events such as pronghorn hunts, gathering of ponderosa pine nuts, and trapping of rabbits and mud hens. A "boss" was often in charge, but his authority ended with the event, which usually lasted no more than a day. Except for these brief, occasional events, each family acquired foods by the labor of its members, who hunted and gathered just for their family.[13]

Subsistence living in the Great Basin, then, rewarded small groups and punished large groups, leading to the disbursal of political authority to many autonomous family units. While this was an efficient way to gather food, it was not effective for much of any other purpose. If, for example, dozens of Paiute families fishing and gathering seeds and roots at Malheur Lake were intruded upon by Klamaths, the Paiutes had no spokesperson who could communicate with the Klamaths on behalf of the many affected Paiutes. The sovereignty of the kin-clique also limited Paiutes' ability to manage difficult or dangerous tribesmen. As long as the problem individual was on good terms with his own family unit, little could be done.

Compared to Paiutes, indigenous people to the north were more prosperous, politically organized, and socially integrated with their neighbors. Umatilla and Walla Walla, side by side on the Columbia River, abutted Cayuse to the southeast. East of the Cayuse and closely allied with them were the Nez Perce, an advanced, populous, powerful, and respected tribe. In winter Walla Walla and Umatilla lived in mat houses sixty feet

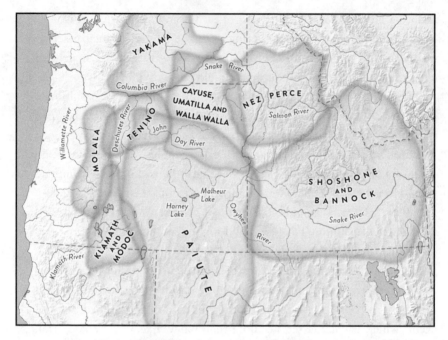

MAP 2. Great Basin tribes of the Oregon Country. Cartography by Erin Greb.

long, with up to ten families, each with its own fire. Intermarriage was common, as were villages of mixed populations. Mounted hunting parties, also mixed, would seek deer and elk in the Blue Mountains, surrounding their prey in the snow. Men caught steelhead from the shore and other fish from canoes. Unlike the Paiute, the multiple Walla Walla and Umatilla families in a lodge selected a single headman to represent the lodge in the village council. The council selected its own headman.

Preeminent headmen became band chiefs who, along with headman, raised war parties, which could be as large as several hundred and could include Palouse and Nez Perce. Warfare was common against Shoshone, Bannock, Northern Paiute, and Blackfeet.

In the first half of the nineteenth century Umatilla, Cayuse, Walla Walla, and Nez Perce had an additional advantage in that they were adjacent to or near the routes of fur trappers on the Columbia and Snake Rivers, providing regular opportunities to trade furs for guns, ammunition, and other valuables, to keep or to barter for horses. Horses strengthened them militarily and enabled them to reach a broader range of food sources.

West of the Umatilla were Tenino, a Paiute enemy since prior to 1800. Once the Tenino began trading with fur trappers, acquiring horses and weapons, they attacked their eastern neighbor, the Molalla, and drove them west, over the Cascade Mountains, never to return. The Tenino also turned on the Paiutes, their traditional foe, and drove deep into Paiute territory, killing Paiutes and taking them for slaves.[14]

Tenino, Umatilla, Cayuse, Walla Walla, and Nez Perce had access to rich Columbia River salmon runs as well as the reliable winds and dry heat that allowed salmon to be easily preserved and transported. These neighbors lived in relative prosperity under central leadership, without the relentless, unforgiving bondage to hunting and gathering that scattered the Paiutes into a loose affiliation of autonomous families.[15]

East of the Paiutes were three groups that were more likely to be aligned with the Paiutes than against them: Bannocks, Shoshone, and Weiser. Bannocks were close to Oregon Paiutes genetically as well as geographically. Both were Northern Paiute. There was considerable social interaction and intermarriage between them, yet there were significant differences. Before about 1850 Paiutes lived peacefully, unmounted, on a diet that depended on plant-based foods as a staple; Bannocks hunted buffalo, stole horses, and did not shy from a fight. Bannocks were closely allied with Northern Shoshone, another Numic-speaking tribe. Like Oregon Paiutes, Shoshone originated in the Great Basin and lacked central authority. Although Northern Shoshone outnumbered Bannocks, Bannocks were favored for leadership positions in joint Bannock-Shoshone groups.

Bannock head chiefs and band chiefs organized horse-stealing raids and buffalo hunts, directed food-gathering sorties, and supervised food and fuel in winter. Their structured, hierarchical organization allowed them to become, in the words of one Indian agent, the "most powerful and warlike tribe that dwell between the Rocky Mountains and the Pacific."[16]

Weiser Indians resided on the Weiser River, which originates in the Seven Devils Range in Idaho and flows through forests, then grassy meadows into high desert sagebrush before emptying into the Snake River about sixty miles northwest of Boise. Only fifteen miles up the Snake River from the mouth of the Weiser is the outlet of the Malheur River, an Oregon tributary of the Snake and an important source of salmon and recreation for the Paiutes.[17] Weisers and Paiutes resided on opposite sides of the Snake yet were close neighbors. The definitive ethnological study of Northern Paiute, by anthropologists Julian H. Steward and Erminie Wheeler-Voegelin, puzzles over the tribal affiliation of Weisers, concluding that they were not Bannocks, were possibly Paiute, but were probably Shoshone.[18]

Weisers are uniquely connected to the Paiutes' story through Ezich'guegah, whose anglicized name is Egan.[19] He was raised by Weisers but became an influential Paiute chief.

What little is known of Egan's early life is from the writings of General Oliver Otis Howard. He did not reveal his source, but it is almost certainly Egan's niece Mattie. According to Howard, whose writings were of inconsistent reliability, Weiser warriors came upon a scene in the foothills of the Blue Mountains in northeast Oregon in which they took an intense interest—a group of Cayuse families camped in a meadow, gathering seeds and roots. The Weisers descended on the meadow, killed all the adult Cayuse, and made off with the Cayuse children to the warriors' home on the Weiser River. Among the children who were forever separated from their natural parents that day was Egan, who was taken in and raised by a Weiser family. As Egan matured, he excelled as a hunter, fisherman, and athlete. He attracted growing respect for his leadership and judgment, became a war chief, and married the sister of Shenkah, the primary Weiser chief.[20] He is at the heart of this narrative.

CHAPTER 3

"Wholly and Completely Different"

Trappers' sporadic forays into Paiute country took a heavy toll on game but otherwise had little immediate impact on the Natives. The trappers' diseases spread quickly among Indians on both sides of the Cascade Mountains, catastrophically on the west side, but had minimal impact on Paiutes, who had little contact with whites and, for most of the year, were widely dispersed in small groups in remote locations.[1]

Beginning in the early 1840s, however, a different kind of white began to arrive. They were enticed by visions of land, free for the taking, beautiful, moist, and fertile land, sprouting plump and luscious fruits, grains, and legumes in a climate that bathed them in dew, showers, and sunlight. The 1850 Donation Claims Act accelerated the migration. Under that law, for 640 acres of paradise, it seemed, all a man and his wife had to do was fell some trees, notch and stack them in a rectangle, roof it, plant a garden, and take in the bounty of the black, moist soil for four years. Many found the offer irresistible.

At first the great migration into Oregon had little impact on Oregon Paiutes and their lands. Settlers crossing Oregon saw nothing of interest in the sagebrush, greasewood, and alkali east of the Cascade Mountains. They had had their fill of desert and saw eastern Oregon as the last obstacle separating them from the dreams that had been luring them onward for so many months: "The vision of the green valley of the Willamette with its tall firs and meadows was in their eyes, and they pressed on."[2]

As the 1850s drew to a close, however, the forty-three thousand immigrants who had arrived in that decade had snapped up the choice lands in the Willamette Valley. Increasingly newcomers were drawn to the dry side of the mountains. For their farms they took the best land in the valleys and on the borders of lakes and streams, blocking Paiutes from the sites where they had long gathered grass seed, caught fish, and killed wildfowl. To build houses, barns, fences, sluices, and bridges, the newcomers felled forests in a land of few trees, depriving Paiutes of ponderosa pine nuts and destroying habitat for deer, rabbit, quail, and grouse. Fields where Paiutes had gathered the roots of sego lily, wild onion, biscuitroot, and yampah were now fenced, trampled, and fouled by cattle.

Minerals also drew whites into Paiute lands. Unremarkable discoveries of gold throughout the Northwest in the early fifties were followed by significant strikes in 1855 at Fort Colville in northeast Washington and on the Kootenai River in British Columbia.[3] This gold excitement resurrected memories of an emigrant wagon train camped in eastern Oregon in 1845. Children brought to their parents a bucket of water with yellow pebbles at the bottom. The bucket was blue. The pebbles drew little attention at the time, partly because the group was plagued by troubles and illnesses and partly because before the California gold rush few expected to find gold in such a place. After the Colville and Kootenai discoveries, however, tales of "blue bucket" gold attracted many to Paiute country in southeast Oregon.[4]

Paiutes were already too familiar with hunger and starvation. They could ill afford the loss of resources caused by the whites moving onto their lands. "These Indians are almost forced into collisions and hostilities with the whites," Major General Halleck wrote, "and from their shiftless habits in regard to subsistence, they have scarcely any other alternative than to *rob* or *starve*."[5]

After observing immigrants overrun, fence, plow, and mine their lands, Paiutes did not have to puzzle over the cause of the hunger and starvation that beset them. On occasion the cause contributed to the solution. The cattle grazing in the meadow that they destroyed were almost like finding a robber still counting his booty in the bank. The Indians' taking of settlers' cattle evoked rage from whites, yet brought satisfaction to Paiutes as infants who had been suckling dry breasts began to draw milk and show flesh beneath skin that had been taut against ribs. In a speech in San Francisco Sarah Winnemucca, Paiute daughter of Chief Winnemucca, explained, "Necess[ity] made them go and take a cow or a steer to feed their little ones and wives. . . . My people think as much of their wives and daughters as you think of yours."[6]

Paiutes had a legal right to their lands, unless and until the United States took the lands by force or by treaty. In the words of the country's highest court, "The title by conquest is acquired and maintained by force."[7] A people whose lands were invaded had no obligation, legal or otherwise, to capitulate. They had every right to fight back and defend themselves and their land. The Paiutes' rights were especially critical since the nourishment available from their lands was scarcely enough to sustain them.

With neither horses nor guns, however, Paiutes were no match for mounted, armed ranchers. Gradually during the 1850s Paiutes like those who traded with Peter Skene Ogden metamorphosed into armed, mounted, and hostile Paiutes like those who attacked the Otter Bar miners. The best source on this transformation, as well as Northern Paiute ethnology generally, is *The Northern Paiute Indians*, by Erminie Wheeler-Voegelin and Julian H. Steward. This study of over three hundred pages on a relatively obscure indigenous people owes its existence in large measure to an equally obscure Catholic priest, Father Peter Heuel.

Twenty years before *The Northern Paiute Indians*, Erminie Wheeler-Voegelin and her husband, Charles ("Carl") Frederick Voegelin, both graduate students at the University of California, spent an evening at the home of an Indiana businessman with a passionate interest in Indiana's archaeological past. Eli Lilly had recently inherited the presidency of the Indianapolis pharmaceutical firm bearing his name. Believing that the young couple's work would advance the studies that were his focus, Lilly funded graduate fellowships at Yale, first for Carl and later for Erminie. She was the first woman to receive a doctoral degree in anthropology from Yale. A decade later both won Guggenheim fellowships.[8]

Wheeler-Voegelin's career took another abrupt turn following the establishment of the Indian Claims Commission in 1946 to hear over four hundred treaty claims by Indian tribes against the United States. To defend itself from those claims the United States, through the Department of Justice, hired Wheeler-Voegelin to conduct the needed research. Among the hundreds of claims was one brought on behalf of Oregon Paiutes by Father Heuel, who devoted his last two decades to this people. Wheeler-Voegelin and Steward's research for the Department of Justice defense of the Paiutes' claim, published in 1974 as *The Northern Paiute Indians*, is the richest ethnological source on Paiutes in the Oregon Country.

Steward and Wheeler-Voegelin described the formation of groups of armed, mounted warriors and the rise of leaders of those groups. These new bands and chiefs were "wholly and completely different from anything known in pre-white days." According to Steward and Wheeler-Voegelin, they were "predatory, military, and mounted."[9] Historian Hubert Bancroft wrote that "a change had come over these savages with the introduction of fire-arms and cattle." From "cowardly, skulking creatures, whose eyes were forever fastened on the ground in search of some small living thing to eat," they had become "as much feared as any savages in Oregon."[10]

There were two phases of intense treaty-making in the Oregon Country, 1850–52 and 1854–55. Although Paiutes participated in neither, they, and all tribes, were profoundly affected by both. The first phase was initiated by Samuel Thurston, the Oregon territorial delegate to Congress. (States have representatives and senators; territories have a single, nonvoting delegate.) Thurston initiated a new law appointing three commissioners to make treaties with Natives on the west side of the Cascade Mountains, removing them to the east side of the mountains.

The three commissioners appointed under that law discovered that, as they wrote to Commissioner of Indian Affairs Luke Lea in Washington City, west-side Indians were "friendly and well disposed," living "peaceably and on friendly terms" by fishing and working for whites. However, they had minimal skills as hunters and warriors. To remove them would "insure their annihilation in a short time whether from want or by the hands of their more warlike neighbors." Moving them over the mountains without the use of force "will be impossible," for they had "manifested a fixed and settled determination not under any circumstances or for any consideration" to make such a move. [11]

Unable to persuade west-side Indians to move over the mountains, the commissioners proceeded to negotiate the remaining treaty terms. There was nothing casual about the negotiations. In most cases the entire band was present; some treaties were signed by every member. The ceded land was described in each treaty, and the payments to tribes, largely in goods, were set out in painstaking detail. The annual payment to the Wahkiakum tribe, just north of the Columbia River, is typical: twenty blankets, ten woolen coats, ten pairs of pants, ten vests, twenty shirts, twenty pairs of shoes, fifty yards of Lindsay plaid fabric, one hundred yards each of calico and shirting, eight blanket shawls, one hundred pounds each of soap, tobacco, and sugar, one barrel each of salt and molasses, fifteen bags of flour, ten hoes, ten axes, fifteen knives, twenty-five cotton handkerchiefs, ten pounds of tea, six eight-quart brass kettles, ten ten-quart tin pails, twelve pint cups, ten six-quart pans, and ten caps.[12]

The granular detail of these terms provides a sense of the gravity of the proceedings. Under no illusions, Natives knew that their lives and the existence of their people were at stake. The three commissioners' communications with Washington City, although professional and businesslike, reflect an unmistakable appreciation of the plight of the people they were negotiating with. Although the objective of the statute that the commissioners were hired to implement was to move west-side Indians east, the commissioners stated that such a move was "[not] very desirable," for it "would in our opinion insure their annihilation in a short time."

After the commissioners negotiated six treaties, their duties were transferred by statute to Superintendent Dart, who negotiated another thirteen treaties, following the pattern set by the commissioners.[13] In April 1851 Dart sent all nineteen treaties to the capital for ratification by the Senate. Over a year later the treaties were tabled permanently without explanation. The most thorough study of these events concluded that the cause of the failure was "the absurdity of the plan. To have moved the western Indians into eastern Oregon would have meant to have exterminated them."[14]

Thurston did not succeed in removing west-side Indians from their homelands, but lack of success does not begin to describe the consequences. He had set in motion one process in Washington City raising expectations that all the Indians in western Oregon would move east; and a second, contradictory process in Oregon leading to negotiations that painstakingly built a mutual trust with tribe after tribe over the minutiae of their new life on a west-side reservation. As a result of Thurston's ill-considered scheme, Northwest Indians' introduction to the territorial government was a process laden with the earmarks of bad faith. What reason could a person of integrity possibly have, tribesmen may well have puzzled, for niggling over the number of pint cups per year until agreement was finally reached, then niggling over the number of tin pails until agreement was finally reached, then the number of caps, then handkerchiefs, then vests, and so on until agreement was finally reached on all terms, and then doing the same thing again in another treaty and another and another, until all nineteen treaties ended in agreement, only to cast all nineteen to the winds a year later? As Dart's successor, Joel Palmer, put it, the stillborn treaties did "much to destroy [Indians'] confidence in the good intentions of the Government. . . . This want of confidence in the declarations of government agents is not confined to those . . . tribes with whom treaties have been negotiated; it extends through the entire country."[15]

It is puzzling that a man as savvy and ambitious as Thurston would not have foreseen the obstacles to his plan for relocating west-side Indians. He was not a man to take on a fight that he thought he might lose. That, however, may be the explanation. For this was Thurston's third attempt to oust Indians from western Oregon and his third failure. Was the prominence that he expected to gain with his white constituents by his persistent, if unavailing, attempts to cleanse the land of nonwhites his true goal, and therefore a victory delivered in the guise of defeat? Was the destruction of Indian trust in the United States and its agents inflicted in the cause of Thurston's ambition to appear as the white man's hope for a pure white valley of the Willamette River?

Egotism at such a level should not be lightly inferred. Yet there is more evidence of the reach of Thurston's ambition. He deceived Congress into approving an amendment to a land bill that confiscated a wealth of land from an innocent man. It became known as "the original Oregon land fraud" and established Thurston as "Chief of Liars."[16] In the midst of the battle over this amendment, his wife expressed concern that their son, three-year-old Henry, showed signs of "combativeness." Thurston's response, superficially about young Henry, was that he wanted his son to be "a distinguished lawyer." His wife should not, he instructed, weaken the trait of "combativeness" in the boy but "strengthen it, for it is a giant in this world of war." Guided by "moral obligations," their son should "plant his battery of combativeness and storm the very citadel of his enemies." He should be cautious and considerate but able to "summon a spirit to his aid that will spread dread & terror at its approach."[17] Ruthlessness and unrestrained ambition do not appear to be out of character for Thurston.

Whatever his motives, though, the result was a legacy of deep and widespread Native distrust.

Any traces of trust that endured after Thurston were dealt another blow by Isaac Stevens, governor of the Washington Territory with responsibility for territorial Indian affairs. Stevens and Joel Palmer scheduled back-to-back treaty councils in Walla Walla in May 1855 and in The Dalles, Oregon, in June. Most tribes east of the Cascade Mountains participated in one of these two treaty councils.

Although treaties were concluded at both venues, the Walla Walla council was a contentious affair. Among the lessons Indians had learned from the nineteen failed Oregon treaties was that signatures by all parties did not bring the document to life. Until it was ratified by the Senate, the document remained a legal nullity. Or so the tribesmen thought until, immediately after the Washington treaties were signed, Stevens published announcements opening to white settlers all Indian lands ceded in the treaties, even though the Senate had not yet ratified them.[18] The white men's laws seemed to shift meaning to assure that the Indians always lost. The Washington tribes could see that settlers would immediately begin claiming their land, even though the tribes had no treaty and, like the Nations that negotiated the nineteen lifeless instruments in Oregon, might never have one. Congress did not ratify any of the 1855 treaties until 1859 and failed to fund them until 1860, further solidifying Northwest Natives' distrust of the Great Father.[19]

Palmer had attempted to open communications with Paiutes and to include them in the June 1855 treaty council at The Dalles. However, the agents he sent to Paiute lands faced many challenges, fear of the Paiutes not least among them. No contact was made and the treaty council at The Dalles was conducted without Paiutes. Major General Halleck was sympathetic to the Paiutes, but also realistic in observing, "These Indians have no general chief whom they all obey, and most of the bands act entirely independently of each other. It is therefore not possible to make any formal treaty with them. . . . The small communities or families into which they are divided have no fixed abodes, and are scattered over an immense extent of country."[20]

The 1855 treaties were a watershed event in Northwest Indian relations. Under these treaties tribes moved to reservations and ceded most of their lands to the United States. Gradually, in fits and starts, and despite delays and broken promises, these Indians began to receive treaty benefits. They varied from one reservation to the next, but could include a sawmill, flour mill, schoolhouse, blacksmith shop, tools for farming and building, houses and private plots for chiefs, instruction for children, agricultural instruction, medical care, rations for a limited time, clothing, cloth, and more.

After 1855 Paiutes were on an entirely different path from treaty tribes. With no agent, no reservation, no benefits, and no relationship with the United States government, Paiutes continued their food-gathering practices of the past, all the while developing the military capability to protect their land, their sources of nutrition, and their people.[21]

CHAPTER 4

Paiute Power

On a morning in mid-March 1856, Robert Thompson awoke to the here-again-gone-again sounds of Shitike Creek threading through rushes, stones, and cottonwood roots. He emerged from one of a dozen or more tents and was soon enjoying breakfast with Billy Chinook (Wasco chief), Stock Whitley (Deschutes chief), Alexsee (Tenino chief), and fourteen other leaders of Northwest tribes and bands, all of whom had signed the June 1855 treaty at The Dalles. That treaty had created the Warm Springs Reservation on the west bank of the Deschutes River in central Oregon. Thompson was the eastern Oregon agent of the Oregon Territorial Indian Superintendency. Expecting that the treaty would be ratified by the Senate, Thompson and the Indian leaders with him were on their sixth day of a journey to select a location within the Warm Springs Reservation for a community where the federal government would build the structures required by the treaty—not unlike the public and business buildings in any rural community.

Thompson was just months away from the end of his first decade in the Northwest. By his own admission, when he arrived he did not know "anything at all about the Indian character" and was more interested in Democratic Party politics.[1] But it was politics that led him to Indians, through Joe Lane, Oregon's first territorial governor. Thompson had helped Lane out of a financial bind by purchasing from Lane partial interest in a pair of mills on the Willamette River that were damaged by a flood. In return Lane, a Democrat, called in a favor from Democratic president Franklin Pierce, who appointed Thompson eastern Oregon Indian agent in 1853.[2] Thompson was now approaching the end of his third year on the job—three years of such tumultuous Indian-white relations that he had recently notified superintendent Joel Palmer of his resignation in June 1856, just three months away.[3]

After breakfast the chiefs began by affirming yesterday's discussion that this location was well suited for a sawmill and a flour mill. They had found nothing better in six days. The chiefs had concerns, however. They were keenly aware of the Yakama War, in progress north of the Columbia River. To the tribes caught up in that conflict, the horses and cattle provided by the federal government to the Warm Springs tribes could be a tempting target.

The chiefs wanted a location that could be defended. The lay of the land should force an enemy to approach uphill, through rough or rocky terrain, or around a lake. The location should favor the defender, not the attacker. If the U.S. government placed them on this land, so difficult to defend, it should protect them, the chiefs urged. Tenino chief Alexsee may have been concerned as well about Paiutes bent on revenge for years of Tenino aggression against Paiutes and their land.

Inscrutable behind a salt-and-pepper beard, convinced by the chiefs' arguments, Thompson assured them that they were not expected to move to a reservation that was not safe and that once Thompson returned to The Dalles, he and Palmer would make the chiefs' case to Colonel Wright. Thompson was true to his word but to little effect. Despite Warm Springs' vulnerability, the military was never persuaded to protect it with more than a temporary post.[4]

The peaceful Paiutes Peter Skene Ogden met on the John Day River in 1826 were typical of that era. Before the arrival of whites in Paiute country, "normally, intertribal relations were peaceful," according to Steward and Wheeler-Voegelin. "Where there was warfare other than individual raids for revenge or woman stealing, it was largely provoked by the aggression of a stronger group."[5] By 1859, however, much had changed. White incursions on Paiute territory and white interference with Paiute food sources had given rise to war chiefs. Family units remained autonomous, but, much like a group pronghorn hunt, an attack on Warm Springs was a collective effort. Multiple families combined to launch the attack and afterward shared the horses, cattle, and other plunder and returned to their families and traditional life. Family autonomy remained intact.[6] However, unlike the boss of a rabbit or antelope hunt, whose authority was limited and ended when the hunt ended, war chiefs remained in power as long as they had followers. The bands of war chiefs did not supplant the family units; rather, the families engaged in warfare through the war chief that each chose to align with.

The Paiutes' growing militarism became evident with their raids on Warm Springs. On a spring evening in 1859, one hundred mounted Paiutes descended on Warm Springs. The occasional Warm Springs Indians who attempted to oppose the Paiutes lost their lives as well as their stock. The reward of the attack was so rich and the resistance so minimal that Paiutes returned for more later that same month. This raid yielded another fine crop of horses, but at a price. Two Paiutes were captured. Their captors did not know who they had.[7]

The two captives figured into a plan of the commander of the U.S. Army's Oregon Department, General William S. Harney. He wanted a wagon route into Oregon from the east that could be traveled year-round. Existing routes through the Blue Mountains were impassable in winter. Harney appointed Captain Henry D. Wallen to open a wagon road from The Dalles south, through central Oregon, then east to Salt Lake City. Since the route would traverse untamed, little-traveled lands, Wallen wanted Indian scouts. The capture of the two Paiutes fit his plans nicely. Wallen left Fort Dalles on June 4, 1859, with the Paiute captives, who "appear[ed] to be well disposed," perhaps appreciating the military horses, the official look of the uniform, the regular meals.[8]

The Paiute raid on Warm Springs in which the two prisoners were taken prompted the reservation physician, Thomas L. Fitch, to lead a retaliatory attack on a Paiute winter camp. The Paiutes struck back on August 6, 1859. By this point they were wealthy enough in horses and arms to mount a significant response. Two hundred and fifty Paiutes, many on mounts acquired from Warm Springs, rumbled through the reservation again. Fitch sent a message to The Dalles: "Directed to any White man—For God's sake send some help as soon as possible. We are surrounded with Snakes—they have killed a good many Indians, and got all our stock—don't delay a single minute." The Paiutes killed thirteen Indian women and children and one white man and made off with 150 horses and forty cows. Fitch was captured but escaped during a war dance. Terrorized, the residents, both Indian and white, fled the reservation and could not be coaxed back for months. The military blamed Fitch for inciting the retaliatory raid.[9]

Captain Wallen's search for a wagon road led him to southeastern Oregon, where he camped one afternoon just east of Harney Lake, an expansive bed of alkali. Wallen was probably unaware that this was the heart of Paiute country, the native land of his scouts, who vanished along with several horses and two good rifles. The scouts turned out to be Chief Tsanumad and his half-brother, Chief Weyouwewa. Tsanumad's enemies at the Warm Springs Reservation called him "Paulina," meaning crazy or deranged.[10] (Since that name has lasted through the years and made its way into history books and maps, it is used here.) Newly armed, schooled in the ways of the white military, the two rejoined their people.[11]

As the Paiutes were gaining economic and military strength through their attacks on Warm Springs, nearly every other tribe east of the Cascades was in the midst of profound change of a different nature. On March 9, 1859, the Senate ratified the 1855 treaties, confirming the relocation of these tribes to reservations and the opening of their ancestral lands to settlers. The opening of lands yielded by treaty east of the Cascade Mountains, just as the last of the prime property of the Willamette Valley was being claimed, accelerated the movement of settlers into eastern Oregon and Paiute territory even before gold became a lure.

CHAPTER 5

Keeping Up Appearances

The slaying of eleven miners was the deadliest Paiute attack on whites in the Northwest and among the most serious by any Northwest tribe. The United States' response had enduring repercussions.

On the morning of March 9, 1862, when one of the miners, probably Lewis, reported the deaths at Fort Dalles, Captain George B. Currey had few good options. It is likely that one of his first acts was to send word to William Rector, the superintendent of Indian affairs in Portland, boxing Rector into the same quandary that Currey faced—an apparent Indian atrocity that would arouse public expectations of an instant and effective response, at a time when there were no soldiers capable of such a response.

Rector was born in Virginia to a well-to-do father and a mother of humble origins. He left an "autobiography" in which he noted that the Rector family looked askance on his father's choice of "the schotch blacksmiths daughter." (All quotes from the autobiography preserve Rector's spelling.) But, to young William Rector, his mother "was a strong minded woman and spereted enough to not like to be concidered an inferior to the Rector family." She convinced her husband to move to Ohio. There were few churches in Ohio, but, churches, Rector wrote, "we did not kneed father brought religion enough from Virginia to last him his lifetime and mother was god enough to live without religion." Rector did not recall ever doing anything wrong as a child, but he was "possessed of a quick temper full of life." "Father believed that he could whip that temper out of me and that it was his duty as a christan man to do so or he would be responsible for it heare after." Rector thought the whippings were unjust.

They "inclined me to think for my self at a very tender age I doubted the truth or justis of his duty to punish me for no offence and became skeptical of all immaterial things that was talked of so common believing in nothing but what was material and tangible."[1]

Before he became superintendent, Rector had already shown that he was no more swayed by popular sentiment against Indians than he was by the Christian dogma so deeply rooted in the culture. As a representative of Champoeg County in the Provisional Legislature during the Cayuse War, Rector was in no hurry to send troops: "With all the facts before me I was unwilling to hazard a contest with the Indians all for glory. besides all this I was in doubts whether the Indians was so much to blame for what they had don and with all that has com to light since I am still of the same belief but there was not a few of the members but what wanted noteriaty as cournals captains, &c."[2]

Almost a decade and a half later as the Civil War was erupting, Rector stepped into the Oregon superintendency, skeptical, agnostic, only partially literate, yet fully and deservedly confident in his abilities. He wrote of the Paiutes (apparently with clerical help) that "no attempts have ever been made to obtain their friendship or goodwill."[3]

Although Rector claimed to be guided by only the tangible and material, he said of the Paiutes: "I have every reason to believe that amicable relations can be entered into with them, and that they will faithfully observe them." If Rector was correct in this assessment, it was not for "material and tangible" reasons, for he probably never met a Paiute and he was aware of the Paiute attacks on Warm Springs. For some intangible, nonmaterial reason, he nevertheless believed that a friendly relationship could be formed with them.

When word of the deaths of the Otter Bar miners reached Rector, he was in no more a rush to judge the Paiutes than he had been to blame the Cayuse for the deaths at the Whitman mission. That severe winter of 1861–62 had taken many miners. Since Rector's responsibility was limited to Indian matters, the Otter Bar deaths would be outside his jurisdiction if they were caused by weather.

There may have been a hint of these thoughts in Rector's conversation with J. M. Kirkpatrick, who he assigned to investigate the deaths. For in his travels to investigate the disappearance of the miners, Kirkpatrick gave a wide berth to any location that might harbor a Paiute. He then reported to Rector: "I am still of the opinion that the greater part, if not nearly all, of this unfortunate party perished in the snow and cold. I am quite fully satisfied that the Snake Indians had nothing to do in this matter; that the Indians engaged in the matter belong on the Columbia River, and are renegades who have never been removed to any of the reservations."[4]

Based on Kirkpatrick's report, Superintendent Rector concluded that "there were no Snake Indians on this side of the Blue Mountains, and that the lost party had, in all probability, perished from the effect of the severe cold weather which prevailed at that time."[5] Three pages earlier in the same document, Rector pointed out a "serious drawback" of the Warm Springs Reservation, which was about 120 miles due west of the Blue Mountains. The problem with Warm Springs, in Rector's view, was that "its close proximity to the Snake country renders it liable at any moment to be invaded by some roving band of these [Snake] Indians."[6] In Rector's view, then, Warm Springs Indians 120 miles from the Blue Mountain home of the "Snakes" were "liable at any moment" to be invaded, whereas miners only thirty miles from the Blue Mountains could not have been attacked by Snakes because there were "no Snake Indians on this side of the Blue Mountains."

While Kirkpatrick and Rector were investigating the fate of the miners from the standpoint of the Indian superintendency, Captain Currey and the twelve troops of Company E crossed the Columbia to the north shore and continued north in an effort to explain the disappearance of the miners well south of the Columbia. Currey reported that his company "put spurs to the horses," charged into a village of Yakamas "at full speed," "made prisoners of several old consequential looking individuals, and held them hostages."[7] These captives claimed innocence but, apparently sensing an opportunity, were happy to send Currey fifteen miles to the camp of another band of Yakamas, evidently not on good terms with the first. As Currey entered each village along the way, he took a new hostage/guide and released the old. Currey arrived at dusk at the camp of the second band and took the chief hostage. He searched the camp and questioned the people, but found no sign of Yakama involvement. At the end of their five-day sortie Company E rode back to Fort Dalles "wet to the skin, without tents or supper and with saddle blankets for pillows, mattresses, cover and roofing."

Currey thought it odd that he was sent to the Yakamas, about fifty miles north of the Columbia River, to pursue Indians encountered about fifty miles south of that river. In his report he explained that his commanding officer had heard a rumor that members of the Yakamas had crossed to the south side of the Columbia near the John Day River and returned with articles resembling possessions of the Otter Bar party.

Still, it is hard to understand how the commanding officer could have given the rumor any credence.[8] The Yakamas had been at peace with whites for three and a half years, since the end of the Yakama War in September 1858. Paiutes, in contrast, had made at least five attacks on whites and on other Indians since early 1858, including raids on the Warm Springs Reservation and another near the main stem of the John Day River. The ambushes of the Otter Bar party occurred in territory rarely, if ever, visited by the Yakamas.

Currey returned from the Yakama Reservation in the firm belief that the Yakamas were not involved. Although this conclusion left little doubt that Paiutes were responsible, Currey declared that his work was done. "The first scout of the Regiment and Company 'E' was over," he reported.[9]

The predicament faced by the army and the Indian superintendency was that a proper investigation of the eleven deaths would require a foray into Paiute country. With all experienced troops away on Civil War duty, it was not possible to assemble a force capable of such an undertaking. Yet officials did not wish to be seen as idle in the face of such a loss. In misguided efforts to escape this dilemma through guile, the Currey and Kirkpatrick expeditions were concocted.

More significant than the cover-up of the decision not to pursue the Paiutes was the decision itself. Indians who took white lives could expect with near certainty a prompt and firm response, particularly if there were multiple innocent victims. The United States' inaction in the face of so many deaths gave a convincing, if erroneous, appearance of irresolution and weakness. This was not an image that the United States wanted to project at this time, for the need for a treaty with the Paiutes was becoming increasingly apparent. Paiutes had become a force of consequence as a result of the wealth of horses and arms accumulated in their attacks on

Warm Springs. As the attacks strengthened the Paiutes, they also threatened the very foundation of the reservation system. Indians could not be expected to occupy reservations that were magnets for deadly assaults. While a treaty with the Paiutes was perhaps the most obvious way to make Warm Springs safe, there were obstacles to a treaty. The Paiutes had to be convinced to give up nearly all of their land, forever. A key component of the inducement to make such a sacrifice was peaceful relations with the United States. Yet, the totality of Paiute tribal land was a steep price for peace with a nation too meek to respond to the killing of its citizens.

CHAPTER 6

Dark Dawn

Robert Thompson, the Indian agent who joined the Warm Springs chiefs in selecting the site for the Warm Springs community, had arrived in Oregon in 1846 from Ohio. He had been a successful carpenter and mechanic in Ohio, but brought his family to Oregon in the belief that the wealthiest members of a community tend to be those who were there from the beginning, when the community was in its earliest, formative stages. He would find such a place in Oregon, he believed.[1]

As an Indian agent in 1855, Thompson had witnessed the frenzy that followed the discovery of gold in northeast Washington Territory. "The influx of immigration is such," he wrote in August of that year, "that it can be but a few years when this hitherto comparatively unknown region will be teeming with a dense population."[2] It was not lost on him that the Columbia River provided the most direct waterway for that projected population and for the freight needed to sustain it.

With the help of a steamboat pilot, John Ainsworth, Thompson calculated expected freight, ridership, capital expenses, payroll, and other costs and earnings. The projected profits, Thompson found, were irresistible. "It is an undertaking that requires some little nerve," he said later, "but I had made up my mind to run a steamer on that section of the river."[3] Once the steamer was completed Thompson put a novice at the helm who impaled it on a rock before its engine had ever turned the paddlewheel. Thompson ran his calculations again, reached the same conclusion, and promptly built a second vessel, the *Colonel Wright*. Once it proved its worth by steaming from the mouth of the Deschutes River to Wallula and back, Thompson started building his next, the *Tenino*.

In August 1861 a tree downed by wind in the Clearwater Mountains over-looking the Salmon River in Idaho caught the eye of a prospector named John Healy. Gravel in the root system looked promising. Healy filled his pan with the gravel embedded in the roots and swirled out the rocks and dirt, revealing a rich glow that no miner could mistake. He and his companions tested more samples, with similar results. They set out for Elk City to buy supplies and share the news with the other fourteen in their group. Their pact to keep the discovery to themselves was short-lived.[4]

For most, the route to the place of Healy's discovery, which came to be known as Florence, was up the Columbia River. Before Thompson launched the *Colonel Wright* in April 1859, all upstream steamboat travel from Portland stopped at 115 miles, the foot of Celilo Falls—only about one-fifth of the way to Florence. By the time of the Florence discovery there were two Thompson-built steamboats on the upper river, the *Colonel Wright* and the *Tenino*; a third, the *Okanogan*, was built by the Oregon Steam Navigation Company, which Thompson had by then joined. Thompson's steamboats had converted the journey to Salmon River country from mountains, sweat, and mule dung, to deck chairs, brandy, and cigars. These vessels allowed miners and their suppliers to travel 114 more miles to Wallula in low water; in higher water (which came quickly in the heavy rains of the fall of 1861) they could travel all the way to Lewiston, only about eighty miles from Florence on a direct line.[5]

News of the gold strikes on the Salmon River reached Portland that fall. The November 9, 1861, *Oregon Argus* forecast a "great rush in the direction of Salmon River in the coming season from twenty to fifty thousand people." The excitement intensified in response to reports of claims that yielded thirty to eighty dollars per pan; of another that generated $1,800 in three hours with two men and a rocker; of a single dip of a single pan that produced $1,500; of a dig with three rockers, each producing $1,000 per day. All manner of vessels, including yeast powder boxes, oyster cans, and pickle bottles, were in demand as receptacles for gold. The *Oregonian* told its readers: "Neither California [n]or Caribou [British Columbia] ever presented such gold prospects as are now found on Salmon River." The *Portland Times* interviewed miners who "pronounce the [Salmon River] mines to be the richest ever discovered." The earnings of a lifetime, it seemed, could be had in days.[6]

Paiutes had their eastern Oregon territory largely to themselves until the gold rush to the Florence and other Salmon River mines in the spring of 1862. Aided by Thompson's steamboats, thousands of miners fanned out over every ravine of every drainage, every bar of every river, every moraine of every glacier. Few were poor.[7] They purchased mining equipment, clothing, provisions, camping gear, horses, saddles, and more at Portland, The Dalles, Wallula, and Lewiston. According to one observer, the business done at those four towns "was entirely out of proportion to their populations and fabulously remunerative."[8] Properly capitalized and equipped, the miners knew how to coax the treasure from the land. Pacific Northwest gold production jumped from $1.75 million to $9 million between 1861 and 1862.[9] Forecasts that in spring 1862 miners would inundate the Northwest, intended more to promote than predict, succeeded in both.

The Oregon Steam Navigation Company (OSNC) had the delightfully vexing challenge of more customers placing more orders for more shipments of more freight and more passengers than it could possibly provide. On a single trip in April 1862 a steamship from San Francisco landed one thousand passengers in Portland—about a quarter of the city's population. Drays delivering goods to docks in Portland for shipping upriver had to wait nearly twenty-four hours just to unload. The portage roads at the Cascades and Celilo were lined with freight waiting to be transported. That year the OSNC enjoyed a "prosperity beyond all precedent."[10] The gold rush was "the largest business boom ever to strike the Oregon country."[11] Steamboats could not keep up with demand.[12] Until the rush to the Klondike in 1897, the "rush to Idaho, as chronicled in 1861–64, exceeded in eagerness and volume any mining rush in the Pacific Northwest."[13]

Two years later the rush was still a force. In February 1864 the OSNC had eight steamboats on the upper river. In early March a thousand miners arrived in The Dalles in the space of two days. On Court Street a "hurdy-gurdy" establishment opened where miners purchased tickets for a few minutes twirling with a young damsel to the bagpipe-like music of a hurdy-gurdy.[14] Hotels turned away scores of customers nightly. OSNC launched the *Oneanta*, a luxurious new vessel with velvet carpets, marble washstands, gilt mirrors, baths, a barber shop, and saloons with "retiring rooms."

According to Bancroft, 1862 brought ten thousand immigrants to Oregon, mostly to Paiute country. This influx pushed the Paiutes off the lands where they had hunted, fished, and gathered seeds and roots. Pasture was scarce, and in the main river valleys "the settlers were slowly taking over grasslands which the Indians needed, not only for their own subsistence but to feed their growing stock of horses." The result was a state of hostility beginning in about 1862, growing with each year, and evolving into the Snake War.[15]

Before this gold rush the Oregon Country had been, in large measure, a collection of isolated, self-sufficient homes, ranches, and farms. In the space of a few years the rush stimulated stagecoach services, roads, bridges, river transport, improved mail service, markets, trade, and newspapers. Connections within and between communities and with other regions of the nation blossomed. For immigrants this rush was in many respects the dawn of Oregon and the Northwest. For Paiutes, it was a different dawn—the dawn of a new, dark era.

CHAPTER 7

A Messenger to My Heart

Robert Thompson's steamboats were in place on the upper Columbia just in time to meet the explosive demand touched off by the Salmon River gold strikes. The speed and capacity of the steamboats allowed the OSNC to pump miners and their supplies into the land of the Paiutes at an unprecedented rate. In response Paiutes launched a guerilla campaign led by Paulina, Weyouwewa, Howluck, and other chiefs. To suppress the Paiutes Oregon deployed two companies of volunteers, one of which was led by Captain John Drake. On April 20, 1864, Drake embarked from The Dalles with 160 men and their mounts, eight six-mule teams, and ninety-five pack mules.

After Lieutenant Watson and sixteen soldiers from B Company joined Drake's command, he moved south for three weeks with no sign of the enemy until he reached the Crooked River on May 17. Warm Springs Indian scouts under their chief, Stock Whitley, accompanied by Donald McKay, discovered a Paiute camp. McKay, son of a fur trader and a Cayuse woman, was a translator for the U.S. Army and Indian Affairs as well as a soldier. He told Drake that a force of sixty would be needed to attack the Paiutes. At dusk Drake ordered McCall, Watson, and Whitley to mount a surprise attack on the Paiute camp at dawn. Drake chose to remain at base camp. He had no particular need for men at base camp, but sent only forty to attack the Paiutes, not the sixty that McKay recommended.

The following morning McCall led the platoon to a point just west of the Paiute camp of nine lodges. Huddled with Watson and Whitley, McCall whispered his plan. Watson would lead his troops up the center, with McCall on his right and Whitley and his Indian scouts on his left.

The huddle broke. Each of the three joined his men and led the stealthy advance toward the Paiute camp. The light of a nearly full moon, however, forced them to keep more distance from the sleeping Paiutes than was comfortable. McCall paused to capture Paiute horses and was slowed further by soggy ground. Watson and Whitley advanced deliberately, cautiously, attempting to maintain silence. Then a canteen or a rifle struck a boulder. A few of the sleeping Paiutes stirred. Suddenly all the Paiutes were on their feet, guns and bows in hand, fleeing upward into a jumble of rocks.

John Drake had come west at age nineteen, looking for gold in California. After three years in the mines he switched to farming, but abandoned that too after three years and moved north to Oregon in 1856. In 1861 he enlisted for three years in the Oregon Volunteer Cavalry. He was accepted as an officer, probably because of his education at Stroudsberg Academy in Pennsylvania.

Like Drake, Watson came to California for gold, then tried farming. He must have been an engaging and adventurous sort because, although his farm was in heavily Democratic southern Oregon, he won a seat in the Provisional Legislature as a Republican. When the Civil War led to a call for volunteers, he abandoned farming and politics for fighting. By 1864 he had a command of sixteen troops from Company B, nine of whom were with him in the early morning hours of May 18, watching Paiutes vanish into a field of boulders.

Watson responded at once to the Paiutes' retreat. Unlike Drake and McCall, he led from the front. He ascended a slope to the left of the boulder field in a flanking action, designed to catch the enemy immobilized among boulders. Bullets and arrows rained out of the eastern sky, bright from the impending sunrise. Watson's men fired back wildly. As Watson topped the boulder field, he rushed the enemy's flank, yelling, "Pour it into them, boys!"—his last words. The apparent boulder field was an elaborate fort. It was not the Paiutes' flank. Paulina and his men were shielded behind stone walls awaiting Watson, who was greeted with the muzzle of a gun at point-blank range. Watson and two of his men were killed. Five were wounded.

Stock Whitley and his scouts had a similar reception as they mounted a futile assault on the rock wall. Paiutes disemboweled one of the Indian scouts. Whitley, "though almost shot to pieces, walked off to where he could receive assistance, like an old *grizzly*."[1] Thus ended the soldiers' first encounter with Paulina.[2]

As McCall watched his plan come to grief, he decided to send for reinforcements and rescue the wounded rather than join the battle. If he expected reinforcements to turn the tide of the contest, he was disappointed. Drake did not arrive for three hours. He had left base camp that morning "pursuing the march as usual," as if dispatching forty men to attack an unknown number of Paiutes on their home ground was routine. He claimed to be puzzled by the sight of two men approaching from the direction of the battle at full gallop until he noticed the "sheen of their gun barrels, carried on their shoulder, [giving] them the appearance of soldiers." After hearing the grim report and collecting reinforcements, Drake rode hard. The healthy distance that he had maintained between his camp and the battle assured that by the time he arrived Paulina and his band had vanished into the sagebrush and arroyos that had concealed Paiutes for generations. Stock Whitley soon died of his wounds. Paiutes hovered about the fringes of Drake's camp for long after this battle, harassing, stealing, insouciant in the face of the white man's military might.[3]

For two years the volunteer cavalry gave chase to the Paiutes, "with about the same success that the house-dog pursues the limber and burrowing fox."[4] For centuries Paiutes had found ways to survive and even flourish among militarily superior enemies. Familiarity with every thicket, cave, and canyon empowered them to scatter like quail and disappear at will. Accustomed to eluding Columbia River Indians in territory familiar to them, Paiutes found that these soldiers, who knew the land not at all, were easily duped and shaken. Oregon Paiutes got the better of the conflict in which Watson died and were never drawn into any other fighting on that scale during the remainder of the Civil War years.

The warfare between volunteers and Paiutes did not go unnoticed by the new Oregon superintendent of Indian affairs, John Webster Perit Huntington, who succeeded William H. Rector in 1863. Thirteen years earlier Huntington and fellow investors from the East Coast had purchased a ship, loaded it with mining supplies, and, on their arrival in California, sold all at inflated gold rush prices. Huntington then settled in Yoncalla, a small community in southwest Oregon, home of the three Applegate brothers, Jesse, Charles, and Lindsay, who arrived in the Oregon Country in 1843. Jesse played a lead role in forming the Provisional Government of the Oregon Country in 1845. Huntington married Mary Applegate, daughter of Charles. The Applegate connection, his legal training, and his service as a state legislator helped persuade Lincoln to appoint Huntington to the superintendent position.[5]

When he took office in April 1863, Huntington made the Paiute situation an early priority. In his first annual report he urged that it was "of the utmost importance that treaties be made with these bands," and recommended that twenty thousand dollars be appropriated for this purpose.[6] Congress obliged, appropriating the exact sum that he requested. Huntington invited Modocs, Klamaths, Yahooskins, and Paulina's Walpapi band of Paiutes to a treaty council in early October 1864 at Fort Klamath in southern Oregon, east of the Cascade Mountains. Huntington sought treaties of cession—that is, treaties under which Indians gave up land in return for specified benefits provided to them on a reservation.

One advantage that a treaty would have brought to Paiutes was an end to the fighting with the United States. Before 1866, however, Paiutes had little respect for U.S. soldiers. "Snake" Indians told Robert Thompson that the United States had threatened that if they continued their depredations "an army would come and destroy them"; that no army had come; that the Americans were afraid to fight them; and that "if we wish to fight them, to come on." Gifts to Paiutes "only tend to impress . . . [them] with a belief in their superior power and our cowardice," according to another Indian agent. Shoshones, another Numic-speaking tribe, told Major Granville Haller that whites had threatened them with chastisement and war. Haller continued, "But they ask why has it not come? Are not the Americans afraid? Our inactivity has been constructed to fear."[7] Bannocks, who were Northern Paiute, attacked a Mormon mission at Fort Lemhi, Idaho, killing three and wounding five. A historian of the Bannocks observed: "The fact that almost no effort was made on the part of the Mormons or of the United States troops to punish the Bannock emboldened all the other tribes." Indians began stealing and threatening Mormons, saying "the Mormons are squaws, they won't fight."[8]

The halfhearted military response to the Paiutes' repeated raids on Warm Springs from 1859–62 did nothing to change this perception of American impotence. But allowing the killing of eleven Otter Bar miners to pass with no perceptible response may have done more than any other single event to convince Northwest Paiutes that the United States feared them. The failure to respond to the Paiutes' killing of these miners appeared all the more remarkable in comparison to the vigorous U.S. responses to attacks by the Cayuse (Whitman massacre), Coquilles, Shoshone (Ward massacre), Yakama (Cascades massacre), and Rogues (Rogue war).[9]

Warriors are practiced at judging the strength of their adversaries. Decisions whether to fight, when to fight, when to retreat, and when to make peace all begin with an assessment of the strength of the other side. If the Paiutes had killed eleven Tenino or Cayuse, retaliation would have been certain. Indians generally considered whites to be another tribe.[10] A tribe that did not respond at all was a weak tribe that presented no threat. There was no reason to make a treaty with such a tribe.

Paiutes were probably aware in a general sense that the United States claimed that its primary fighting forces were unavailable because they were engaged in a conflict elsewhere. To the Paiutes the possibility that the United States had a powerful army that could overwhelm them but that was temporarily detained in some mysterious, distant place was unprovable and suspicious. The United States' failure to respond to the Paiutes' attacks on the Otter Bar miners, on the other hand, was a certainty and a reliable sign of a weak and irresolute opponent. A treaty with such an opponent provided little apparent benefit and exacted a steep price—land and freedom.

At the time that Huntington invited Paulina to a treaty council in 1864, Paulina had five years or more of success in evading and occasionally battling volunteers. His experience against volunteers had very likely convinced him that these soldiers were more of a nuisance than a threat.

Indians throughout Oregon, on both sides of the Cascade Mountains, were aware that the United States had refused to ratify any of the nineteen treaties negotiated during Anson Dart's administration. As Dart's successor, Joel Palmer, put it, the nineteen stillborn treaties did "much to destroy their [Indians'] confidence in the good intentions of the Government. . . . This want of confidence in the declarations of government agents is not confined to those tribes with whom treaties have been negotiated; it extends throughout the entire country."[11] Equally well known was the United

States' four-year delay in ratifying the 1855 treaties. Signing a treaty may have appeared to Paiutes, and other tribes as well, as an immense concession by Indians that left the United States free to do whatever it pleased, whenever it pleased.

Paulina declined Huntington's invitation. The three other tribes, Yah-ooskin, Klamath, and Modoc, accepted and made a treaty with Huntington on October 15, 1864.[12] Huntington and his entourage of Warm Springs Indians then started back to The Dalles, believing that treaty-making was done.

Just over two weeks later, on November 1, 1864, Shytiattitk, a Yah-ooskin, and Klamath chief LaLakes, met with Captain William Kelley at Fort Klamath in south-central Oregon. Shytiattitk conveyed to Kelley a message from Paulina about Huntington's return to The Dalles with his Warm Springs scouts. Riding behind Huntington, the Warm Springs Indians came upon Paiutes and captured four women, a boy, and, later, five men. The Warm Springs killed four of the men. The fifth got away and reported the event to Paulina. Paulina sent Shytiattitk to convey his offer to kill no more whites, provided that Huntington return the women and children held by the Warm Springs.[13] Shytiattitk did not reveal, although Kelley may have guessed, that one of the captured women was Paulina's wife or that the boy was his son.

At Fort Klamath on November 10, 1864, a solitary rider emerged from a forest of lodgepole and ponderosa pine into an expansive meadow, leached of its greens by winter's first frosts. Soon Captain Kelley and a translator were sitting with Chief Paulina, in a tattered military overcoat, appearing "very sullen, his brows knit heavily." He told Kelley that he was tired of fighting, that he wanted the women and children taken by the Warm Springs, and that he would live peacefully. They agreed that the terms of a peace would be settled the following summer. Paulina rode out of Fort Klamath looking cheered by the prospect of regaining his wife and child and by Kelley's gift of rice and sugar.[14]

Impromptu and casual as it was, the November 10, 1864, meeting between Kelley and Paulina was nevertheless epochal. Despite Superintendent Rector's 1861 statement that "amicable relations can be entered into with them [Paiutes], and that they will faithfully observe them,"[15] the only exchanges between the two peoples for the next three years had been bullets and arrows. Paulina's disconsolate, unannounced appearance at Fort Klamath that November, therefore, was the first occasion on which an Oregon Paiute chief and a military officer discussed peace.[16] The long silence between the two peoples was ended, not by victory or defeat in battle, not by the gaining of military advantage, not by political upheaval, but simply by a father's bonds with his wife and son.

Paulina and forty members of his Walpapi band rode into the fortress of his enemy a second time on August 10, 1865, four months after Lee's surrender at Appomattox. Paulina's wife and son were awaiting him. Lieutenant John McCall, who had been so ignominiously whipped by Paulina in the skirmish in which Watson died, wrote a mostly literate description of the scene: "They are a miserable lot of looking rascals. Apparently capable of committing almost any fiendish act. There wardrobe is in a seedy condition, giving evident token that they have either been very unsuccessful in their recent plundering excursions or else they have a cache in the mountains."[17]

Two days later Paulina met with Superintendent Huntington. Donald McKay and his half-brother William, physician at Warm Springs, translated from English to Chinook.[18] A Klamath translated the Chinook to Numic. Huntington described Paulina as "a man of very powerful physique," "stern determination," and "very powerful intellect." Paulina and his band sat on flour sacks in two semicircles, as unarmed soldiers and Warm Springs and Klamath Indians stood in the background. Among the observers was an officer stationed at Camp Klamath, William V. Rinehart, who, starting eleven years later, would play a central role in the climax of the Paiute chronicle.[19]

Huntington explained the benefits that would be provided under the treaty, including $4,000 in seeds and tools, rations until they were able to raise crops, and noncash annuities for fifteen years. When Huntington finished, Paulina spoke. "I have nothing bad to say," Paulina began. After agreeing to the treaty terms, he added: "Your sending back my little son went

FIG. 2. (*opposite*) Paiute chief Paulina, at Camp Klamath in August 1865 to make treaty. Courtesy of Oregon Historical Society, neg. # OrHi 85543-A /0363P040.

like a messenger to my heart, and what evil I intended to have said, the sight of him killed it all." Paulina promised as well to send a messenger to Paiute Chiefs Howluck and Weyouwewa, "telling them how good you have treated me . . . and on hearing from me they will come right in and make peace."[20]

Since Paulina did not need to make this prediction to stay in Huntington's favor, it had the ring of candor. McCall thought that Paulina "was apparently sincere in his professions and may possibly stick to what he has said and agreed to."[21] Huntington was more optimistic. In his nearly breathless report to the commissioner in Washington, he wrote that Paulina's band "will be the means of bringing all the others [i.e., other Paiute chiefs] in." Huntington therefore "confidently expect[ed]" to make similar treaties with all Northwest Paiute chiefs. He attached a long list of Paiute depredations and calculated that his two treaties placing Indians on the Klamath Reservation (this Paiute treaty and his 1864 treaty) did "include a greater number of Indians, cede a larger extent of territory, and anticipate smaller expenditure than any other treaties ever negotiated in this region."[22]

Huntington had good cause for his barely stifled exuberance. When he concluded the treaty in October a year earlier, there had appeared no hope of a treaty with Paiutes. Now he had a treaty with the Walpapi, and the fiercest of Paiute chiefs had confidently declared that the other Northwest chiefs would join in a global treaty. If Paulina's word and his forecast were good, a seemingly endless war would end, and Indians who were among the last holdouts would move to a reservation.

Huntington's breakthrough came at a critical moment, four months after the end of the Civil War, as the Union army was in the early stages of shifting its focus from fighting the South to fighting Indians. If Paulina succeeded in convincing Weyouwewa and other chiefs to sign a treaty that fall, he would deliver peace to his people just in time to avoid confrontation with bluecoats of a caliber that Paiutes had not yet seen.

In the months that followed the treaty Paulina appeared to be committed to peace. When the Klamath agent, Lindsay Applegate—Huntington's wife's uncle—asked him to keep his people on the reservation, Paulina agreed. He also acted as an intermediary in Applegate's effort to make peace with Paiute chief Howluck, albeit unsuccessfully.

In December 1865 Applegate issued subsistence to the Walpapi Paiutes sufficient to last until spring.[23] But in April 1866, when cottonwoods lining the rivers of the Klamath region were veiled in the ephemeral green of leaves just uncurling from the bud, Paulina and his people were gone. Paulina never returned.

Huntington's confident predictions in his 1865 annual report were awkward for him when it came time to explain in his 1866 annual report that no other chiefs had made a treaty, that Paulina and his band had abandoned the Klamath Reservation, and that the "Snake War" persisted. The Indians who he "confidently expect[ed]" to sign treaties, had become instead Indians "always having their hand against every man, and every man's hand against them. . . . *Now*, nothing is to be done but fight and exterminate them." To attempt to make a treaty with them "is simply folly."[24]

Huntington's reference to extermination was out of character; in any case, nothing of the sort occurred at the Klamath Agency. Applegate was one of those rare Indian agents who, like William Rector, believed in the Paiutes. He continued to manage the Walpapi Paiute situation with patience and restraint for the next three years. After the Walpapi left the reservation in April 1866, a number were captured and returned. By October 1866, sixty were in custody at the Klamath Agency, but all escaped en masse. A year later nineteen were captured. Applegate did not punish them for violating the treaty or for escaping. He did not make them examples so that other Indians would be frightened into obedience. Instead he took them to a location in the eastern portion of the reservation that later became known as the Yainax Station. There he broke ground for farming and began building two log houses. More Paiutes began to settle at Yainax, including a group of nearly one hundred that arrived in December 1868. Yainax became the permanent location for Walpapi Paiutes and Yahooskin Paiutes (who were parties to the 1864 treaty made at the Klamath Agency).[25]

In April 1867, a year after Paulina left the Klamath Reservation, he and others were making off with cattle from a ranch on the John Day River as a stagecoach happened by, driven by Jim Clark. Clark had not been a stagecoach driver for long. Until September 1866 he had been a rancher on

Bridge Creek, near its outlet into the John Day River. He and his brother-in-law, George Masterson, had been gathering firewood that September in preparation for winter. When they looked back at the ranch and saw it in flames, surrounded by Indians, they mounted their horses and fled. Clark kept a pace just out of gunshot range of the pursuing Indians, but Masterson pushed his horse too hard. When it slowed Masterson jumped into the John Day River and hid under water, breathing through a reed. Both escaped.

Seven months later Jim Clark took a lively interest in the Indians he saw from his stagecoach. He turned the coach around and raced eight miles to the home of Howard Maupin. Maupin was soon in the saddle, a new Henry repeating rifle in the scabbard, and fifteen rounds in the magazine. Maupin led Clark and Ragan, a passenger on the coach, in pursuit of the Indians, but not on their trail. They would leave a man to ambush anyone following, Maupin said. He set out on a different route to a ridge overlooking a basin where he expected the Indians to camp. Clark was the first to the ridgetop. He saw an Indian, fired, and missed. Immediately seven Indians were on a dead run for an opening leading out of the basin. Maupin then reached the top, dismounted, and fired. An Indian dropped. He fired again. A second Indian dropped but regained his feet and resumed his flight. Maupin fired several more shots without effect.

When only the cattle and the body remained in the basin, the three whites approached. Maupin unsheathed his knife and looked down on the chief. Some might say that Paulina resisted until the end because he was too inflexible to adapt to the new reality brought by the whites. Others might say that he resisted to the end because he could foresee, with a clarity that few others enjoyed, that a treaty would only whet the white appetite for Native lands, that white crimes on Natives would never be punished, and that Indian youths would struggle to avoid stagnation on reservations. Apparently untroubled by such thoughts, Maupin stabilized his grasp on Paulina's head, still warm to the touch, drew the blade along the hair line, lifted the skin, and peeled away his prize.[26]

Written references to Paulina begin with his capture at Warm Springs in 1859. By then settlers and miners had infringed on Paiute lands to the point that their ability to sustain themselves on their traditional food sources was threatened. Forced to find nourishment to make up for losses caused by settlers, Paiutes had every reason to take settlers' cattle as compensation for the destruction of grasses and other plants essential to the Paiutes. Paulina had the same permission to take the settlers' cattle as they had to take Paiutes' lands.

Settlers reacted with rage to the taking of their stock and the killings of those who invaded Paiute lands, denouncing Paulina as "a blood-thirsty savage [guilty of] crimes, . . . killings and robberies," "cunning and unscrupulous," and a "cutthroat."[27] Yet, as between Natives and the settlers who appropriated their land, most would consider the settlers to be the wrongdoers. But since settlers had exclusive control of the press during these events, those who lost their land, rather than those who took it, were portrayed as bloodthirsty criminals and cutthroats. A few contemporary observers, however, saw past racial differences to the heart of the matter. Among them was Courtney M. Walker, a member of Jason Lee's missionary party of 1834 and later in charge of Fort Hall in eastern Idaho. Walker saw unarmed strangers walk alone through Paiute lands and encounter only kindness and generosity. Another, Major General H. W. Halleck, saw that the rapid advance of white settlements had limited the sources of food, reducing Paiutes "to the verge of starvation," leaving them "scarcely any other alternative than to rob or starve."[28] The choice was not difficult for Paulina.

CHAPTER 8

The Snake War

From the early 1860s Paiutes and Shoshones had resisted the miners, ranchers, and settlers overrunning their lands, and soldiers had pursued the Indians to little effect. These intermittent hostilities, which came to be known as the Snake War, ranged across northern California, northern Nevada, southern Idaho, and eastern Oregon. Paiute chiefs swept up in the fighting included Weyouwewa, Paulina, Oits, Ponee, Winnemucca, and, from the Weiser River in Idaho, Chiefs Shenkah and his brother-in-law Egan, the Cayuse orphan raised by Weisers.

Paiutes saw no need to make peace with an opponent so easily eluded. However, dark clouds were forming on the Paiutes' horizon. In the last year of the Civil War, when Oregon's volunteer cavalry was the principal military presence in eastern Oregon, roughly a dozen Paiutes were killed. The following year, as Civil War regulars began replacing volunteers in eastern Oregon, about 186 Paiutes were killed, a fifteenfold increase from the prior year.[1]

The "Snake War" became an issue in the 1866 Oregon gubernatorial race, which George Woods won by just over two hundred votes. He had arrived in Oregon as a teenager, with his parents. Later he married a doctor's daughter, took a land claim, cleared, plowed, and planted, but did not take to farming. He sold the land and worked as a carpenter as he studied law, which turned out to be his calling and eventually led to his governorship.

Learning more about Indians or the causes of the Snake conflict, however, was not Woods's way. "The only [way that] lasting peace . . . can be procured with hostile Indians," he declared, is to "whip them into submission."[2] He met with a joint session of the Oregon legislature and came away with authority to raise a volunteer force if the federal government did not send troops in sufficient numbers within thirty days. Armed with this ultimatum, Woods met with General Frederick Steele, commander of the Department of the Columbia, who granted Woods's request and began recruiting for the Eighth Regiment of the United States.

Emboldened by this success, the governor went a step further. Under an 1866 federal law, one hundred Indian scouts were allotted to the Department of the Pacific (Oregon, Washington, and Idaho). Woods applied to General Steele under this law to form two fifty-man companies of Indians under commanders to be appointed by Woods. While Indians had often been used as scouts for regular troops, Woods asked that the two new companies be independent fighting units.

Now the governor had crossed the line into the military's bailiwick, Steele concluded, and denied the application. Woods appealed to the division commander, Major General H. W. Halleck, who curtly rejected it. Woods appealed again, this time to U.S. secretary of war Edwin Stanton, who overruled his two generals and granted the upstart governor's requests, authorizing him to appoint commanders for the two companies. Soon the two new commands were in the field tracking Paiutes.[3]

Woods's audacity had served him well so far, but whether there was any judgment to keep it in check was cast in doubt by his next move, which is best seen in light of an event that had occurred nine years earlier, in 1857. Woods had been with a party of six, led by his father-in-law, James McBride, on their way to the Malheur River in southeast Oregon to search for gold. They were deep in the wilderness on the eastern slope of the Cascade Mountains, the sun was low, and they were looking for a place to camp. Cresting a rise, they came upon a sight that surely stayed with each man for the rest of his days. As McBride later described it, "we became suddenly conscious of the observation of about one hundred pairs of savage eyes, directed toward us." All were in war paint, gesticulating, brandishing weapons, obviously excited by the easy prey that had just fallen into their hands.

After a brief consultation, the miners rode forward, dismounted, and began to set up camp. The Paiute headman—probably Chief Ochoho—gestured that he wanted to meet with McBride.[4] In their private conference,

McBride later reported that he explained to the chief that he and his companions were "children of the great father of the Bostons, who are traveling through your country to see its beauties and its excellence" and that they came in peace but were brave and not afraid to die. Impressed, the chief returned to his camp and quieted his men. The miners slept little and left before dawn. To avoid any more such encounters, they forged a new route over the Cascade Mountains and returned to the Willamette Valley.[5]

Nine years later as governor of Oregon, Woods had a range of choices on how this conflict would be managed. The fate of members of the tribe that had spared his life on that summer evening hung in the balance. He did not equivocate. He directed that the two lieutenants he had placed in charge of the Warm Springs scouts be ordered "to impress upon the scouts the necessity of exterminating their old enemies [that is, the Paiutes] as the only means of securing their peace and safety."[6] Men were to be killed because they were warriors, boys because they would become warriors, and women and girls because they would deliver more.

The mercy that Ochoho had shown was not extraordinary; it was a simple act of decency. Woods's order, superficially intended to rid the land of savagery, instead made it official.[7]

Commissioner of Indian Affairs Perit Huntington reported on the consequences of Woods's extermination order. On a small fork of the Crooked River in central Oregon, the two Indian companies surprised a camp of Paiutes, killed seven men, and took fourteen women and children prisoner. The officers then directed the Indian scouts to kill the prisoners. They objected, but "finally, reluctantly, killed and scalped all the women and children, they offering no resistance."[8] Although Huntington's report overstates the number of women and children killed, there is little question that Woods's extermination order led to the slaying of Paiute women and children.[9]

Woods's rhetoric and his extermination order were not inconsistent with mainstream views at the time. It was not unusual for community leaders to advocate and applaud the death of Indians. In 1858 the Democratic *Oregon Statesman* editorialized that treaties and the idea that Indians have title to land "are downright, unmitigated humbugs." The effect of treaties, the paper warned, "is to raise the downgraded and bestial savages, at least

FIG. 3. Paiute women, by Thomas Woodliff, courtesy of Mathewson-IGT Knowledge Center, SCUA and Bilbao Basque Library, University of Nevada, Reno.

in their own estimation, to a political equality with the whites." Although the U.S. government should extend care to the Indians, as a people they are "in the very nature of things . . . compelled to give way to the 'manifest destiny' of a superior race."[10] "Manifest destiny" began as an expression of belief that the United States would, on the strength of its superior form of government and its rapid, prosperous growth, subsume much of the remainder of the continent. By the time of the *Statesman* article, the manifest destiny of the nation had subtly, insidiously metamorphosed into the manifest destiny of the country's dominant race. Indeed, seventy years later an article in the *Oregon Historical Quarterly* described the "destruction of the Indians of the Pacific Northwest" as a "source of thanksgiving" that "spared the pioneer settlers the horrors of a strong and malignant foe."[11]

Late in 1855, as a result of the Rogue River War in southwest Oregon, superintendent of Indian Affairs Palmer made plans to relocate the Rogue Indians to a reservation in the Willamette Valley. A memorial to Congress was introduced in the territorial legislature opposing the reservation and censuring Palmer as "foolish and visionary." In the debate over the memorial, Representative Brown of Multnomah County proclaimed: "The Indians here have always been barbarous . . . and the only argument that is worth anything with an Indian here is powder and ball." The Indians have "the manifest destiny of the Anglo-Saxon race to conquer . . . Civilized man has taken a stand, and the savage must retreat before him. . . . The red man must be pushed back—because he must be killed." Linn County representative Smith urged: "The whole history of settlements upon this continent proved that the destiny of the Indian race, was to fade out of existence before the advance of the Caucasian, or Anglo Saxon race—that sooner or later religion and civilization shall possess the earth, as the waters do the deep."[12] The memorial was approved. Palmer was removed from office a year later.

These Oregon legislators were not out of step with the rest of the nation. Indeed they were parroting beliefs that by midcentury were gaining wide acceptance, sweeping aside the understandings that had held sway since the earliest days of the republic. In 1785 Thomas Jefferson wrote: "I believe the Indian then to be in body and mind equal to the whiteman."[13] The reason that whites were more advanced than Indians, Jefferson believed, was that Europe "was swarming with numbers; because numbers produce emulation, and multiply the chances of improvement, and one improvement begets another."[14] Once Indians were exposed to whites, they would achieve the same level of civilization, and, "our settlements and theirs [will] meet and blend together, to intermix, and become one people."[15]

Jefferson's views were widely accepted, but by the time of the Snake War a distinct shift had occurred. Concepts of Indians as a different and inferior race, as a race that was bound to fade from existence before the favored, "most perfect," Anglo-Saxon race, had moved from the fringe to the mainstream and gained acceptance in respected journals and among community leaders.[16] An early figure in this racial "science" was a Viennese physician at the beginning of the nineteenth century. Dr. Franz Joseph Gall first suspected that a person's character might be revealed in the shape of his head when he came to believe that those with good memories had large foreheads. He began investigating other personal qualities by hiring subjects who were acquainted with one another. To determine whether a person was quarrelsome or peaceable, for example, he interviewed each subject about the quarrelsomeness of the others and assigned a rank to each, from the most quarrelsome to the most peaceable. He then took measurements of different regions of their heads, looking for a region that produced measurements that, in rank order, corresponded to the ranking on the peaceable-quarrelsome scale. In this way he believed he had identified the part of the skull that reflected the sector of the brain that controlled quarrelsomeness. Using this method he identified twenty-seven traits and the corresponding region of the head for each, including "amativeness" (sexuality), "philoprogenitiveness" (parental love), and "adhesiveness" (love of friends). As the twenty-six letters of the alphabet combine in thousands of permutations to create a vocabulary as capacious and flexible as the mind itself, so the twenty-seven traits or faculties measured by phrenology were believed to be capable of producing every variation of the human character. Because each faculty was reflected in the shape and size of the skull, all the information needed to unearth the character within was available without. By feeling or "reading" the skull of a living person, properly trained phrenologists, it was believed, could divine the ingredients of her character.[17]

J. G. Spurzheim, a student of Gall's who probably originated the term *phrenology*, lectured and published on the so-called new science throughout Europe. During a similar tour in America he died unexpectedly, but not before his lecture at the Athenaeum in Boston, attended by an Amherst student, Orson Fowler. Spurzheim's talk ignited a passion in Fowler, whose brother Lorenzo followed him through Amherst and joined him in the phrenology business. The brothers gave free lectures but charged for "reading" heads. The lectures regularly drew skeptics who, for example, demanded that each Fowler read the same head in his brother's absence, then compared the two readings. Another tactic was to attempt to mislead the Fowlers by bringing for head-reading clergymen and physicians disguised in wildly colored clothing and spouting off-color invective.[18]

The Fowlers were able to muddle through these challenges and by 1842 had moved their business to New York City, where they opened the Phrenological Cabinet, a display of skulls, casts, and charts. Their sister Charlotte and other relatives joined them and helped form a publishing company for hundreds of phrenological tracts to spread and lend authenticity to the doctrines that fueled their growing prosperity.[19]

Others had embraced the same ideas. An English physician, Charles

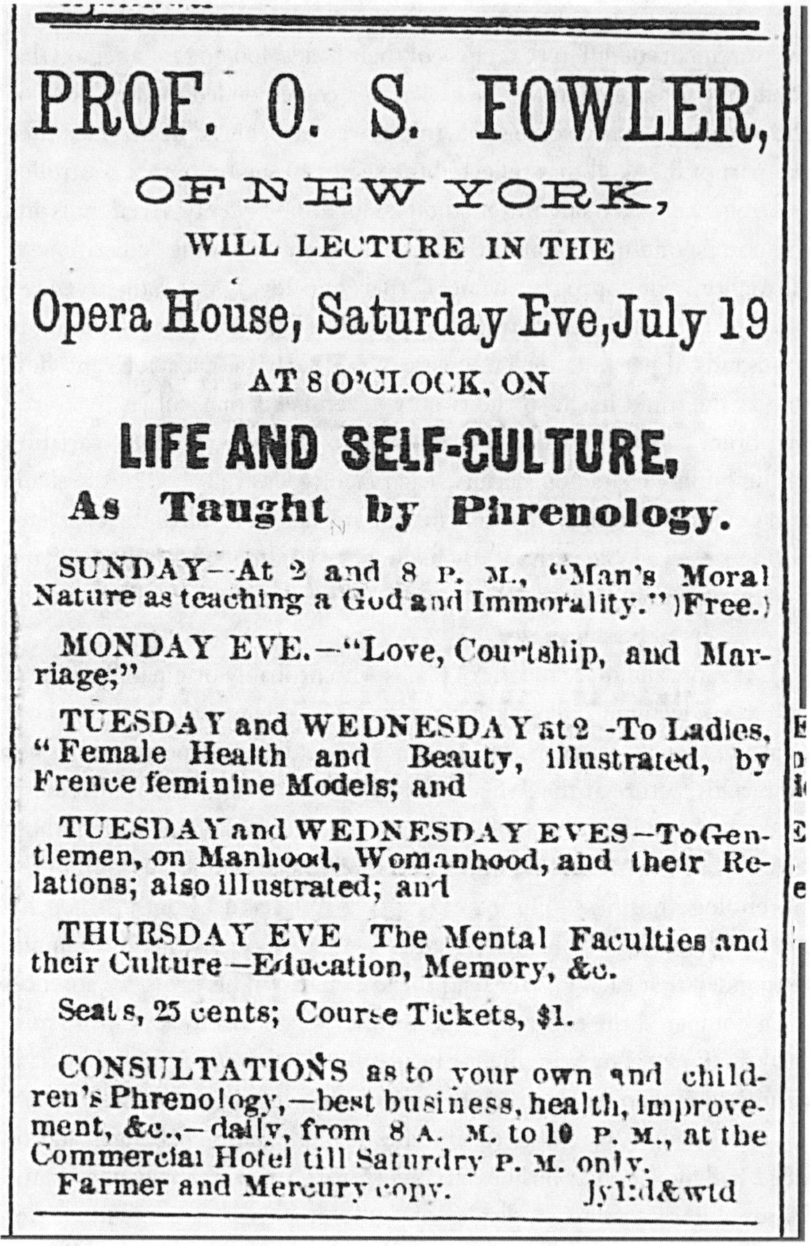

PROF. O. S. FOWLER,

OF NEW YORK,

WILL LECTURE IN THE

Opera House, Saturday Eve, July 19

AT 8 O'CLOCK, ON

LIFE AND SELF-CULTURE,

As Taught by Phrenology.

SUNDAY--At 2 and 8 P. M., "Man's Moral Nature as teaching a God and Immorality.")Free.)

MONDAY EVE.—"Love, Courtship, and Marriage;"

TUESDAY and WEDNESDAY at 2 -To Ladies, "Female Health and Beauty, illustrated, by Frence feminine Models; and

TUESDAY and WEDNESDAY EVES—To Gentlemen, on Manhood, Womanhood, and their Relations; also illustrated; and

THURSDAY EVE The Mental Faculties and their Culture—Education, Memory, &c.

Seats, 25 cents; Course Tickets, $1.

CONSULTATIONS as to your own and children's Phrenology,—best business, health, improvement, &c.,—daily, from 8 A. M. to 10 P. M., at the Commercial Hotel till Saturdry P. M. only.

Farmer and Mercury copy. Jyl:d&wtd

FIG. 4. Ad for Fowler lectures in Salem, Oregon, July 1873, *Weekly Oregon Statesman*.

White, did not look to the skull alone to differentiate the races. Only in Caucasians, White wrote, could one find "that nobly arched head, containing such a quantity of brain. . . . In what other quarter of the globe shall we find the blush that overspreads the soft features of the beautiful women of Europe, that emblem of modesty, of delicate feelings . . . where, except on the bosom of the European woman, two such plump and snowy white hemispheres, tipt with vermillion."[20] What phrenology lacked in intellectual rigor it more than compensated for by providing an apparently scientific justification for subjugating Indians and Blacks, the two minorities that were critical to unlocking America's wealth.

Phrenology found its warmest reception in the South. Southern journals were drawn to the claims that African American brains were inferior, that they had a large "tune" organ of the brain but "smaller reasoning organs," as the Fowlers put it. Partial proof lay in their songs, described as "glowing with vivacity and . . . containing many words . . . with but few ideas." Informing whites in terms that sounded scientific that they had intellectual gifts while their slaves had "small reasoning organs," "little depth . . . of intellect," and "feeble judgment" proved to be lucrative.[21]

There was also an audience for the Fowlers' assessment of Indians, who, the Fowlers claimed, were limited in the "coronal region of the head," the locus of the intellectual and moral organs. The "extreme development" of the faculties of destructiveness, secretiveness, and cautiousness explained their "cruel, blood-thirsty, and revengeful disposition," which steeled them "to such acts of barbarity as they are wont to practise in torturing the hapless victims of their vengeance." Given their traits, we may expect them "to glory in dark deeds of cruelty . . . in butchering helpless women and children."[22]

Phrenology remained a fringe movement until the publication in 1839 of *Crania Americana* by Samuel G. Morton, a bookish Quaker physician who had studied in Edinburgh and Paris before opening a practice in Philadelphia. In preparing to give an anatomy lecture on the differences in skulls among racial groups, he was surprised to find that he could not buy or borrow skulls. So, he began his own collection, which eventually included specimens from much of the planet. Caucasian, American Indian, and African American skulls dominated the collection. Morton believed that the brain was revealed by its container—the larger the skull, the larger the brain, and the larger the brain, the greater the intelligence. He experimented with methods of measurement, settling on pouring granular material or a liquid into the cranial cavities to determine volume. Drawing on the principles of phrenology, Morton believed that brain size revealed not only intelligence but also moral traits and cultural development.[23]

American Indian skulls, Morton claimed in *Crania Americana*, had remained relatively constant for centuries, according to his measurements, demonstrating that Indian skull size, and therefore intelligence, was not affected by the environment. From the shape of the skull he deduced that "the structure of the mind appears to be different from that of the white man," and that American Indians were "adverse to cultivation, and slow in acquiring knowledge."[24] The Caucasian race, he concluded, has attained the "highest intellectual endowments" and, through its "spontaneous fertility," has migrated in every direction, populated the finest lands on earth, and given birth "to its fairest inhabitants."[25]

His analyses of American Indians and African Americans, seemingly based on empirical data, lent an air of scientific legitimacy to phrenologists' alchemy. Morton wrote that Indians are "crafty, sensual, ungrateful, obstinate and unfeeling, and much of their affection for their children may be traced to purely selfish motives. They devour the most disgusting aliments uncooked and uncleaned, and seem to have no idea beyond providing for the present moment. . . . Their mental faculties, from infancy to old age, present a continued childhood."[26]

Morton's attempt to correlate mental capacity and behavioral traits with skull volume and shape through painstaking measurement of many specimens represented a scientific methodology well ahead of his time. For that he was seen as a significant scientific figure. However, his capacity to keep his conclusions within the strictures of his methodology, or even in the same ball park, came up short.

In *Bone Rooms* Samuel J. Redman argues that "Morton's presentation of detailed skull measurements alongside striking illustrations projected scientific rigor, limited only by tantalizingly incomplete data. Morton's work seemed only to beg the collecting of more evidence. Morton hesitated before stretching his data to present whites as a superior race."[27]

Many of Morton's conclusions, however, suffered from considerably more than lack of evidence. His claim that all Indians "seem to have no idea beyond providing for the present moment" is untrue for many, possibly all, tribes. Before the arrival of whites, Northern Paiutes' very existence depended on their capacity to collect and store foods for nine months, and then ration their supplies to last the winter. They provided for beyond the present moment daily for most of every year.

Morton's study included the Cherokees, who, he acknowledges, were "far more intelligent" than the surrounding tribes, as demonstrated by their development of a written language.[28] Morton did not mention the uses to which the Cherokee put their language, including the drafting of a constitution and publication of a newspaper.[29] Twenty-first-century readers who struggle to understand how Morton could claim that Cherokees, along with all other Indians, had the mental faculties of a child are not guilty of holding nineteenth-century scientists to twenty-first-century standards of racial equality. Rather, they are guilty of expecting a scientific conclusion to make sense.

Historian Reginald Horsman argues in *Race and Manifest Destiny* that *Crania Americana* fueled a growing interest in and respect for phrenological racial views, which then began to find their way into respected northern publications.[30] "One did not have to read obscure books," Horsman writes, "to know that the Caucasians were innately superior, and that they were responsible for civilization in the world, or to know that inferior races were destined to be overwhelmed or even to disappear. These ideas permeated the main American periodicals and in the second half of the century formed part of the accepted truth of America's schoolbooks."[31] No less a figure than Supreme Court justice Oliver Wendell Holmes wrote to Morton that he was "delighted" with the "severe and cautious character" of his research on race. The results of Morton's research, Holmes wrote, would provide "permanent data for all future students of Ethnology, whose leader on this side of the Atlantic" Morton had "happily constituted himself."[32]

As Morton's influence grew, white superiority gained currency in mainstream publications and among the respectable. A growing portion of the population came to regard Indians as a distinct, inferior race, with origins that differed from that of whites. This concept, however, offended the Christian belief that all humankind descended from Adam and Eve. It was for this reason, according to Francis Paul Prucha, a leading scholar on Indian affairs, that scientific racism carried little weight in the Office of Indian Affairs, which was predominantly Christian.[33] Yet, whether or not it masquerades as scientific, racism is a seductive and insidiously contagious affliction—a proposition for which the United States is Exhibit A. Since racism is rarely if ever driven by science, removing its fatuous scientific underpinning leaves it solidly ensconced on its familiar, seemingly unmovable foundation. Assurance that there were no scientific racists in the Office of Indian Affairs is no assurance that racism was less prevalent there.

When the Oregon Paiutes turned down the opportunity to make peace in 1864 and abandoned the Walpapi treaty of 1865, they did not know, and had no way to know, of the likes of Lieutenant Colonel George Crook. "Exceedingly non-communicative" was how the congressman who recommended Crook for West Point saw the reclusive lad: "He hadn't a stupid look but was quiet to reticence."[34] His biographer described the youth as "a stolid, thick, solid farmer's son."[35] A classmate edged Crook out for last place in his West Point class. But young Crook made his mark; a classmate described him as "a big Newfoundland dog among a lot of puppies. He would never permit injustice or bullying of the smaller boys."[36]

His next nine years after West Point were in the Pacific Northwest among Indians, protecting the peaceful, hunting down the disorderly. In addition to traditional military duties, he and several other officers worked with four local tribes to learn their languages and compile vocabularies. He developed an ability with these languages that, although rudimentary, won Indian confidence and invitations to Indian homes and ceremonies. He especially enjoyed fishing trips, where the simultaneous, silent thrust of bow and stern paddles and the aroma of rainbow trout on a spit dissolved for a few hours or a few days the vast gulf between the two peoples.[37] As an Indian fighter as well as a friend and admirer of Indians, Crook typified the ambivalence that marked military attitudes toward the Indians—"fear, distrust, loathing, contempt, and condescension, on the one hand, curiosity, admiration, sympathy, and even friendship, on the other."[38]

Crook arrived at Fort Boise in mid-December 1866 to replace an ineffective commander. The *Owyhee Avalanche* welcomed him as "a splendid Indian exterminator."[39] He consulted Donald and William McKay. (Donald had advised Drake to send sixty troops, not forty, to surprise Paulina. His half-brother William, physician at Warm Springs, was appointed by

GENERAL GEORGE CROOK ON THE TRAIL.

FIG. 5. General George Crook, by Frederick Remington. Cornell Digital Library.

Governor Woods to lead Warm Springs scouts against the Paiutes.) The McKays told him that the Paiutes were most vulnerable in their winter camps.[40]

Crook also drew on his own experience in the Shenandoah Valley, where he had a cavalry command under his West Point roommate, General Phil Sheridan. General-in-chief Ulysses Grant ordered Sheridan to take all provisions, forage, and stock that he wanted for his command and to destroy the rest. After defeating Confederate general Jubal Early, Sheridan confiscated thousands of sheep and cattle, and burned mills, factories, railroads, and over two thousand barns, rendering four hundred square miles nearly uninhabitable. Crook's cavalry corps was not assigned destruction duties but for weeks was in the midst of the smoky maelstrom.

Crook sensed that in winter Sheridan's "scorched earth" tactics could be effective against the Paiutes. Paiute food, clothing, weapons, implements, and shelters came from the bark, needles, leaves, stems, seeds, and roots of plants and trees and from the fur, feathers, skin, meat, and bones of fish and wildlife. With considerable industry these essentials could be found and gathered in adequate quantities in spring, summer, and fall. They were nearly impossible to find and gather in adequate quantities in winter. After the destruction of a winter camp, including its shelters, tools, weapons, fuel, clothing, and food supplies, Crook expected that Paiutes would be too overwhelmed with the business of staying alive to mount a military threat.[41]

The army had another advantage in winter campaigns. It could resupply a command in remote locations, providing its horses with grain that saved them from grazing. While Crook's horses rested and took in nourishing feed in each camp, Indian ponies grew weaker foraging on dying range grasses.[42]

Crook's success depended on minimizing weight and maximizing speed. He was a consummate hunter and fisherman, inured to the rigors of spartan winter travel. On some missions he took no tents. Soldiers put a rubber pad on the snow and blankets on the pad, then lay on the blankets, and pulled a second rubber pad over themselves. The warmth of their bodies sank the bed out of the wind.[43]

Within a week of Crook's arrival Indians mounted an attack twenty miles from Fort Boise. He packed a toothbrush and a change of underwear for a trip to reconnoiter the area. He estimated that the trip would take a week. He did not return for over two years.[44]

Crook's first battle against Paiutes presaged his entire campaign. From Fort Boise he rode to the scene of the attack and deployed his Indian scouts, ten from Warm Springs and ten friendly Paiutes. The Warm Springs scouts were eager to avenge the killing of Wasco chief Queapama, shot under a flag of truce by a member of Paulina's band.[45]

Scouts led the command up the Owyhee River through a violent snowstorm, with no tents. At daylight on December 18 they located the Indian camp of about eighty and attacked. In a battle of several hours Crook took the camp, killing about half the Indians at the cost of one man. No action of the volunteer companies under Drake and Currey that had stalked the Paiutes so ineffectively during the Civil War years had given any hint that the U.S. military was capable of a nocturnal approach so stealthy, or of an attack so lethal. Crook ignored Governor Woods's orders to spare no one. He took nine women and children prisoner.[46]

Crook's Indian scouts next picked up a trail leading west and guided Crook and his command toward Steens Mountain. From the west, Steens Mountain does not look at all like a mountain. It appears to be a long—more than a mile, more than two miles—gentle rise through barren terrain. But those who ascend from the west quickly discover that it is not two miles, but twenty, rising to almost ten thousand feet above sea level. From the east, Steens is unmistakably a mountain—steep, broken slopes towering a mile above the Alvord Desert.

Crook approached the Indian camp from the east. Just as the sun topped the horizon on the morning of January 29, Crook nodded, signaling the start of another dawn attack. First light illuminated the backdrop to the Indian camp—sepia-brown foothills, bright against the slate-gray cliffs and deep shadows of the upper mountain. Once they were aroused by the attack, Paiutes stood out crisply against this scene, presenting sharply defined targets. To the Paiutes, the attackers were elusive silhouettes against the sun and glare from the alkali desert and snow. Sixty Paiutes died, including twenty-seven women and children. Another twenty-seven women and children were taken prisoner. One white died.[47]

Once the echoes of the last shots finished resounding off Steen's east wall, and the calculus of who would be taken by this battle and who would not had run its course, the participants began to absorb the consequences of this event. Civil War veterans among Crook's soldiers, inured to killing and death had never experienced in that war a battle like this one. Instead of a field of dead and injured soldiers, they now stood over a field of dead and wounded families.

The twenty-seven Paiute women and children who survived this battle had no frame of reference in their own experience or in the oral history of their tribe for a catastrophe so monumental. Breaches of the peace within the tribe were unusual and mostly limited to disputes between individuals.

Before the late 1850s intertribal conflicts were reliably initiated by a stronger, more aggressive opponent, to which the Paiutes' typical response was to scatter and hide.[48] Except in winter, it was rare for more than a few families to gather at one location; since Paiutes were almost always widely dispersed in small family groups, there was rarely an occasion for so many to be slain at once. In any case, group warfare was unknown to the Paiutes before war chiefs and war bands evolved in about 1859.[49] Between 1859 and 1865 Paiute Indian enemies were on reservations and no longer a threat except as scouts for U.S. troops. Paiute losses in battles with U.S. troops prior to 1865 were minimal.[50] Paiute losses to white diseases were also minimal because of their limited contact with settlers and miners.[51]

The bloody battles of the Snake War were, therefore, entirely outside of the experience of Paiutes. At the Steens Mountain fight, these twenty-seven survivors experienced a lifetime or two of tragedies all condensed into a fraction of an hour. In traditional Paiute rituals following a death, relatives and friends gathered, cried, wailed, cut their hair short, and, for those most deeply affected, gashed their arms and legs. The deceased was wrapped in tanned deer skin and taken to the final resting place, usually nestled in a bed of rocks. All of the possessions of the deceased were burned to guard against nocturnal visitors looking for what they left behind. The name of the deceased was never mentioned again.[52]

Death rituals can provide the comfort of the familiar in a time of grief. But the survivors of the battle were captives and were far too few to manage so many corpses. In any case, death rituals were of secondary concern. A barrage of bullets sufficient to kill sixty surely left many wounded. The women survivors were overwhelmed by the needs of the injured and of the newly orphaned babies, toddlers, and teens, all the while doing their best to contain their own grief for husbands, children, and parents whose fresh corpses were lying nearby. The experience of the survivors seared them too profoundly to have lost its edge when, ten years hence, another war against the soldiers loomed.

In May 1868, as the lopsided war was nearing its end, troops from Camp Harney made a reconnaissance of the Malheur country. They surprised ten lodges of Paiutes on the North Fork of the Malheur River, near Castle Rock (which is fifty-three miles northeast of Burns), capturing a number, including Chief Egan and his following. According to Bancroft, Egan "professed a great desire to live thereafter in peace, and offered to send couriers to bring in his warriors and the head chief Wewawewa [Weyouwewa], who, he declared, was as weary of conflict as himself."[53] Although conciliatory statements made at the point of a gun are of doubtful credibility, Egan did bring in his warriors and Weyouwewa did surrender.

Among the reasons for Egan's weariness of conflict was surely the death of Chief Shenkah, his brother-in-law. After Shenkah's mortal wounding, his daughter Mattie and Egan had been with him in his final moments. At Shenkah's request, Egan had agreed to take Mattie into his family, which, by the time of his surrender in 1868, included a boy of about twelve, Honey.[54]

Egan's surrender and his commitment to bring Weyouwewa as well caused word to be sent to General Crook, who made his way to Camp Harney to meet with the Paiute chiefs. At a grand council on June 30, Crook asked the chiefs: "Do you see any fewer soldiers than two years ago?" The chiefs answered: "No. More." "Have you as many warriors?" "No; not half as many." "Very well, that is how I mean to have it until you are all gone."[55]

Crook had been hamstrung by his superior, General Halleck, commander of the Division of the Pacific, who forbade the making of any treaty without his prior approval. Unable to make a treaty, Crook instead warned that Weyouwewa was responsible for the good conduct of all. Crook had a notice published in multiple newspapers announcing his agreement with Weyouwewa that the Paiutes could return to their territory and that "while they remain peaceable and do not meddle with citizens or their private property they shall not be molested." The Paiutes' desire for peace is sincere, the notice continued, "and they will keep it, provided bad white men do not, in their turn, commit outrages upon them."[56] Not given to overstatement, in his military report Crook stated: "I feel satisfied that with proper management by our troops they [Paiutes] will not willingly enter into hostilities with us again."[57]

Nothing in any of the Paiute chiefs' experience with whites had prepared them for the tightly orchestrated, ruthless attacks that Crook mounted, surprising them on lands that Paiutes believed they knew as no one else knew. Nothing in their experience had prepared them for hundreds of

Paiutes to be swept up, tsunami-like, and united in the soil with their ancestors; or for the soil that Paiutes believed had nourished and sheltered the Paiute people from the beginning of time to be wrenched away by strangers to be farmed, mined, grazed, logged, bought, and sold—slowly, inexorably, it seemed, defiling all that was ever Paiute.

CHAPTER 9

A Home on Their Native Soil

The Paiutes were committed to fulfill their promise to General Crook to maintain peace. Their challenge, they knew, would be troublesome whites. If a fight broke out, regardless of who was at fault, the Paiutes believed from long experience that the blame would fall on them. To keep such whites at bay, Paiutes settled adjacent to army camps. But peace came at a price. The arid land yielded nourishment only to those consistently on the move, in small groups. To sustain themselves, then, Paiutes needed to be scattered and mobile. The protection of the soldiers' camps, however, required them to be congregated and stationary. Forced to choose between hunger and danger, the Paiutes more often than not chose hunger over the risk, however remote, of incurring the wrath of the dreaded General Crook. The result, as described by the chaplain at Camp Harney, was that the Paiutes became "miserably poor, and in need of both food and clothing." While Paiute lands, he added, were "continually contracting from the invasion of the whites," the Indians "suffer, if not some of them perish, without help."[1]

On November 6, 1868, a solitary rider with a drill sergeant's chin and a shock of dark hair that reached for the heavens like maple shoots rode into Fort Klamath in south-central Oregon. Indian superintendent Huntington was on a 1,300-mile journey to assess the condition of Paiutes in the aftermath of General Crook's campaign. Huntington and his wife, Mary, had moved from Yoncalla, where Huntington had met her and the rest of the Applegate family, to Salem, fifty miles south of Portland. Mary was watching over their Salem household and their two young sons, Perit and Ben, as Huntington endured the onset of winter at four thousand feet above sea level.

After meeting Captain Kelley at Fort Klamath, Huntington rode fifty miles southeast to the agency's Yainax Station, home of Walpapi Paiutes and Yahooskin Paiutes. Here Huntington found "130 souls . . . in deplorably destitute condition." Despite hard freezes, the children had few clothes and the adults were next to naked. They had a small supply of roots and seeds that would not last until February.

From Yainax Huntington rode north to Fort Warner, where he found 250 Paiutes lacking adequate clothing, although not so destitute as those at Yainax. Huntington's last two stops were at Warm Springs, where he found fifty Paiutes, and at Fort Harney, where seven hundred more were encamped, all as deprived as those at Fort Warner. He estimated that there were 1,980 in total and that twice that number had died in Crook's campaign against the Paiutes. Steward and Wheeler-Voegelin claim that Huntington's number is an exaggeration and that the Paiute death toll was closer to five hundred.[2]

At Fort Harney Huntington met seven Paiute chiefs, including Weyou-wewa, the principal chief, Oits, Egan, and Ponee.[3] Huntington presented the chiefs with a treaty, which they signed. The treaty stated that it was preliminary and that a more complete version would follow. No treaty followed. The document was never ratified by Congress and was therefore not a valid treaty. Yet this apparently stillborn nontreaty, unilaterally imposed on the seven chiefs by Huntington, turned out to have a legal life and to be of modest benefit to the Paiutes over almost a century.

Huntington's treaty was one of his last official acts. On March 31, 1869, the secretary of the interior replaced him with Alfred B. Meacham, for reasons that became apparent when Meacham walked into the office vacated by Huntington to find that it was bare of records of any kind—no lists of employees, no contracts for supplies, no payroll records, no correspondence, no reports. (In May, two months after Huntington was removed from his position, his son Perit died at age seven of an unknown disease. A few weeks later Huntington himself died at age thirty-eight. Mary lost her two Perits in the space of a month. Of the six males in her family, one son remained.)[4]

Meacham and Major Elmer Otis, commanding officer of the District of the Lakes, met with the Paiute chiefs at Fort Harney in November 1869 in an effort to persuade them to move to the Klamath Reservation.

Weyouwewa, Egan, Ponee, and Oits refused, relying on the language of the Huntington treaty, which required them to reside on a reservation "in their own country."[5] The Klamath Reservation was not in the Paiutes' own country, the chiefs pointed out. On the strength of the Huntington treaty, the Indians had their way.

Major Otis and T. B. Odeneal, who replaced Meacham in early 1872, set about drawing the boundaries of a new reservation. With the eastern third of the state largely unsettled, they had near-divine powers to choose features of this vast and varied terrain that would become the home of the Malheurs. While many reservations are the discarded scraps left after whites snapped up the choice lands, Otis did not see his task in that light. "I have been stationed where I have had intercourses with a large portion of these Indians since October of 1864," he wrote early in 1872. "This is a country which these Indians have inhabited and that they know, and where the majority desire to stay."[6]

The features that Otis had to choose from included Malheur Lake to the south, a sixty-mile-long belt of ponderosa pine to the north, the Malheur River to the east, and the Silvies River to the west. The ponderosa pine was of a superior quality, a junction of branches of the Malheur River was the favorite resort of the Paiutes, winter and summer, and the Silvies Valley provided fowl hunting and rich sources of seeds, roots, and bird eggs.[7]

Wary of proposing a reservation too large, and believing that the ponderosa stand should be included, Otis drew the southern boundary above Malheur Lake, so that it, Harney Lake, and Steens Mountain were excluded. For the west boundary he chose Silvies River, which established a reasonably precise line as protection against encroaching settlers. With the boundaries defined, Otis seemed positively exuberant in declaring, "This country is the exact country [where] the Piutes are desirous of remaining."[8] In 1872 President Grant approved Otis's boundaries.

Almost two decades earlier Oregon territorial superintendent Joel Palmer wrote that, if Indians were to survive, "there appears but one path open. A home remote from the settlements must be selected for them. There they must be guarded from the pestiferous influence of degraded whitemen."[9] Now Paiutes had that home—vast, remote, and off limits to whites. It was all the better because it was the land that they knew and that had sheltered and nourished their people for generations.

CHAPTER 10

A Troika

As Paiutes moved onto the Malheur Reservation in the fall of 1873, three events coincided with their arrival that would play defining roles in their time at Malheur—President Grant's Peace Policy was reduced to specific requirements, the Modoc War reached its finale, and the nation descended into its worst financial collapse since the Panic of 1837.

"The proper treatment of the original occupants of this land—the Indians—[is] deserving of careful study. I will favor any course toward them which tends to their civilization and ultimate citizenship." President Grant's vague ideal, stated in his first inaugural address in March 1869, spawned his "Peace Policy," which gradually took shape during his first term. Early in Grant's second term, as the Malheur Agency structures were nearing completion, interior secretary Columbus Delano sought to reduce the Peace Policy to specific provisions, two of which were of particular significance to the Paiutes. First, the Peace Policy sought "to place the Indians upon reservations as rapidly as possible." Any Indians who "persistently refuse to go upon a reservation" would be treated "with all needed severity." Second, "through the instrumentality and by the advice and assistance of the various religious organizations" the government would procure "competent, upright, faithful, moral, and religious agents to care for the Indians."[1]

Before the Malheur Reservation opened there were troubles about two hundred miles to the southwest involving the Modocs and Klamaths, historic enemies on adjacent lands with extensive marshes in southern Oregon and northern California.[2] A Modoc band led by Kientpoos (known to the settlers as Captain Jack), living on Modoc native lands on the Lost

River, made a treaty with the United States that, Kientpoos claimed, allowed them to remain on the Lost River. The government claimed that the Modocs were required to move to the Klamath Reservation on Upper Klamath Lake. Eventually fighting broke out and developed into one of the earliest "Wars of the Peace Policy." A conference conducted by peace commissioners was arranged for April 11, 1873. As it began Kientpoos repeated his request for a reservation on the Lost River. When this was denied, Kientpoos shot dead General Edward Canby, Boston Charley killed one of the peace commissioners, and Schonchin John shot Alfred Meacham, chair of the commission, four times, but not fatally. Over the next several months the Modocs, divided and outnumbered, surrendered piecemeal, ending with Kientpoos. In October 1873 at the Klamath Reservation, Boston Charley, Black Jim, Schonchin John, and Kientpoos were hanged.[3]

As the executions were carried out at Fort Klamath, the Malheur Reservation was in its opening stages. Buildings had been erected for a commissary, office, mess house, dwelling for employees, and a slaughter-house.[4] A special commissary, Samuel Ball Parrish, had supervised the construction and acted as unofficial reservation agent over the growing population of Paiutes.[5]

When Chief Weyouwewa passed away at Malheur during the opening phases of the reservation, Paiutes paid homage to the head of the Paiute nation with fires on high peaks and ridges.[6] To some the ceremonies marked not just the passing of a respected leader, but also the opening of an opportunity. Particularly attracted to the vacuum in leadership was Weyouwewa's cousin Oits, a chief who also claimed shamanic powers.[7] (Chief *Oits* should not be confused with Major Elmer *Otis* or with General Oliver *Otis* Howard.)

Chief Winnemucca was older and more respected than Oits, but was unlikely to compete with Oits because he feared the younger man's claimed black powers. While shamans were believed to have curative powers, they could also inflict harm, as Oits was not hesitant to remind his fellow Paiutes. When misfortune occurred, Oits tried to enhance his perceived power by claiming that he was the cause. Possibly it was the combination of the power vacuum and the murders at the Modoc peace conference that inspired his plot to kill Samuel Parrish.

In 1839, when Samuel Parrish was two years old, his parents, Josiah and
Elizabeth, boarded the *Lausanne* in New York with Samuel and his two
older brothers. The fifty-one passengers of the *Lausanne* were to be the
"Great Reinforcement" for an Oregon community of Methodists established by Jason Lee in 1833. The *Lausanne* rounded Cape Horn, stopped
at the Sandwich Islands (Hawaii), and arrived at Fort Vancouver on June
1, where Chief Factor John McLoughlin gave them a warm welcome and
hosted them for two weeks. Then the Parrishes loaded little Samuel and
his siblings into a Chinook canoe and ascended the Willamette River fifty
miles to the mission, just north of present-day Salem.

The reinforcement was called "Great" not for what it had done, but
for what it hoped to do. Four years later, however, the mission was dissolved, after ten years during which "nothing was done that ever in the
least benefited the Indians," in the view of Bancroft. While the Natives
took little in the way of religion from Jason Lee's mission, it could not
be said that they took nothing, for, according to Josiah, in the year that
his party arrived, "500 Indians . . . died in this valley with chills and fever
and typhoid fever."[8]

Samuel was seven by the time the mission closed. The record of Samuel's
life is sketchy, but his father's interview with Bancroft reveals that Samuel
was among Indians and religion for much of his early life. Religion did
not "take" with him. Indians did.

Samuel's rejection of the religion that was at the core of his father's
life demonstrated that he was neither meek nor subservient to his father.
His decision to pursue a career as an Indian agent, as his father had, was
therefore likely an informed choice rather than a matter of blind obedience or reflexive imitation. That Samuel learned about the duties of an
Indian agent from years under the same roof with his father is suggested
by a certain congruity in their relationships with Indians.

Josiah Parrish's account of his work as Indian agent in his interview with
historian Bancroft covered a range of events, but one had the finespun
precision of a tale that had become as much of a fixture in the Parrish
household as the raconteur's overstuffed chair. As Bancroft recorded Josiah's
story, Superintendent Dart asked him to meet with Coquille Indians on the
southern Oregon coast to attempt to lure them to Port Orford to answer
questions about a battle that they had fought with miners. Dart offered

Josiah as many armed men as he wanted. Josiah accepted the assignment, but not the armed men. Instead he made his way to the mouth of the Coquille River with an Indian translator, a second Indian, gifts, salmon, and bread. Josiah had his translator bring the Coquilles to his camp. Many arrived armed with something between a machete and a sword. According to Josiah, he showed no fear and spent a day talking with the Coquilles, never mentioning the battle or the five dead miners. After feeding them copiously with bread and salmon, he told the chief that he wanted to exchange presents. He explained that the exchange would allow him to show that his heart was kind toward them and—undoubtedly of far greater importance to Josiah, although he tried not to reveal as much—to allow them to show that their hearts were kind toward him. He tied a brilliant silk belt around the chief's naked body. The chief then reciprocated with an otter skin. "This is my pledge," the chief said, "that I will deal fairly with you." Parrish returned to Port Orford the next day. He brought no Coquilles with him, but he had walked into a den of hostile Indians and walked out with the beginnings of a friendship.[9]

Like his father, Samuel Parrish had a rare talent for respecting Indians in a way that inspired in them a respect for him and his authority. He knew that Oits had been telling Indians that bullets passed through him harmlessly. Parrish summoned him the next morning. He told Oits that he had three hundred dollars, and that the money would belong to Oits once Parrish sent a bullet harmlessly through him. Oits was reduced to sniveling, begging for his life. As Major Otis described this event, Oits's troublemaking "was quelled on the spot by Mr. Parrish in such a firm and decided way that Oits has feared him ever since."[10]

The ease with which Parrish parried Oits's threats, converting him to a terrified thrall and, later, a friend, capped off the proof of Parrish's unusual capabilities as an Indian agent.[11] Under Grant's Peace Policy, however, the source of "competent, upright, faithful, moral, and religious agents to care for the Indians" was religious organizations. Not being religious, Parrish was not qualified.[12]

In accordance with the Peace Policy, the Committee of the Christian Denomination designated a candidate. Born in Tennessee, Harrison Linville arrived in Oregon in 1847 and settled in Polk County near the Luckimute

River. He was the first postmaster of the Luckimute post office and ran a ferry service, store, hotel, and stagecoach stop. His home on the Luckimute River served as the Luckimute Church, providing the Christian credentials that apparently led to his selection. The Indian Affairs inspector for the Northwest approved the appointment of Linville despite his inexperience, but recommended that Parrish be retained as commissary and as informal mentor for Linville. But this recommendation was ignored.[13]

Sensing that Linville was no Parrish, Oits began scheming again. The weather strengthened Oits's hand by burying the hills surrounding the agency in six feet of snow, limiting access to the soldiers at Fort Harney. Despite the snow, Linville was able to get two letters to Major Otis at Fort Harney that winter. The letters leave an impression that Linville's nights were haunted by visions of the Modoc peace conference.

In his letters Linville explained to Major Otis that Oits was trying to induce the Indians "to join him and his band in a plot to massacre the Agent [that is, Linville] and Employees." Oits "has tried to induce Eagan . . . with his men," Linville wrote, but "Eagan has so far persistently refused to have any connection with Oytz, and professes to maintain friendly relations with the Agent." Linville fairly begged for Otis to come and arrest Oits.[14] Spring brought soldiers to Malheur, but they found no trouble.

The Paiutes liked Linville. Indeed, three Paiute leaders—Winnemucca, Egan, and Jerry Long—submitted a joint statement to the commissioner of Indian affairs acknowledging that "Oitz has given our people much anxiety and trouble," but declaring that "we are well satisfied and pleased with Mr. Linville as our agent. [We hope] he may always remain with us; he is a good man."[15] Linville's bond with the Paiute leaders boded well, but his inability to manage Oits did not. On Major Otis's recommendation, Parrish was recalled to replace Linville at the end of July 1874.[16]

After the Snake War Chief Egan and his followers went to Nevada, where they became acquainted, or possibly reacquainted, with the Winnemuccas— Chief Winnemucca and his children, Natchez, Lee, and Sarah. Egan's niece and adopted daughter, Mattie, had married Lee. Sarah's cousin Jerry Long had married Egan's daughter.[17] Despite Egan's deepening ties to the Winnemuccas, the opening of the Malheur Reservation lured him and his band away from Nevada.[18] He explained his decision to his band in words that Mattie later put in writing:

> The white men are taking away from us all our land here in Nevada. They are driving off all our ponies. . . . The red man and white man did fight many suns, many soldiers and many braves fell in battle, and the young men are buried all along the creeks and rivers. My brother, Chief Shenkah has passed on to the better land. We see very plainly that the red men cannot fight the white men. We have not such good rifles and good horses as they have. Our bows and arrows are nothing. And now the white men say *Peace*. They say, take a home in Malheur, Oregon. There is good land, good water, and plenty of food over there. The red man and the white man must eat bread together. I now say this is good,—let us go.[19]

Egan led his band to Malheur, including his wife, Sally, her brother Charlie, her and Egan's teenage son, Honey, and their niece and adopted daughter, Mattie.[20]

Not long after Egan and his followers reached Malheur, Agent Linville and his son Willard arrived. Willard wrote a short piece about Malheur in which he described Egan as the primary Indian spokesman and "a fine specimen of his race, tall and muscular and straight as an arrow, with head well poised." After Linville first addressed the Indians at Malheur, Egan rose to speak. Egan's words, according to Willard, were that "he had fought the white people with all his might, but now he was tired of war and would do all he could to help to carry out the plans of the government."[21] After he replaced Linville, Parrish wrote that Egan had the eastern part of the Silvies Valley (on the Malheur Reservation) under his charge, and "is now cultivating and improving a portion thereof under my direction," and that he was "one of the strongest and best chiefs on this reserve." He gave no such praise to any other chief.[22]

Samuel Parrish learned that Chief Winnemucca was at Fort Harney with his daughter Sarah, who had worked as a translator at Fort McDermitt in northern Nevada. Parrish sent a letter to Sarah at Fort Harney offering to hire her to translate at Malheur. She accepted and with her father moved to Malheur. (Because Chief Winnemucca is widely referred to as "Winnemucca," his children are usually referred to by their first names.)

Sarah was born Thocmetony in about 1844. As a child she was terrified of "owls," the Paiutes' term for white people because of the hair on men's faces, leaving little more than eyes showing. Thocmetony's grandmother and her father told her that the white people would kill little children and eat them, an apparent reference to the cannibalism of the Donner party, trapped by winter in the Sierra Nevada Mountains. Thocmetony had a vivid recollection of a panicked flight of many Paiutes from approaching whites. She could not keep up, so her mother buried her in sand, with only her face showing, so that the whites would be less likely to find and eat her.[23]

Thocmetony's fear of whites put her at odds with her grandfather, Chief Truckee, who believed that the Paiutes' future lay in cooperation with the whites. He had guided the first immigrant party to cross the Sierra Nevada Mountains in wagons. Later groups that he led came to call him Truckee—Paiute for "very well"—possibly for the response that he made to their requests. He met and possibly guided John C. Fremont, an explorer, officer in the Mexican-American War, and a U.S. senator from California. Truckee's most precious possession was his "rag friend," a letter from Fremont asking all who read it to treat Truckee well. Truckee put his rag friend to regular use and marveled at its powers.[24]

Truckee never tired of recounting to his people the accomplishments of the whites. He taught them to sing the "Star-Spangled Banner." He told a traditional Paiute tale in which the first man and first woman had both dark and white children. The children quarreled so relentlessly that the father told them to leave. Only the white pair left. The dark boy and girl remained and became the original Indians. Now, Truckee proclaimed, the descendants of the two whites who were siblings of the original Indians had arrived.[25] Whether Truckee took the tale literally or not, he was not hesitant to exploit it to convince his people that their future lay in friendship with the whites and learning their ways.[26] (In an interview with the *New York Times* in her later years Sarah recounted the legend and added, "My people still believe in this tradition, and are warmly friendly to the whites.")[27]

The most daunting obstacle to Truckee's claim that the whites were the Paiutes' friends was the whites themselves. They felled pinyon pine trees, source of nuts that were a staple of the Paiute diet in Nevada. They grazed their cattle on meadows and fields, destroying important Paiute foods. They torched the Paiutes' winter food supplies.[28]

Immigrants fired at Paiutes peacefully fishing the Humboldt River, killing six, including one of Truckee's sons. Furious young men intent on revenge prepared to kill the settlers at the nearby Humboldt Sink, an intermittent lake. Addressing a gathering of his people, Truckee warned that nothing of the kind would be done while he lived. As he spoke, Thocmetony recalled, "he wept, and men, women, and children, were all weeping." "I know," he said, "and you know that those men who live at the sink are not the ones who killed our men." After he spoke, Thocmetony was alarmed to see her parents cut their hair and slash their arms and legs, as did other relatives, including her uncle's widow, who would not remarry until her hair grew back to the length it was at his death or wash her face or apply any kind of paint until her father-in-law approved.[29]

Thocmetony's father, Chief Winnemucca, was among the most difficult for Truckee to persuade. Chief Winnemucca's skepticism of whites intensified after he dreamed three nights in succession of whites killing Paiutes. When a shaman confirmed Winnemucca's vision, few doubted that whites would bring ill fortune.[30]

Truckee's most obstinate, stubborn skeptic may well have been Thocmetony. When he finally succeeded in leading his family to the San Joaquin Valley in California to introduce them to the world of the whites, Thocmetony wept, buried her head in a blanket, squeezed her eyes shut, and did all within her power to keep the whites from registering in any of her senses.[31]

In 1857, at age thirteen, Thocmetony began learning English when she and her sister Elma, eleven, lived with William and Margaret Ormsby and their daughter, Lizzie, in Genoa, a small town in the valley of the Carson River in western Nevada. In an era of widespread animosity toward Indians, the Ormsbys showed remarkable independence in their kindness and respect for the Winnemucca girls. Both were quick to learn English. It is likely that Mrs. Ormsby educated her Indian guests along with Lizzie, possibly in return for performing household duties.[32] The next decade brought sorrow, beginning with the Pyramid War in which both Paiutes and soldiers suffered heavy losses. Then Truckee passed away. Five years later soldiers slaughtered twenty-nine Indians, including Thocmetony's mother and a baby brother.[33]

By 1870 Thocmetony had become Sarah and was working as interpreter at Camp McDermitt, Nevada, commanded by Major Henry Douglas. She wrote to Douglas:

> If proper pains were taken, they [the Paiutes] would willingly make the effort to maintain themselves by their own labor, providing they could be made to believe that the products were their own, for their own use and comfort. . . . If the Indians have any guarantee that they can secure a permanent home on their own native soil, and that our white neighbors can be kept from encroaching on our rights, after having a reasonable share of ground allotted to us as our own, and giving us the required advantages of learning, I warrant that the savage (as he is called today) will be a thrifty and law-abiding member of the community.[34]

Impressed by the letter, Douglas forwarded it to Commissioner of Indian Affairs Ely Parker. It then made its way to *Harper's Weekly*, where it was praised as "very sagacious." "If there are savages who will not be tamed," *Harper's* continued, "at least there are a multitude of Indians of whom what this letter says is true."[35] The startling power and simplicity of her prose announced the arrival of a new force of gravity in the Paiutes' realm.

After Sarah and her father moved to Malheur, Parrish met with the Malheur Paiutes. With Sarah translating, Parrish said that he would work hand in hand with the Paiutes: "I can't kneel down and pray for sugar and flour and potatoes to rain down as [the previous agent, Linville] did. . . . I will try and do my duty and teach you all how to work. . . . The first thing I want you to do is to make a dam and then dig a ditch."

Chief Egan responded, "Yes, we will work." Chief Oits responded, "I and my men have our own work to do." Sarah's father said, "I will take the rest of the men and go to work upon the ditch."[36]

Parrish soon had the strongest Indians digging an irrigation ditch every day. There were only forty shovels, so some threw dirt out of the ditch with their bare hands. After the Indians excavated two and a half miles of ditch, Parrish wrote to the commissioner in April 1875. He had promised the Indians that they would be rewarded for their work. Now all his promises "must be lived up to, to the spirit and the letter," he told the commissioner. The goods purchased for the Indians had to be of good quality, unlike the six-foot-long blankets that had arrived recently—too short for the men. Parrish asked permission to purchase the goods himself at stores in Portland where he had found better quality at lower prices than Indian Affairs had been paying. The commissioner should grant this and other requests, Parrish argued, because "no agent can control [Indians] and raise them up, unless he has the hearty support of the Department."[37]

Parrish did not let up. Three months later he insisted on fencing, essential for protecting crops. He wrote to the commissioner that he "must have" a school building, hospital, additional storehouse, and another house for employees.[38]

General Oliver Otis Howard, commander of the Columbia District, had been to Malheur, met Parrish, Sarah, Egan, and others, and shown an interest in Parrish's efforts for the Paiutes. Parrish wrote to Howard in March 1876 and in April brought the general up to date again. By the end of the month, he explained, "we will have broken up about *ninety* acres of new land." One teacher at the reservation was Parrish's sister-in-law, Annie Parrish, whom the Indians called "our white lily mother." Her assistant was Sarah Winnemucca. In addition to academics they taught the Indian girls to make clothing. Each had made a dress and a skirt. The teachers had cut out dresses and skirts for all of the women. The savings realized by Indians making their own clothes would pay the teachers' salaries. Parrish had his eyes on another teacher who would fulfill his desire for one "who will go into the matter with his whole soul." In the coming winter Parrish intended to have vegetables enough to give these Indians all they wanted. "I believe I can do it. . . . The Indians all seem, and I am satisfied are, contented and happy," he told Howard. He hoped that the Office of Indian Affairs would send an inspector.[39]

The formula that Sarah had prescribed in her letter to Major Douglas for the independence and prosperity of her people was being fulfilled in her presence. Her people had a home on their native soil. When seventy-eight settlers filed a petition, endorsed by the governor, to carve the Silvies Valley out of the reservation, Parrish, acting as the Paiutes' scrivener, responded that this tract was the subject of a hereditary claim by Peccoihee and Tonnat. The land was never given up by treaty. Legally, then, the Paiutes were on firm ground. But they had more to say: "Let those white men who have not ground enough already and think they must have some of that belonging to the Indians, go and whip out the Sioux and take some of their country and settle upon that. The Sioux are bad Indians and are fighting the whites continually, while we have stopped fighting and are trying to settle down and learn how to do something for ourselves and children."[40] The Paiutes had come to believe that the land was theirs and that the product of their labor was theirs, because Parrish told them so. Under Parrish's tutelage they were learning to draw nourishment from the soil, and their children were learning the fundamentals that could empower them to partake in the abundance of the white way of life. In response to Parrish's support and encouragement, the Paiutes were acting as Sarah had forecast—they had learned to work. They had made a strong start on the foundation of a self-sufficient community for themselves and for future generations. Under the developing leadership of Egan, Parrish, and Sarah, all of whom appeared to be committed for as long as necessary, the Paiutes appeared to be progressing steadily, reliably, on the path that Sarah charted in her 1870 letter to Major Douglas.

But there was a glitch. It harkened back to Samuel at age seven.

CHAPTER 11

A New Agent

In May 1876 William Rinehart replaced Samuel Parrish as Malheur agent. Sarah Winnemucca believed that Parrish lost his job because Rinehart was appointed by a religious organization under the authority of the "Peace Policy." In no conventional sense of the term was Rinehart more qualified than Parrish. Rinehart's primary experience with Indians was shooting at them during the Snake War. He had also worked as a miner and a retail clerk.[1]

The difference between Parrish and Rinehart is best understood in their own words. In his first annual report after the arrival of Nevada Paiutes at his reservation, Parrish wrote that success seemed "doubtful until I saw with what a will these Indians took hold of the matter." They were awkward and slow at first, but determined and eager to learn the reason for each step in the procedure. They had to be taught each step over and over, but "perseverance has finally won." They "now see the result of their labors in a field full of corn, potatoes, squashes, onions, and turnips, which will be their sustenance. The question is settled: the Piute *will work*."

The report continued that Parrish joined the Paiutes in digging the irrigation ditch: "The Indians took hold of the matter with great zeal, and persevered until they had finished a ditch a mile and a quarter in length. . . . The Indians did all the work on this ditch, except the plowing of it, without any compensation other than their subsistence and annuity goods."[2]

In contrast, Rinehart's first annual report states: "The first act of disobedience and disrespect, wherein an Indian cursed me and sullenly refused to obey me, was promptly punished by putting the offender in irons and locking him up in the commissary building over night." (Rinehart did

FIG. 6. William V. Rinehart, Malheur Indian agent, 1854. Courtesy of Oregon Historical Society, Neg. 56820.

not mention in his report that the disobedient Indian, Johnny, was a boy who had said to Rinehart, "What in hell do you want?"; or that Rinehart chased him fruitlessly; or that he threatened to shoot the lad before imprisoning him.)[3]

"The notion prevalent among them," Rinehart continued in his first annual report "[is] that labor is disgraceful." That notion is "strengthened . . . by their natural indolence." He was knowledgeable about the Paiutes, he claimed, because he had fought against them: "[A] more abject race of beings it was never my lot to behold. . . . They merited the hated appellation 'Snakes' absolutely living in the grass."[4]

Parrish had assured the Paiutes that the reservation was their land, but now Rinehart said that it was government land.[5] Parrish had kept his promises to pay for work. Rinehart said he would pay, but when payday arrived, he said that the rations, cloth, and clothing already issued to them was their pay. Rinehart had no more clothing for Paiutes, but his employees, who showed up in rags, were soon wearing new clothes like those that Parrish used to provide to Paiutes. Sarah had forecast that Paiutes would become good citizens if they had land of their own to produce crops of their own. The Paiutes' assurance from Agent Parrish that the land and the crops they grew were their own vanished under Rinehart.[6]

Not long after Rinehart arrived, Sarah heard a scream and turned in time to see him throw a little boy to the ground by his ear and kick him. Rinehart fumed that the boy had laughed in response to his order. Sarah explained that the boy did not understand English and thought that Rinehart had praised him. In a separate incident Rinehart beat a man for failing to respond to an order with sufficient speed.[7]

In response to these and other incidents, Chief Egan confronted Rinehart. Asking Sarah to translate, Egan rose. He was dressed simply in a farmer's suit of light linen over a muscular frame. His black hair was without braid or ornament, parted in the middle, cut short at the neck. Nothing in his unadorned appearance distracted from his handsome looks, his resonant voice.[8] "Did the government tell you to come here and drive us off this reservation?" he began. "Did the Big Father say, go and kill us all off, so you can have our land? Did he tell you to pull our children's ears off, and put handcuffs on them, and carry a pistol to shoot us with?" Egan's strategy for protecting his people from Rinehart's excesses was to seek a solution under the laws and rules of the government. He told Rinehart, "Tomorrow I am going to tell the soldiers what you are doing and see if it is all right."[9]

The next day Egan and Sarah rode south along the North Fork of the Malheur, then west to the southwest corner of the reservation. After twenty miles they arrived at Fort Harney, which spilled over a meadow of lush grasses, sage, and rabbitbrush, divided by Rattlesnake Creek. They passed the cavalry stable, backed by a jailhouse of stout logs, then the soldiers' barracks and officers' quarters, some painted, some whitewashed.[10]

According to Sarah, the officer heard their grievance, advised Sarah to write to Washington, which she did, and promised that he would do the same. But she received no response to her grievance other than Rinehart's order expelling her from the reservation.[11]

Rinehart claimed that he did not fire Sarah for reporting him at Fort Harney. In a letter to General Howard, commander of the Department of the Pacific, he explained that Indians who did not work earned no supplies. Sarah "is believed to have counselled and encouraged disobedience to this law; for which, and other sufficient causes, she was discharged," he claimed.[12] But the rule simply provided that Indians who did not work would receive no supplies. Rinehart did not explain how Indians could have disobeyed a rule that did not require them to do anything.

The Paiutes' discontent at Malheur was not all Rinehart's doing. He had taken office in a depression during which Congress cut the reservation budget from $50,000 in 1873 to $15,000 in 1878. After other obligations were met, the 1878 funding allowed only one and a half cents per meal per person. Each morning, in hunger, the Indians could look out over the many acres they had cleared, sitting fallow; the endless irrigation ditch they had excavated, bone dry; and their reservation land, illegally overrun by white men's cattle. They could not farm because there were no posts to build fences to keep out animals that would feed on their crops; there were no posts because Congress failed to fund a sawmill. The reservation could produce no crops, but if Paiutes hunted off the reservation they took their lives in their hands.

An experience of Egan and his followers in 1876 in the valley of the Powder River just east of Baker City was probably typical. Egan was in camp while his men were hunting. A platoon of whites approached on horseback, led by Tod Merwin, who had persuaded the governor to allow his group to form a military unit and to arm it with twenty-one Winchester rifles and thousands of rounds of ammunition. Merwin led his men into a circle around Egan and the Paiute women and children, Winchesters at the ready. Deaf to the irony even as he repeated this story fifty years after the fact, Merwin explained that he scolded Egan that he "was off his reservation and was scaring our women and children. . . . I told him he must get out immediately." After the Indians packed up their camp and prepared to leave, Merwin "ordered him not to camp until he reached Little Lookout," ten miles away.[13] .

Aware of the skimpiness of rations on the reservation and of the challenges of seeking food off the reservation, Rinehart eloquently championed the Paiutes' cause. Was it fair and reasonable, he asked in his 1877 annual report, to take a people who "God made as free as the deer on the mountains," confine them on a reservation where they were unable to obtain food in their traditional ways, and allow them a "ration so scanty" as to put them in the position of "half-fed pauper[s]?"[14] Yet the apparent compassion for the Paiutes in Rinehart's report to the commissioner stands in jarring contrast to his physical and verbal abuse of the Paiutes behind the commissioner's back. The impoverished plight of the Paiutes appeared to matter to Rinehart more as a ploy to leverage funds into his budget than as a condition to be alleviated.

After Rinehart expelled Sarah from the Malheur Reservation she moved north to the John Day River valley. In April 1878 three Paiute men from Malheur appeared at her door with a request. They described the minimal rations and clothing that Rinehart distributed and pleaded with her to go to Washington DC on their behalf. Sarah declined, believing that she lacked the resources to make the trip and the clout to help.

In late May the same three Paiutes returned, this time with three others. With nothing to eat at Malheur, they explained, they had moved to the fish traps on the Malheur River, twenty-five miles east of the Malheur agency. At the fish traps they met about fifteen Bannock families from the reservation at Fort Hall, Idaho, under Bannock Jack.

Sarah's visitors explained Bannock Jack's story, which began with a drunken Bannock at Fort Hall who shot two whites that, he believed, had molested his sister. Tensions mounted and did not dissipate in the least when soldiers took all of the Indians' guns and ponies. The Indian who shot the whites was "the cause of all our trouble," Jack's people said, "and caused us to lose our horses and everything we had, and we all left there thinking your good agent [Samuel Parrish] was with you yet. We have come to make us a home with you, but we see that your new agent [Rinehart] is very bad indeed."[15]

When Sarah's visitors finished their tale, Sarah relented. She would go to Washington DC, she promised, at the end of May. She would take passengers to Silver City, Idaho, and sell her horse and wagon there to help fund the journey. But what Sarah expected to be a routine trip to Silver City was not at all routine and not to Silver City.[16]

CHAPTER 12

The Bannock Uprising

About sixty-five miles east of Camp Boise, Big Camas Prairie produced a lush crop of camas bulbs that Bannock Indians had harvested for decades. Bannock women with sticks and elk horns pried bulbs to the surface and arranged them in shallow holes lined with stones, where they were cooked for days. By treaty Bannocks had exclusive right to the camas harvest, but settlers ignored the treaty, grazing cattle and hogs that damaged the camas bulbs and plants. In the spring of 1878 Bannock chief Buffalo Horn confronted the settlers and instructed them to leave. The settlers agreed and seemed to be preparing to move.

On the morning of May 28, 1878, two young Bannocks, Charley and Jim, rode through the camas to the cattlemen's camp. They had spent much of the previous day with three cattlemen, William Silvey, Lew Kensler, and George Nesbet. On this morning the young Bannocks returned to the same three cattlemen, who were at breakfast. They served Charley and Jim. After they finished eating, Silvey walked to a rise overlooking the horses and cattle. Nesbet began to clean the eating area. When he leaned over to pick up dishes, Charley drew a pistol and shot him through the jaws.[1]

Like the Malheurs, Bannocks were a Numic-speaking Northern Paiute people of the Great Basin. But, unlike other Northern Paiutes, Bannocks had adopted the lifestyle of Plains Indians, who made their living on horseback hunting buffalo. Bannocks were also one of the most warlike tribes in the West.[2]

Chief Taghee had been an inspirational leader who united the Bannock tribe, but his death in 1871 on a trip to the plains for buffalo had destabilized his people. His sixteen-year-old son, also Taghee, would be his successor, but a struggle developed over who would have control until Taghee was of a suitable age.[3]

During the 1877 Nez Perce War soldiers had limited Bannocks to their reservation at Fort Hall (near present-day Idaho Falls). Since the Fort Hall Bannocks made a living by hunting and gathering off the reservation, restricting them to the reservation limited them to the rations funded by Congress at four and a half cents per day per person.[4]

The Bannocks were still confined on the reservation in August on a starvation diet when rumors of an impending attack led to disturbances, one of which was a shooting by Nampeyogo. The Bannocks were ordered to produce Nampe, but were either unable or unwilling to comply. Eventually the cavalry found and arrested him and then surrounded two Bannock villages, where they captured fifty-three warriors, thirty-two guns, and three hundred ponies. The *Idaho Statesman* reported that throughout the affair the Bannock displayed no fear and "they were in no way backward in using threats and insults toward the soldiers performing this duty."[5] The subsequent freeing of the warriors and return of the ponies did not undo the insult or turn bad blood to good. That spring the Fort Hall agent, William Danilson, allowed the Bannocks to leave the reservation. By about May 1, two hundred Bannocks had convened at Big Camas Prairie.

Charley's shot cast Nesbet to the ground. He crawled several feet into his tent for his gun. Kensler started for the tent, too. Indian Jim then shot Kensler in the head. The bullet glanced off, knocking Kensler down and lodging in his horse. Charley and Jim turned and began firing at Silvey. Their shots went astray. While Charley and Jim's attention was on Silvey, Kensler regained his feet, reached for Nesbet's gun, and opened fire on the two Indians. They turned and ran. One was hit but continued. Kensler and Silvey saddled two horses. Silvey helped Nesbet onto the back of Kensler's horse. They rode as fast as Nesbet could tolerate, regularly looking back. After five miles they appropriated a third horse. After twenty miles they reached the settlement of Dixie Station, where Kensler's horse promptly died. They told their story. Their listeners soon had listeners of their own. In a few more minutes it seemed that all of Boise knew, and in not much longer, all of the Northwest. Nesbet soon had medical attention. He survived.[6]

Bannock warriors convened a war council that evening. Many Bannocks had foreseen what was coming and, wanting no part of it, had started back to their reservations at Fort Hall and Fort Lemhi.[7] At the war council Buffalo Horn, tall and angular, long black hair held in cords by beaded rings, fixed the Bannocks with intense black eyes that dominated a face of startling magnetism.[8]

Just a year earlier Buffalo Horn had led Bannock scouts in support of U.S. troops under General Oliver Otis Howard in the Nez Perce War. Buffalo Horn's position exposed him to General Howard's tactics, his strengths and his failings, and the army's weak showings in the battles at White Bird Canyon, the Clearwater, the Big Hole, and Camas Meadows. After the war Buffalo Horn returned to his reservation in relative anonymity. In January 1878 came the confiscation of Bannock guns and ponies. Soon he was laying plans for an alternative to life under the boot of the bluecoats.

At the war council at Big Camas Prairie, Buffalo Horn reminded his followers of the agent's warning that the entire tribe would be held responsible for the misdeed of any member. Because of the shootings that morning they were already guilty in the soldiers' eyes, he argued; they should get something in return for the guilt—horses or cattle or whatever else the warpath might yield. Buffalo Horn persuaded about two hundred to join him.[9]

The following day Buffalo Horn led his warriors west toward Boise City and raided a stagecoach station at King Hill, making off with eight horses. The proprietor of the station saw the Indians in time to flee into the hills. On June 2 they crossed the Snake River at Glenns Ferry, set the ferry adrift, and captured two large freight wagons laden with groceries, revolvers, cartridges, and powder.[10]

On May 31, 1878, General Oliver Otis Howard looked up from the telegram that had just arrived at his home in Portland, Oregon, and remarked to his wife, "Is it possible that we must go through another such ordeal as that of last year?"[11] It had been a year nearly to the day since he was notified that hostilities had broken out between nontreaty Nez Perce Indians and settlers in the Idaho Territory. He had spent the summer and early fall of 1877 locked in a war in which he led the U.S. forces to success against the Nez Perce. For Howard personally, however, it was well short of a success. After the war he had endured bruising and, he believed, unfair attacks in the press. While he surely did not welcome another war, the Bannock uprising was nevertheless a chance to restore the reputation he believed he had earned in his years of service to his country as a soldier and public servant. On June 7 Howard and his aide, Charles Erskine Scott Wood, boarded a train in Portland for Boise, to take command of forces gathering to suppress the uprising.[12]

Howard first met Erskine Wood in the winter of 1876. Wood's commanding officer at Fort Vancouver had sent him across the Columbia River to army headquarters in Portland. Wood could not hire a boat because no one would risk their vessels in the running ice. He found an empty skiff and shoved off, pushing his way through ice floes until he discovered that the joints of the skiff had been watertight only because they were frozen. By midriver they were melting. The boat sank just as he reached Hayden Island, where he persuaded a pair of woodchoppers to ferry him across the final stretch of the Columbia. Then a walk through a dense fir forest led to Portland, where he delivered his dispatches to General Howard.

"I rather think that was our first meeting," Wood wrote in a diary. "Anyway he took a fancy to me." Nearly everyone did.[13] A biographer described him: "With resolute chiseled features, curly black hair, and keen, penetrating eyes he cut a dashing figure. He was cultured, self-assured, immensely charming."[14] Wood grew to know Howard's family, which filled the many gaps left by his own. Wood had emerged from West Point without enthusiasm for the army. He could talk openly with Howard about his aimlessness, a subject that stoked a cold fury in his alcoholic father. When Wood discovered that Howard was publishing in religious papers and eastern magazines, he began seeking advice on writing from the general. Howard's children, from Guy at Yale and Grace at Vassar down to four-year-old Bessie, also fell under Wood's spell. Soon a "Wood" bedroom materialized in the Howard home.[15] After serving as Howard's aide in the 1877 Nez Perce War, Wood grew even closer to Howard in their joint campaign to defend Howard's conduct of the war in the press and within the army.

As Wood and Howard made their way toward Camp Boise, a cavalry platoon led by Captain Reuben Bernard pursued Buffalo Horn. Bernard had come to soldiering by happenstance. He was the second of fourteen siblings in a family that barely scratched out a living in the mountains of eastern Tennessee. It was not a sense of adventure that drove him from home, but the coughing and sneezing that was triggered every time his hoe shook the pollen off a corn tassel. To escape his allergy symptoms, he set out for Knoxville and wandered into the shop of a blacksmith, who quickly discovered that the lad was a quick, eager study and every bit as powerful as his commanding physique promised. The blacksmith hired Bernard, who took his first pay in advance in the form of a nearly endless meal, his first in days. It was not long before Bernard had mastered the skills of the job. Yet he took no satisfaction from it. When he stumbled on an opportunity in February 1855 to enlist in First Dragoons, he leapt at the chance without bothering to quit his blacksmith job.

He ended up serving under a West Point graduate, Second Lieutenant Richard Lord, in New Mexico. Lord struggled to maintain discipline among a rough lot of dragoons. He decided to look for a man with the leadership skills that he lacked. Although Bernard was a green recruit among veterans, Lord promoted him to first sergeant. It was not long before a veteran undertook to discuss Bernard's order before deciding whether to obey it. The veteran suddenly found himself in the dirt, smarting in a way that was still fresh in his memory on the next occasion that the green kid gave him an order. After several others had similar lessons in respect for the new officer, Lord found that through Bernard he had gained a disciplined company. Bernard had found his calling. He continued in positions of cavalry command in conflicts with Indians and in Civil War battles (for the North) at Culpeper, Charlottesville, Spotsylvania, Cold Harbor, Chickahominy, Halltown, Winchester, Bunker's Hill, Five Forks, and Appomattox, to name a few.[16]

As Bernard was gathering his forces at Camp Boise to respond to the outbreak, he happened upon army surgeon John Fitzgerald, who was in town to refit his supply of medicine. Fitzgerald had served under General Sherman in his March to the Sea in the Civil War, and may have come to know General Howard at that time. Now the doctor dropped his plans and joined Bernard's command. On June 5, with no ferry to cross the Snake, Bernard, Fitzgerald, officers, and troops crossed on a small skiff, horses swimming alongside, and resumed their pursuit of Buffalo Horn.[17]

CHAPTER 13

Exodus

On June 3 a horse of uncommon bearing burst into Camp Harney with a rider who appeared to have the handle of a shovel projecting to the side. Only when the rider dismounted, and gracefully at that, did the apparent shovel handle reveal itself as a peg leg that rose almost to his hip. He showed no fatigue despite his 150-mile ride from Camp Boise. He carried a message for the Camp Harney commander that Bannock Indians had attacked settlers and that Camp Boise needed all troops that could be spared.[1]

The Harney Valley had remained unsettled while hostilities of the Snake War were erupting unpredictably. Once the Paiutes surrendered to General Crook and camped peacefully near Camp Harney, interest in Harney Valley began to percolate. In 1869 the first permanent settler, John S. Devine, arrived on a silver-trimmed saddle, sporting a wide-brimmed hat and a bolero jacket. With the backing of W. B. Todhunter, a wealthy California cattleman, Devine began building a cattle empire on a ranch just south of Steens Mountain and another along the Silvies River near its outlet into Malheur Lake.[2]

Among the Willamette Valley settlers who were lured to Paiute country after the Snake War were three generations of the Smyth family. George and Margaret Smyth and family had departed Missouri in 1853 for Oregon, settling near the town of Junction City in the Willamette Valley. Twenty years later George and Margaret, with their children and their children's families, retraced about 250 miles of the 1853 journey to a hot spring near present-day Burns. On September 29, not long after their arrival, Candace

Smyth, wife of the oldest child, John, gave birth to Margaret ("Maggie"), the first white child born in the Harney Valley.

At about noon on Thanksgiving Day, two days short of Maggie's second month, a snowfall began. For the next three days it continued, burying Harney Valley under a three-foot blanket that threatened the Smyths' livestock. While others rescued the animals, Stilley Riddle, young husband of Sarah Smyth Riddle, journeyed south in search of a better location. A few days later Stilley returned with news of a fertile crescent where the snow was minimal and good grazing grasses drew their moisture from what are now known as Smyth and Riddle Creeks. The families drove their stock south and settled in the seemingly perfect cattle country that Stilley had discovered.[3] He had no way of knowing that farther upstream on Smyth and Riddle Creeks, just above the newly claimed Smyth family ranch, was a flat that was a favorite location of many Paiutes.

The rangeland where the Smyths settled took on an optimistic name, Happy Valley. Perhaps it was an antidote for the ubiquitous Malheur: Malheur Lake, Malheur River, Malheur Reservation, Malheur Paiutes. There may have been a touch of defiance, of contrariness, in placing "Happy Valley" on a map where the other works of man were known as Folly Farm Flat, Poverty Flat, Brokendown Waterhole, and Dead Horse Reservoir, and where the works of nature inspired such names as Raw Dog Creek, Poison Basin, Disaster Peak, Skull Creek, Bastard Spring, and Little Stinking Water Basin.

In early June 1878, word reached the Smyths at Happy Valley of an Indian uprising in Idaho that appeared to be heading west. George and Margaret Smyth, their sons John and Darius, John's wife Candy, their four children, and Stilley and Sarah Riddle loaded a few essentials in wagons and hastened north to Camp Harney, where most of the area population gathered.

At noon on June 5 William Rinehart, the Malheur agent, began to notice Indians leaving the reservation in droves. In the report that he later made to the commissioner, he did not describe any details—what the Paiutes carried with them; whether they left in haste or at leisure; whether their mood was gay or grim.[4] Within twenty-four hours all Indians were gone.

Sarah's cousin Jerry Long, Rinehart's translator, spent June 5 on a long ride to pick up the agency mail, which he delivered to Rinehart that evening. When Rinehart told him that the Indians were leaving, Jerry appeared to Rinehart to be "greatly alarmed—gave no hint of having learned the news from other sources." The next day Jerry, too, was gone.[5]

Rinehart was in a fix. His concern about the gradual decline of the Malheur population was now eclipsed by the sudden, baffling disappearance of the population in its entirety. The press, the public, and the Office of Indian Affairs in Washington DC would all expect an immediate explanation. Among possible causes of the Paiutes' disappearance, Rinehart himself was the leading candidate, for the discontent of the Malheur Paiutes was widely known. That summer the *Owyhee Avalanche* would declare, "We believe that his [Rinehart's] mistreatment of the Indians under his immediate supervision at Malheur, has caused them, one and all, to leave the reservation" and, later, "If reports from Piutes and other sources are true, Indian agent Rinehart is to a great extent responsible for this state of affairs."[6]

In fact Rinehart's oppressive rule was not the sole cause of Paiute discontent at Malheur. Congressional appropriations for Indian reservations had plummeted. After the Civil War railroad construction boomed, attracting seemingly unlimited capital, which fueled even more growth. The building of railroad infrastructure, however, produced little short-term return. Investors became more skittish as Indian troubles attracted headlines. Prominent among the troubles was the Modoc War and Kientpoos's murder of General Canby in April 1873, followed by his trial and execution. On September 18, 1873, Jay Cooke & Co., a major financial firm heavily invested in railroads, folded, brought down by a conspiracy of junior partners. The collapse triggered a cascade of more than one hundred bank failures and almost twenty thousand business failures, plunging the nation into its worst depression to that time.[7]

Over the life of the depression, 1873–78, congressional appropriations for the Malheur Reservation dropped from $50,000 to $15,000. Under the $15,000 appropriation, Rinehart calculated that, after other expenses were met, the balance left for food was the equivalent of four and a half cents per day per person. The same was true at Fort Hall. "The Indians Starved into Fighting," announced the June 13, 1878, headline in the *Morning Oregonian*. The starvation of the Indians provided "additional proof of the assumption that invariably some wrong done to Idaho Indians has been the cause of their wars with whites," according to the *New York Times*.[8]

Yet these global causes for the unrest at Malheur were unlikely to distract attention from Rinehart himself as the principal suspect. Other reservations experienced budget cuts but still retained their Indians. Rinehart had lost his amid suspicions that he mistreated the Paiutes. He did not know why his Indians had left, but he surely knew that if he had no explanation for their departure, the blame was all the more likely to fall on him. It was not in Rinehart's character to allow such a thing to happen.

CHAPTER 14

Truth Management

By noon on June 7, Rinehart's reservation had been empty for twenty-four hours. Waiting much longer to notify the commissioner and explain why the Indians had left could raise eyebrows. As he began composing a letter to the commissioner, the uprising was limited to Idaho and appeared likely to remain so. Therefore, an Indian leaving Malheur in the direction of Boise would incur suspicion. If the Indian claimed that he was going elsewhere but then turned toward Boise, suspicion would begin to approach conviction.

In his letter to the commissioner Rinehart described a sequence of events beginning with the issuance of rations on May 20. Among those who appeared for rations that day, he wrote, were forty-six Bannocks from Fort Hall, Idaho. Rinehart noted that one of the Bannocks had a permit to hunt from the Fort Hall agent (implying that the forty-six were armed). Rations were next issued on June 1. On that day, he continued, the same forty-six arrived and "Chief Egan begged me to issue [rations] to them . . . and upon my refusal he divided his own with them." On June 2, "Egan got my permit to buy some ammunition and asked me to say on paper that he wanted to trade his horse for a gun, which I did." Egan then left "in the direction of Boise claiming to be going to the fish traps" but was later seen past the fish traps. On June 7 Rinehart sent a telegram to General McDowell's office in San Francisco, with much the same information, adding, "Indians commenced stealing away on 2d instant, Eagan going first."[1]

Rinehart had not directly accused Egan of anything, but the implied accusation was unmistakable. Egan's close ties to the forty-six apparently armed Bannocks led by Jack, Egan's sudden desire for ammunition and a gun, his pretense of going to the fish traps to conceal his true destination—all combined to produce the intended result. Indeed many decades later Rinehart's allegations are still alive and well. In 1974 Steward and Wheeler-Voegelin urged, "When the Bannock War broke out in Oregon . . . , after 46 Bannocks had . . . been refused food by Agent Rinehart, Egan interceded for the Bannock, and failing this, shared his supplies with them, joined forces, and left the reservation. . . . No other Northern Paiute leader showed such close affinity with the groups designated as Bannock."[2] Egan "became one of the leaders in the Bannock war."[3] In her 2004 biography of Sarah Winnemucca, Sally Zanjani wrote: "A party of forty-six Bannocks arrived to speak of Buffalo Horn's plan. . . . Not long after these talks, Egan, Oytes, and their bands joined the Bannocks."[4]

It is true that hostile Bannocks arrived at the Malheur Reservation in early June, but they were no friends of Egan. The forty-six Bannocks who appeared in the mess hall on May 20 and June 1, with whom Egan shared his rations and whom Egan accompanied to the fish traps, were peaceful Bannocks led by Bannock Jack. Since they were families, it is unlikely that more than one-third were men. The hostile Bannocks who arrived in early June, in contrast, were all men, or nearly so.[5] The Bannocks under Jack came to Malheur to avoid the hostilities, not to join them. Sarah Winnemucca first learned of Bannock Jack's group in May from the Paiutes who visited her in the John Day Valley. From these Paiutes Sarah learned that Bannock Jack had led his forty-six people to Malheur in May to escape the impending violence at the Bannock-Shoshone Reservation at Fort Hall, Idaho, and to make a peaceful home at the Malheur Reservation under its benevolent agent, Samuel Parrish. Only after Jack's Bannocks reached the Malheur River fish traps did they discover that Parrish had been replaced by William Rinehart.[6]

Jack's forty-six Bannocks were only a portion of the peaceful Bannocks who came to Malheur to escape impending troubles at Fort Hall. In April, a time when the Malheur population usually declined as Indians left to hunt and gather, Rinehart reported that the Malheur population was growing rapidly, as a result of "the threatened difficulty at Fort Hall." The influx of Fort Hall Bannocks at the Malheur Reservation "must be taken as an index to their [Bannocks'] fears . . . that there is real trouble abroad in the near future."[7]

Jack and his people had been at the Malheur River fish traps since mid-May, one hundred miles from Big Camas Prairie, when the outbreak occurred and when Buffalo Horn recruited warriors there. As a result of Rinehart's deceptions, Egan's close relationship with Jack's peace-seeking Bannocks has been misconstrued for over a century as evidence that he was allied with the hostiles.

In early June Bannocks of a different disposition arrived at Malheur. On June 2 Buffalo Horn's Bannock war party crossed the Snake River at Glenns Ferry and captured two wagons there, helping themselves to a trove of weapons and supplies. Twenty-five miles east of Glenns Ferry is the valley of the Bruneau River. The *Idaho Statesman* reported that an Indian rode through the valley warning ranchers. They joined together at one ranch, where they watched in safety as Indians drove about six hundred horses through the valley. "As nearly as they could be counted," the article reported, the Indians "numbered about 150 warriors."[8] Since Buffalo Horn's party began with 200 warriors and only 150 went from Glenns Ferry to Bruneau Valley, about 50 split from the main party, probably at Glenns Ferry.

From the ferry to the small Oregon town of Jordan Valley is a long day's ride. An unremarkable, apparently unnoticed military report stated that on June 2, the same day that 150 Natives rode through Bruneau Valley, a small group of tribesmen surrounded a house in Jordan Valley and demanded guns and ammunition.[9] The considerable distance between Jordan and Bruneau Valleys makes it improbable that any Bannocks participated in both events.

The small advance party's long ride to Jordan Valley on June 2 suggests that it had an urgent mission. From Jordan Valley it was another 120 miles to the Malheur Agency, a distance that allowed them to reach Malheur on the afternoon of June 4. They would then have had time to reconnoiter the reservation and plan their strategy for June 5, the day that began the Paiutes' sudden and unexpected flight from the reservation.

The first of the whites in Harney Valley to learn that Bannocks of unfriendly disposition were about was probably J. G. Abbott. Four years earlier Abbott had opened the Alvord Post Office in the vicinity of the Alvord Desert, an expansive playa in the eastern shadow of Steens Mountain.[10] On about June 6, 1878, a young Paiute had arrived at Abbott's office on a panting pony. After listening to the young man's tale, Abbott wrote a message to the effect that Bannocks at the Malheur Reservation had captured all the arms there and announced they were going to burn the houses and take the stock. The message continued that the Paiutes were asking for guns to defend themselves. Abbott handed the message to the young man, who set a course for Fort McDermitt, fifty miles southeast.

The message came to Captain Thompson, commanding officer at McDermitt. On June 9 he forwarded Abbott's message to the assistant adjutant general in San Francisco.[11] There is no sign that it was ever read. Although it is not mentioned again, it is corroborated by Lee Winnemucca's statement to Sarah several days later at Steens Mountain that "the Bannocks . . . have taken from us what few guns we had."[12]

The Paiutes' unanimous decamping from the Malheur Reservation, their home of the last five years, was out of character. Coordinating the entire reservation meant uniting all of the chiefs and subchiefs, with the many sovereign family units under each, on a single course of action. Such a broad-based unity was at least unusual, perhaps unprecedented. And yet over a twenty-four-hour period starting at noon on June 5, 1878, all Paiutes left the reservation, abandoning permanently all their benefits, including rations, clothing, schooling, and medical care.[13]

Clues to the Paiutes' attitude toward the troubles stirred by the Bannocks are provided by the reactions of other Native peoples. Even though Bannocks were one of the most aggressive, warlike tribesmen in the West, most of them shunned this war. Many fled their Fort Hall reservation weeks in advance to be out of danger.[14] In the end well below fifteen percent of the Bannocks and Shoshones at Fort Hall took part.[15] Even the Bannocks who chose war did not plunge into the conflict impetuously. They canvassed other tribes in search of allies, including Shoshones at the Duck Valley Reservation in Nevada, Shoshones at Carlin Farms Reservation, Paiutes at Pyramid Lake, Nevada, and Umatillas. All refused, despite the Bannocks' heavy-handed tactics.[16]

Only ten years earlier these Paiutes were fighting the last battles of the Snake War, in which Superintendent Huntington estimated four thousand Paiutes died. Probably closer to the mark is five hundred, which represents about twenty percent of Paiutes in the Oregon Country at that time.[17] Twenty percent is a fatality rate ten times higher than that of the United

States in the Civil War, which was the country's bloodiest by far. Deaths in the Civil War exceeded the total American fatalities in the Revolution, the War of 1812, the Spanish-American War, World War I, World War II, and the Korean War combined.[18]

Five hundred deaths left the Paiutes with scores of orphans and widows, and hundreds of wounded carrying the emotional scars of surviving a bath of the blood of those they loved. Most of each group were among those who, ten years later, left the Malheur Reservation on June 5 and 6, 1878, and reached the camp on Steens Mountain about a week later. Any claim that the ten years that had elapsed since the Snake War had dulled Paiute memories of that conflict was answered in April 1878. During that month Paiute leaders confronted Rinehart with accusations that he planned to take their guns and horses, as had occurred to the Bannocks at Fort Hall. Rinehart reported to the commissioner that he had told the Paiute chiefs that if they wanted to make a complaint, he "would invite General Crook to come" and investigate. "The mention of General Crook's name," Rinehart added, "hushed them to silence and ended the conference. No name is better known or more dreaded by them."[19] Surely the dread felt by the average Paiute was no less than that felt by their leaders. The Court of Claims found that by the end of the Snake War Paiutes were "completely terrified" by the soldiers.[20] The theory that these Indians—including the orphaned, the widowed, the wounded, the emotionally scarred—embraced with unanimity another war, against the same enemy that had inflicted such horrific losses in the Snake War and that still inspired dread in 1878, swims upstream against a torrent of evidence.

The rise among four or five hundred Indians of a passion to go to war was ordinarily neither a subtle nor a quiet phenomenon. Rinehart knew from 150 miles away, months in advance, that the Fort Hall Bannocks were on the brink of war. Yet, at the Malheur Reservation over which he presided, he had no inkling that his Indians were on the brink of a mass exodus until the very moment that it began. On June 4, the day before the departure began, he ordered thirty thousand pounds of flour for rations, and he prepared to purchase four workhorses for the approaching harvest.[21] He was expecting an ordinary, uneventful summer. Equally telling is the fact that Jerry Long, an important figure in the Paiute leadership, was just as surprised as was Rinehart.[22] The stark difference between the

Paiutes' sudden, quiet, unexpected departure from their reservation and the Bannocks' long-anticipated and widely predicted outbreak reveals with equal clarity that what drove the Paiutes bears no resemblance to what drove the Bannocks.[23]

Bannocks were regimented, hierarchical, and militaristic, qualities that evolved as a result of the demands of buffalo-hunting and self-defense in Blackfeet country. It is not surprising, therefore, that Paiutes feared Bannocks. General Howard learned of this fear when he asked Captain Reuben Bernard to recruit Paiutes to take a peace overture to the Bannocks. Bernard responded: "So far I can get no Indian or other person to attempt such a thing. The Piutes hereabouts [Silver City, Nevada] and in Duck Valley [Nevada] are all assembled near the whites for protection."[24] Howard's own experience was similar. He wrote in his account of the war: "The friendly Paiutes were so much alarmed, and felt so sure that we would be beaten [by the Bannocks], that no promise of reward could induce them to remain with us or to act as guides."[25] The Idaho City paper reported that "around Silver City are a great many Piutes, who are afraid to move in any direction. Either Bannocks or whites, they fear, are liable to slaughter them."[26]

Uniting four hundred or so Native Americans with little common history and multiple independent leaders to act in virtual unison would require an urgent purpose. The purpose would have to be particularly compelling if it required them to leave their homes of the last five years and abandon all of their governmental benefits. Rushing into the arms of Indian warriors who terrified them to go into battle against a foe that had slaughtered hundreds of Paiutes just ten years earlier is not the kind of purpose that would attract more than a small minority of such Indians, to say nothing of the whole of them.

Rinehart's June 7 letter to the commissioner and his telegram to General McDowell of the same date implied that Egan instigated the Paiute departure from the reservation to lead them into war. This was Rinehart's opening salvo. He had "entered the territory of lies without a passport for return."[27] A week later he sent a telegram to the commissioner and probably to the *Oregonian* claiming that a messenger, Jack Scott, told him that Egan was with four hundred Indians in Barren Valley, and that Egan said "he don't want to talk wants to fight was having a scalp dance . . . several whites have been killed."[28] The next day's *Morning Oregonian* carried a story under the heading, "The War Getting into Oregon." It read in part, "Egan, a Piute chief, was at the head of 400 warriors and resolved to go upon the war path." On June 17 a front-page headline of the *Morning Oregonian* read, "All the Malheurs Gone on the War Path." Tracking Rinehart's June 14 telegram almost word for word, the story read: "On the 2d inst. they [Paiutes] began stealing away on pretense of hunting and fishing but all took nearly the direction of Boise. Chief Egan went away the first. . . . The Malheur Indians, under Chief Egan [are] on the war path."[29] These June 15 and June 17 stories, orchestrated by Rinehart, anointed Egan as the Paiute war chief.

Rinehart's reports on Indians he wished to discredit reliably included claims that the Indians were indulging in a disreputable dance—a "war dance," a "scalp dance," a "brothel dance"—or outright prostitution.[30] Rinehart's telegram claimed Scott had told him that at a meeting between Paiutes and Bannocks at Barren Valley (about fifty miles northeast of Steens Mountain) Egan had said he wanted to go to war. Yet Scott swore in an affidavit that at Barren Valley it was reported to him that "Oits wanted to fight the whites and Egan did not."[31] Rinehart claimed Scott had told him that "several whites have been killed," but none was killed or injured. Nor was Egan leading four hundred Indians at Barren Valley. He was there on his own.[32] Parroting the falsehoods in Rinehart's telegram, the *Oregonian* article became part of the bedrock of white beliefs about the Bannock War.

Two months after the war began, Rinehart sent the commissioner a report elaborating on the statement attributed to Egan that he wanted to fight, not talk. According to this report, Egan said that he knew whites would win, but he would fight as long as he could and then "the Great Father at Washington would give them more supplies, like he did when they quit fighting before, and not try to make his people work."[33]

The Paiutes "quit fighting before" at the end of the Snake War. The "supplies" that Paiutes received after that war were nonexistent. For more than five years after the war Oregon-based Paiutes attempted to eke out a living in the vicinity of army forts, primarily Fort Harney. The chaplain there reported, "These Indians are miserably poor, and need both food and clothing. They subsist at present entirely upon wild cherries," wild rice, and "occasional charity from the garrison." Their clothing is "most pitiable," and they "must suffer, if not some of them perish, without help."[34] Rinehart's claim that Paiutes would go to war in order to repeat the suffering that Paiutes experienced after the Snake War, or that Egan would say such a thing, is consistent with Rinehart's many other attempts to shield himself behind a wall of false accusations against the Paiutes he was paid to protect.

According to Rinehart, the other reason Egan gave for taking his people to war was to spare them from working. Egan had raised this topic eighteen months earlier, suspecting that Rinehart was violating the law by requiring work. Sergeant John Grim was assigned to investigate Egan's complaint. Grim interviewed Egan and advised him that Rinehart was properly requiring Paiutes to work. In his official report Grim stated that Egan "said that he was glad I had come, that he believed I had told them the truth and that he would go to work again with a good spirit. I believe my visit will have a beneficial effect." Egan did go to work with a good spirit. After Grim's report there is no record of Egan or others disputing that report or objecting to working. Rinehart never explained his claim that the war was launched over an issue resolved eighteen months earlier and never again mentioned.[35]

Such were the machinations that led to the false coronation of Egan as leader of the hostile Indians. Once the press had a name for the war chief, that name became the default perpetrator of every Indian act of villainy and of every tactical error, whether there was reason or not to connect his name to the event. One writer mocked the military missteps of the Indians, which he ascribed to "Egan's embecility [sic]" and to missed opportunities that could only have occurred under "a blunderer like Egan."[36] Unrestrained by facts, the stories persisted: "A Party under Egan have burned Diamond Ranch"; "Egan was fully determined to go on the war path"; Egan is "a born devil, having only been restrained from constant murder and pillage by fear"; he will "not fight armed men but his savage propensities" are revealed in "the utmost cruelty to the defenseless."[37] The seeds Rinehart had planted were in fertile soil, sprouting robust limbs that would bear false fruit for decades.[38]

CHAPTER 15

Barren Valley Imbroglio

When news of the Bannock outbreak reached General Irvin McDowell in San Francisco, he sent a telegram to Captain E. F. Thompson, commanding officer at Camp McDermitt, to ask him to tell Chief Winnemucca to keep the Paiutes at peace. Through Thompson, Winnemucca responded to McDowell that he would keep the Paiutes at peace, but that was not the half of it. He would also "talk to the Bannocks there to try to make them keep the peace."[1]

To carry out his promise to preach peace to the Bannocks, Winnemucca first sent a request to his son Natchez to come at once to Camp McDermitt. The timing for Natchez was awkward. Railroad magnate Leland Stanford had promised him land from a railroad right-of-way near the Humboldt River, in Nevada, and in early 1877 Natchez's title to his new property had arrived. In early May 1878, he announced that he would resign his chieftainship and begin planting seeds recently donated to him. Then the message from his father arrived. Setting his plans aside, he joined his father at McDermitt. They embarked for Malheur on June 4. At about the halfway point Winnemucca stopped at Steens Mountain, while Natchez continued north and joined the roughly five hundred Paiutes who had left the Malheur Reservation and were now gathered at the Malheur River fish traps.[2]

It is clear that plans were laid at the fish traps because when the Paiutes left on about June 8 they left in two groups, each with a different destination. The rank and file rode directly south to Steens Mountain, about one hundred miles. The leaders—Natchez, Leggins, Jerry Long, and Egan—rode southeast to Barren Valley to meet the Bannock leaders and Oits. From Juniper Lake Winnemucca rode east to join the other Paiute leaders.

How and why the meeting was arranged is uncertain, but there is reason to believe that Winnemucca had an important role since he volunteered to General McDowell to talk peace to the Bannocks. Given Winnemucca's apparent enthusiasm for this task, it is likely that he had a central role in the decision to meet the Bannocks. Winnemucca's enthusiasm for this task arose from a vision that had long preoccupied the chief. This crisis offered him a chance to fulfill the vision in a more exhilarating way than he could have hoped for.

Winnemucca had discussed his idea with Rinehart in the spring of 1877, just over a year earlier. Rinehart had come to Camp McDermitt to persuade Winnemucca to return to the Malheur Reservation. He eventually found Winnemucca in the vicinity of Steens Mountain, a favorite retreat of the elderly chief. In 1865, for example, after the Mud Lake, Nevada, massacre, in which soldiers killed many Paiutes, he and a small group of grieving followers had found serenity and solace in the vast wilderness of Steens Mountain.[3]

The population of the Malheur Reservation had grown under Samuel Parrish's leadership, but after Rinehart replaced Parrish congressional budget cuts and Rinehart's autocratic rule had driven the population down. A declining population did not reflect well on the reservation agent. Rinehart hoped to improve his standing by persuading Winnemucca to return to Malheur with his people. Winnemucca responded that his goal was to have a new reservation on the upper reaches of the Owyhee River, where his people could farm and raise stock. It would be a "reservation" in name only. It would have no agency—that is, no government officials. Natchez's farm on the Humboldt River, Winnemucca believed, demonstrated that his plan was feasible.

After the meeting Rinehart reported to Commissioner Hayt that Winnemucca had no desire to come to Malheur or any other reservation. Winnemucca's people share his enthusiasm for an Owyhee reservation, Rinehart added, and he "will likely lead most of his people away from this reservation."

In the spring of 1878 Rinehart met Winnemucca again for the same purpose and found the chief had lost no enthusiasm for a reservation on the Owyhee.[4] Indeed Winnemucca had enlisted General McDowell in his effort to establish the reservation. McDowell had urged Secretary of the Interior Schurz and Commissioner Hayt to set aside small reservations for bands under Chiefs Winnemucca, Ochoho, and Natchez. Until the fall of 1878, McDowell believed that the Interior Department had agreed to these reservations and quite probably told Winnemucca as much.[5] In the early summer of that year, therefore, as Winnemucca and Natchez rode north out of McDermitt, Winnemucca had good reason to believe that he would get his Owyhee reservation.

The Paiutes' break from their Malheur Reservation on June 5 and 6, leaving them unmoored on the Malheur River, with no home and no plan, presented Winnemucca with an enticing opportunity. Leading the Paiutes from the Malheur River to Steens Mountain to meet the Bannocks would bring the Paiutes closer to Winnemucca's hoped-for Owyhee reservation. If he could make peace with the Bannocks, or simply persuade them to leave the Paiutes alone, he would be in an ideal position to take his followers, and possibly all the Malheurs, the remaining distance to what he hoped would become their Owyhee home. Winnemucca may have seen his role as peacemaker with the Bannocks as a path to an elevated status that would enable him to unite the disparate Paiute bands at an Owyhee reservation, under his leadership. But leading the Paiutes to Steens Mountain also risked playing into the hands of the Bannocks, who would have difficulty gaining control over the Paiutes if they were free to scatter at will. On the other hand, if the Paiutes, stripped of their arms, were compliant enough to camp jointly on Steens Mountain with their Idaho neighbors, the armed, regimented Bannocks would be well positioned to exert control over the disjointed Paiute clans.

Winnemucca had a limited number of followers, but he was regarded as the leading Paiute spokesman in dealings with other Indian peoples and with whites. Steward and Wheeler-Voegelin described Winnemucca as an "outstanding advocate of peace." Fellow Paiutes said in interviews that "Winnemucca smooth things up in case of trouble with other tribes" and that he was "raised above all others" when "the white people were coming into this particular area."[6] This developing crisis was precisely the type

FIG. 7. Chief Winnemucca. Courtesy of Oregon Historical Society, Neg. OrHi 51003/ 0333P206.

of situation in which Paiutes turned to Winnemucca for leadership. His assurance to General McDowell that he would talk peace to the Bannocks and his trip north toward Malheur with his son Natchez in response to McDowell's request showed Winnemucca's eagerness to step into his role as Paiute ambassador plenipotentiary. The alacrity with which Winnemucca took on the task of dissuading the Bannocks from war suggests, however, that he may have allowed his ambition to blur his judgment.

As the rank-and-file Paiutes left the Malheur River, riding directly toward the Steens Mountain camp, Paiute leaders branched off to the east to Barren Valley. Three groups convened there: the peace-minded Paiute leaders; the Bannock-Oits hostiles; and three whites, G. B. Crowley, a local rancher, Crowley's son James, and Jack Scott, a delivery contractor for Camp Harney. Scott attended at the request of Camp Harney to invite the Bannocks to discuss peace.

When Winnemucca told General McDowell that he would urge peace to the Bannocks, he had specific ideas in mind. He had been to cities in California, including at least two trips to San Francisco. He understood better than anyone in Barren Valley that day the overwhelming numbers and military capability of the people with whom the Bannocks had picked a fight. This was the line of argument that he intended to make to the Bannocks, according to the *Silver State*, which reported that Winnemucca and Natchez planned to invite the Bannocks to travel by train to San Francisco on the Fourth of July to see for themselves the folly of fighting a people as numerous as blades of grass on the prairie.[7]

Winnemucca had collected his thoughts for over a week and was prepared to address the hostiles. When his opportunity to speak arrived, he seized it. But the Bannocks abruptly shushed him. With that brief, decisive shush, his vision of leading a united Paiute people away from Rinehart's cruel regime and out of the clutches of the Bannocks to a new home on the upper Owyhee under his chieftainship dissolved. In its stead was humiliation. He wept.[8]

Winnemucca had miscalculated. Since the Bannocks, like the Malheurs, were Northern Paiute, the inhibition against intratribal strife was undoubtedly the source of his apparent confidence that he would be able to bend the will of the Bannock warriors, or at least have a civil dialogue with them.[9] But the code that he expected to afford him at least a voice in the controversy apparently restrained the Bannocks from shooting him, but little else.

Winnemucca was not dealing with a random selection of Bannocks. These were a self-selected collection of the most militant of the Fort Hall Reservation. Moreover, they had stepped decisively over the line between peace and war. They had had considerable success—they were out from under the rule of their white oppressors and had accumulated a wealth of arms, ammunition, and provisions. Peace to them meant a return to confinement and deprivation—and possibly a noose for the leaders. For these Bannocks the Malheur-Bannock tribal connection represented not a mutual commitment with fellow Paiutes but an opportunity to deceive and entrap them.

After Winnemucca was silenced, the subject of written grievances was raised. As shown in the next chapter, Egan had earlier convinced Bannock Jack to dictate his grievances to Sarah for her to present in Washington DC. It was therefore probably Egan who now steered Bannock anger into this channel to divert them from the hopeless path on which they were so intent. A Bannock leader dictated their complaints, Natchez translated to English, and Jack Scott did the writing.

However, when Scott finished, the wily Bannocks asked the elder Crowley to read aloud what Scott had written. Crowley had been out of earshot. What Crowley read did not match what the Bannocks had said. Scott had toned down or omitted complaints, or so the Bannocks thought. Next, as reported erroneously by the *Morning Oregonian,* "The chief, Egan, stepped up to Scott, and taking hold of his hair, said: 'Me have that in my belt heap soon.'" The Bannocks and Oits then decided among themselves to kill the whites that night.[10] This plan was shared with the Paiutes but not with the whites. Beef was brought and a fire prepared. Natchez told the whites of the murder plan, instructing them to be cheerful and gay, to cut off some beef, and to begin cooking it. While the whites were holding their meat in the fire, Natchez called an Indian council in the tent. When all were gathered, Lee or Jerry lifted a side of the tent and told the whites, "Now go!" Natchez then rose, declared that he was sick, and left the tent. He led the three whites to bushes where he had hidden horses. They were joined by Winnemucca and Leggins. All rode hard, but Natchez's and Winnemucca's horses gave out. All escaped except Winnemucca. Natchez was able to reach Nevada safely despite an actual sickness that immobilized him for three days.[11]

The *Morning Oregonian* reported that Egan protected Scott at the camp, "but when he [Scott] was about two miles out the Indians came after him. Fleetness of his horse saved him."[12]

Egan and his son-in-law, Jerry Long, remained in Barren Valley with the Bannocks. Egan tried but failed to dissuade Eagle Eye's band of Weisers from joining the Bannocks. Next, more warring Bannocks arrived—after having killed a stagecoach driver near the Owyhee crossing and taken guns from the coach. The *Silver State* reported that Egan "talked peace until he became hoarse." Exasperated, he told Jerry to tell the Bannocks to leave the valley. "This enraged them and they took Egan prisoner," along with Winnemucca.[13]

The Paiute leadership was now in disarray. Having saved the lives of the three whites, Natchez and Leggins were in flight, back to Camp McDermitt. Egan and Winnemucca were prisoners of the Bannocks. Lee and Jerry remained at Barren Valley, perhaps not as prisoners, but surely under vigilant guard. Oits and his band, solidly allied with the Bannocks, guarded the Paiute prisoners. The rank-and-file Paiutes, unaware that their leaders' plans had gone so disastrously awry, were approaching the Steens Mountain camp.

CHAPTER 16

Rescue

In late May Sarah Winnemucca had promised the Paiutes who had visited her in the John Day River valley that she would go to Washington DC to explain to Indian Affairs their grievances against Rinehart. Her plan was to take her horse and wagon south to Silver City with two passengers. The fare from her passengers in addition to the proceeds from the sale of her horse and wagon would, she hoped, fund her rail journey from Silver City south on the Virginia-Truckee Railroad to the Central Pacific line, then east across the continent to Washington DC. Having lived off the reservation for months, Sarah planned to stop at Malheur on the way to Silver City to learn about Rinehart's conduct during her absence.

On June 5 at about 6:00 p.m. Sarah arrived at the Malheur Reservation and dropped her passengers, Mr. Morton and his young daughter, Rosey, at the agency office, probably with instructions not to say anything that would identify her since Rinehart had expelled her from the reservation. Sarah continued another two and a half miles to where her cousin Jerry lived. He had just returned from Rinehart's office, where he delivered the mail and where he learned from Rinehart that Indians had been leaving the reservation. Jerry volunteered to Sarah, "A great many of the Bannocks are here with us now, and I don't know what they are going to do here."[1] Tired from her travels, Sarah slept while Jerry sent word of her arrival to Egan at the fish traps on the Malheur River.

Early on the morning of June 6 Sarah was awakened by Egan's voice. She rose and at the council tent met Egan, Oits, and Bannock Jack (who had accompanied Egan from the Malheur River to Jerry's house). She took notes as Egan described to her the recent difficulties with Rinehart. When

Egan finished, he encouraged Bannock Jack to list Bannock grievances for Sarah to present as well. Jack did so. Egan then raised all the money he could, $29.25, to help finance Sarah's journey. She left Malheur for Silver City and Washington DC on about June 8.[2]

Although Rinehart never explicitly stated that Egan had been planning since at least June 2 to take the Paiutes to war, Rinehart's telegrams and letters fabricated an unbroken trail of bread crumbs that allowed for no other conclusion. The Egan that emerges from the historical record, however, is a different character altogether from Rinehart's construct.

When Egan was captured at the end of the Snake War he professed to the soldiers "a great desire to live thereafter in peace"; he offered to send couriers to bring in Weyouwewa, who, Egan said, was as weary of conflict as he was. He led his followers from Nevada to Malheur, because "now the white men say peace. . . . The red men and the white men must eat bread together." At Malheur, he would have nothing to do with Oits's mischief. On his first opportunity to speak before Linville, he vowed that he would do all he could to help to carry out the plans of the government.[3]

Throughout his three years at Malheur, he and Sarah worked as a team. They responded to Rinehart's abuse of the Paiutes with peaceful advocacy. With Sarah translating, Egan confronted Rinehart over his denial that Malheur was Paiute land, over his refusal to pay the Paiutes after promising that he would, and over his beatings of their people.[4] When Egan had believed that Rinehart was improperly requiring Indians to work, he raised his complaint through military channels and graciously accepted the decision that Rinehart's work requirements were proper.

Sarah's meeting with Egan early on the morning of June 6 was a continuation of their teamwork on behalf of the Paiutes. Egan equipped Sarah with the information that she needed, collected the meager funds that he could raise, and sent her to the capital to plead the Paiutes' case. After Sarah left for Washington DC, at Barren Valley Egan argued with the Bannocks against war so relentlessly that they took him into custody.[5]

Egan's commitment to Sarah's mission is palpable, down to the precision of the odd, paltry sum of $29.25. Rinehart's claim that Egan had been planning war since at least June 2 would mean that Egan dispatched Sarah on a three-thousand-mile journey to seek help from the central government of the very people against whom he was about to launch a war. Sending Sarah on an undertaking of this magnitude while plotting a war that would sabotage the undertaking and probably make Sarah appear a fool defies the evidence of Egan's character as well as the strength of his bond with Sarah.

Buffalo Horn's platoon of about two hundred had crossed the Snake River at Glenns Ferry early on June 2, with several days' lead on Captain Bernard's cavalry command. The Bannocks spent some of that lead gathering in whatever stock, supplies, and weapons they happened upon, but then pressed ahead toward Steens Mountain. Watching behind for signs of Bernard, preoccupied with the cattle and horses collected in Bruneau Valley, the Bannocks may not have been fully vigilant when a party of twenty-six volunteers from Silver City approached from the south, near the small town of South Mountain. According to Paiute Joe, a scout for the volunteers, in the ensuing skirmish he discovered that the troops for whom he was scouting had abandoned him to the Bannocks. Realizing that he could not escape by fleeing, he dismounted, rested his rifle on the saddle, and drew a careful bead on Buffalo Horn. If Joe's story is true, his squeeze of the trigger launched the most important bullet of the war, which would end in weeks; of Buffalo Horn's life, which would end in hours; and, probably, of Paiute Joe's life, which was miraculously extended as Buffalo Horn tumbled from his horse, bringing the Bannocks' pursuit of Joe to a halt.[6] While Joe's story was never confirmed, Buffalo Horn's death in the Battle of South Mountain is not in doubt.

It may well have been on the day of this battle that Sarah, Mr. Morton, and Rosey encountered a man who warned that war had broken out and that they should seek safety. Sarah and her passengers took shelter in a stone house along with others, where she happened upon Captain Bernard.[7] Bernard sent a telegram to General Howard, who was now at Fort Boise: "Sarah Winnemucca is in my camp; she wants to go to her people with any message you or General McDowell might desire to send; thinks if she can get to the Pi-Utes with such message she could get all the well-disposed to come near the troops, where they could be safe and fed."

General Howard had been impressed with Sarah when he met her four years earlier at the Malheur Reservation, where she was translating for

FIG. 8. Left of the dark peak, Sarah Winnemucca, George, and John passed over the north ridge of Steens Mountain to reach Indian camp. Author photo.

Samuel Parrish. Howard recalled her English as perfect and her appearance as "neat and tidy." He responded to Bernard's telegram: "Send Sarah with two or three friendly Indians straight to her people." Two of the Paiutes from Fort McDermitt, George and John, agreed to accompany her. Sarah had to explain to Mr. Morton and Rosey that she could take them no further. Rosey burst into tears. Mr. Morton asked Sarah to marry him. She politely declined.[8]

Riding west toward Steens Mountain, George, John, and Sarah found the Bannocks' trail at the Owyhee River crossing. In fifteen more miles they came upon torn clothes, hair, and broken beads, signs of a woman grieving. Sarah thought that this was where Buffalo Horn had died.

After fifty miles they stopped for the night. George and John took turns standing guard. Sarah tied her horse to her arm for lack of a tree, and was tugged out of sleep the night through.

The next day as they approached Juniper Lake on the east side of Steens Mountain, a figure appeared on the ridge above. George called out. A voice came back, "Who are you?" Sarah responded, "Your sister, Sarah." Her brother Lee Winnemucca rode down the slope, as incredulous as was Sarah that an encounter so fortuitous would occur at such a crucial moment. When they reached Lee, he warned that many Paiutes were prisoners of the Bannocks, who had confiscated Paiute guns and horses. Winnemucca was a prisoner. There was also good news: although the Bannocks had condemned their brother Natchez to death, he had escaped.

Once he understood Sarah's mission and her determination, Lee told Sarah to put her hair up and wrap herself in a blanket. He directed John and George to paint their faces and hide their guns. He warned Sarah, "Oytes will know you, for he is their chief now, since Buffalo Horn is killed." Lee led them up the ridge, from which they looked down on a melee of seven hundred Indians. George and John, Sarah's companions, could see that the Paiute camp was below them, but could not see that below the camp was a ranch. Had the ranch been in view, they might well have seen another George and John there. They were father and son. Good men, family men.

Lee led the trio down the slope, where they melted into the scene.[9] Sarah had an emotional meeting with her father, but then plans were made. Lee gathered horses and secured them at Juniper Lake. At dusk the women set out with infants on their backs and ropes in hand as if to gather firewood. Sarah, her father, and the rest crept away in the gloaming. The groups joined at Juniper Lake, including Lee's wife, Mattie (Egan's niece and adopted daughter). Lee turned back to attempt to rescue Jerry, who was nearly blind. The rest set out on horseback with six men as a rear guard, just as a full moon broke the eastern horizon, illuminating their way forward but exposing them to anyone watching for escapees.[10]

After six hours in the saddle they stopped to rest. As they were finishing some lamb, one of the rear guards burst upon them with news that Bannocks were in pursuit and that Egan's attempt to escape had been thwarted by Oits, who drove Egan and his people back to the Steens Mountain camp.

FIG. 9. Sarah Winnemucca. Courtesy of Oregon Historical Society, Neg. OrHi 76236/0333P222.

(A later press report stated that Egan had told both Winnemucca and Jerry that he was going to attempt to escape.)

In response to the report that Bannocks were giving chase, Winnemucca instructed Sarah and Mattie to summon help.[11] The two women pushed ahead to Sheep's Ranch, where General Howard and Erskine Wood, his aide, had set up headquarters. Wood described Sarah's arrival after fifty-five sleepless hours and 220 miles of hard riding: "At sunset three Indians turn the point of a rocky hill just purpling in the shadow of evening. They lash their horses and ride furiously. When they come up they bear a white flag. It is Sarah Winnemucca, her sister-in-law Mattie (Lee's wife), and 'George,' their escort. Sarah jumps from her panting and reeking horse and with tears streaming down her cheeks tells of her approach to the Indian camp."[12]

Howard wrote: "I had sufficient confidence in her story to change my whole plan of movement—a change which afterwards proved to be for the best." Howard's troops rescued Winnemucca and others who escaped with him (about fifteen, according to Wood). Dr. Fitzgerald wrote to his wife that Sarah "says the Bannocks and other hostiles have disarmed the Piutes generally . . . and threaten them if they will not join them." (Later Sarah spoke with reporters about rescuing her father. A window into her abilities with an audience is provided by one of the reports that resulted. She "created considerable merriment among a number of her white admirers," according to the article, when she joked that, to pass unnoticed into the camp of the hostiles, "she had to disguise herself as a squaw.")[13]

The following morning Sarah faced a decision. General Howard sent her a message: "I want you to go with me as my interpreter and guide." If she agreed she would be helping soldiers against some of her own people; she would be aligned with the people who had overrun her grandfather's and father's lands, who shot dead her uncle and other Paiutes peacefully fishing, and who killed Paiute women and children at Mud Lake.

Sarah's grandfather, Truckee, had also experienced wrenching losses at the hand of whites. Yet Truckee did not waver from his belief that his tribe's best chance at surviving this period of change and emerging to a decent new life depended on befriending whites and learning their ways. Truckee's son Winnemucca—Sarah's father—opposed fighting the whites, but he did not trust them. The best path forward, he believed, was to avoid antagonizing whites, but to stay away from them and their reservations.

Now it was Sarah's time to choose. Like her father and her brothers, she knew that this war was wrong for Paiutes. While Sarah was naturally skeptical, especially so of whites, she put soldiers in a different category. Her inclination was to trust them; it had served her well with many. She accepted Howard's offer.[14]

Howard had gathered a command of about 480 men in seven companies on foot and four cavalry troops. Based on Sarah's report after her return from Steens Mountain, he decided, in his words, "that the plan of campaign must be promptly changed, and every available man be brought to bear upon Stein's Mountain as the objective point." He sent out orders the morning of June 16 to coordinate each command in the area for an attack on the Steens Mountain camp.

CHAPTER 17

Steens Mountain

As the Paiutes traveled south to Steens Mountain, they knew that the Bannocks were at war and on their way to Steens Mountain, if not already there. Why did the Paiutes leave their reservation and ride over one hundred miles to meet the Bannocks?

Among those who have weighed in on this question are Steward and Wheeler-Voegelin, who declared that the Paiutes "left the [Malheur] Reservation to join the Bannocks in warfare." In their history of Idaho, Beal and Wells asserted that Steens Mountain "was the appointed place for the Bannock rendezvous with the Paiutes." In the words of Colonel William Parsons, "The Bannocks . . . were joined by a large band of Piutes, under the lead of Egan, their great war chief." Among those who concur are Weatherford ("by the time that General Howard reached the sheep ranch the Bannock Indians had formed junction with the Malheur Indians and were headed for or already were in the Steen Mountain country"), Trenholm and Carley ("Egan, convinced that his people wanted war, joined the Bannocks and assumed leadership of the hostile forces"), and Gregg ("the Bannocks under Buffalo Horn and the Piutes headed by E'Gantz united in Warm Springs valley").[1]

On June 11 and 12, 1878, Paiutes arriving from the Malheur River fish traps flowed into the camp on Steens Mountain, staked their horses, erected simple, fair-weather shelters, gathered roots and fuel, and fed their children. Among them were Egan's wife, Sally, their son Honey, now in his twenties, Honey's infant son, Herbert, and Mattie. Perhaps somewhere in their vicinity was the Adams family and their four-year-old, Annie. A sampling of Egan's followers, with the family size in parentheses, included

Pahnatgee (eight); Dr. Johnson (five); and Blind Oits (eight). Tanwahda's followers included Moothah (five); Tookahpoo (seven); Left Handed (five); and Grandma (seven). Winnemucca's followers counted among them Uncle Sam (thirteen); Uncle Jonathan (seven); and Zeeowits (four).[2]

These Paiutes had been directed to Steens by the leaders at the fish traps—Natchez and Lee Winnemucca, Jerry Long, Leggins, and probably Egan. Since all of these leaders opposed the Bannocks' war, the rank-and-file Paiutes did not expect the gathering at Steens Mountain to be a war council. However, the Paiutes would have quickly realized that the circumstances at the camp were not at all what they had expected. The only arms in the camp were in the hands of Oits, his band, and the Bannocks. Egan and Winnemucca were prisoners. Natchez, who had saved the three whites with Leggins's help, knew that he had made mortal enemies by his deception and therefore had no interest in participating in a Steens Mountain meeting with the Bannocks. Natchez and Leggins were on their way back to Camp McDermitt. Jerry Long was probably in custody with Egan and Winnemucca. Lee Winnemucca was apparently the only Paiute leader who was at liberty, other than Oits. The thirty or forty heads of family, lacking any experience in joint leadership on such a scale, were in no position to coordinate a plan of resistance.

The Paiutes had freely entered into a situation that, it rapidly became apparent, they were not free to exit.

Bannock arrivals at the Steens camp overlapped with Paiute arrivals. Oits, his band, and some Bannocks brought their prisoners from Barren Valley—Egan, Winnemucca, and probably Jerry. The main body of Bannocks, led by Buffalo Horn before his death, rode north from the South Mountain battle to the north flank of Steens Mountain. They ascended to the ridgetop. To the south of their position the ridge climbed to the summit of Steens, just under ten thousand feet. In every other direction the earth beneath them fell away before a panorama of expansive basins—a void uninterrupted by any peak of comparable height for two hundred miles to the west and northeast and for 120 miles to the north. To the northwest they looked down on a plateau alive with Paiutes tethering horses, cooking, and congregating. The Bannocks worked their way toward the camp, sun glinting off the breeches and barrels of new weapons. Many wore at their waists revolvers acquired from a load of freight at the west

FIG. 10. Steens Mountain from the east. Author photo.

landing of Glenns Ferry on the Snake River and Winchester rifles from a shipment carried by a stagecoach near the Owyhee River ferry.[3] Others flaunted fresh scalps, including John Bascom's, taken at the crossing of the Snake, and George McCutcheon's, driver of the stagecoach carrying the Winchesters.[4]

Ten years earlier, surprised by troops near Castle Rock on the North Fork of the Malheur, Egan had surrendered, announcing that he had a great desire to live his life out in peace. About a month later, at Camp Harney on June 30, he and the other Paiute chiefs had given their word to General Crook to remain peaceful. In the decade between wars, his protests against Rinehart's autocratic rule and his campaign to better the Paiutes' lot never flirted with the boundaries of peaceful advocacy. While the onset of Egan's conversion to peace was surely viewed with suspicion, he had been true to those words ever since, all the while emerging as the primary chief of the Paiutes of the Oregon country.

Everything that Egan had worked for during that decade, everything he stood for, was threatened by the Bannock warriors descending into the Paiute camp, adorned to celebrate violence, bloodshed, and death. The emotion in Egan's response to the Bannocks' arrival attests to the clarity of his vision of what their coming foretold. Raising his voice above the din, tears spilling down his cheeks, he cried out to the Bannocks: "Why do you come here among us to bring war to our fireside? Go away. We have done nothing. We are at peace. Why should you bring the soldiers upon us? You have made war and now you come among my people to bring war on them. My people will be killed."[5]

Eagle of the Light, a nontreaty Nez Perce who opposed the whites and the yielding of any land to them, confronted Egan. Egan responded, "I will not fight." Eagle of the Light retorted, "You coward," slashing with his knife but finding no flesh.[6] Running his knife deep into the ground, Eagle of the Light now told Winnemucca and Egan that there was a chance for them to redeem themselves by helping conquer the whites. An *Owyhee Avalanche* story, for which Winnemucca appears to be the source, reported that Winnemucca stood firm but Egan turned out to be a "bad egg." The same edition described an apparently different, later confrontation with Eagle of the Light, in which Winnemucca and Egan asserted that they had made a treaty with the whites and buried their guns and could not consistently take up arms against them now.[7] The same edition declared that Bannocks had imprisoned a large number of Paiutes for refusing to fight. The *New York Times* reported that the hostiles "are determined to retain the Piutes as prisoners until they can get a sufficient number of arms from the white men they kill to arm them." According to the *Owyhee Avalanche*, an Indian who escaped the Bannocks found his way to Captain Bernard's camp and said that "the hostiles had taken horses and everything from Egan and party and were holding them close prisoners."[8] An *Oregonian* story, headlined "Chief Egan of the Malheurs Disarmed," stated that "Egan is rebellious and his horses and arms have been taken from him and his Indians." Natchez Winnemucca, trusted by the soldiers, told General McDowell that Egan was "dismounted and under duress."[9]

Winnemucca's reference to Egan as a "bad egg" had a precedent. In May 1876, shortly before Rinehart took Parrish's position at the Malheur Reservation, Winnemucca had said to an officer at Camp Harney, "All the Indians like him [Parrish] except two, Egan and Oitz who are well known to be restless spirits; and with a less firm man than Mr. Parrish would be likely to create trouble. It was one of them who caused the disturbance, when Mr. Linville was agent." In fact, as far as the written record shows, neither Linville nor Parrish ever had a complaint against Egan. On the contrary, Parrish described Egan as "one of the strongest and best chiefs on this reserve."[10] Linville reported that Egan "refused to have any connection with Oytes, and professes to maintain friendly relations with the Agent [Linville]." Of Oits, on the other hand, Linville wrote that he plotted to kill all whites at the reservation, promising his followers that they would take over all the goods and foods in the commissary.[11]

Despite Winnemucca's claim that he could not remember whether it was Egan or Oits who plotted to kill all the whites, Winnemucca was so terrified of Oits that he and a number of his followers left the reservation when Oits began plotting and did not return until soldiers were posted at the reservation in the spring of 1874. After Winnemucca returned, he, Egan, and Jerry Long signed a statement to the commissioner of Indian affairs supporting Linville and noting that "Oitz has given our people much anxiety and trouble."[12] On another occasion Winnemucca and Egan together approached Samuel Parrish and told him that they were afraid of Oits.[13] Subagent Turner reported in September 1877 that Winnemucca had "an unshaken belief that 'Oits . . . has the power of witchcraft and that he will practice his evil enchantments until every Piute except his own little band is driven through fear from the agency.'"[14] Winnemucca knew precisely who Oits was and that Egan had no more sympathy with Oits and his schemes than did Winnemucca himself.

Winnemucca had his own ambition; it was served by his feigned confusion of Oits with Egan. It was only about twenty years earlier that Paiute chiefs first came into existence as a result of settlers intruding on their lands and interfering with their sources of nutrition. Driven by deprivation, Paiutes began to fight those responsible for their losses. War chiefs evolved to lead Paiute warriors. Some war chiefs learned to leverage their power to settle disputes rather than fight. Among them was Winnemucca, "an outstanding advocate of peace."[15] His strength was the respect he had earned with the military as an honest and peace-loving leader. Paiutes looked up to him when a need arose to deal with the whites.[16]

The Snake War was the beginning of the end of Paiute war chiefs. By 1873, as the Malheur Reservation opened, war chiefs were on the wane. Weyouwewa died that fall. Paulina had died six years earlier. Howluck was apparently dead. As the war chiefs lost influence and passed away, Egan was rapidly stepping into the void. Unlike the war chiefs, Egan was a threat to Winnemucca's position. Egan was as dedicated to peace as was Winnemucca, but he was also charismatic. Thirty years younger than Winnemucca, Egan was gaining recognition in the realm that Winnemucca believed was his.

It was probably not happenstance that the person to whom Winnemucca expressed his confusion of Oits with Egan was an officer at Camp Harney. A key to Winnemucca's prowess as a peace chief was that he had credibility with army officers. Exploiting his own credibility to undercut Egan's helped Winnemucca preserve his dominant position. Winnemucca's "bad egg" comment is suspiciously similar to his feigned confusion of Egan and Oits.

While this drama was unfolding on Steens Mountain, George Smyth and his son John were becoming restless at Camp Harney. With the fruits of years of labor bound up in their Happy Valley property and idle time on their hands, they found their heads swimming with tasks calling them back to their ranch with mounting urgency. Perhaps they should have taken a few more moments to check on the stock—possibly a mare about to give birth; perhaps a pipe into the watering station for the cattle that was inclined to clog. John was the Happy Valley schoolteacher. He may have realized that he should have brought books from the classroom, his lesson plans, and grade book because nearly all of his Happy Valley students were now at Camp Harney. His younger brother Darius had remembered his violin; with that many settlers in one place and nothing else to do, there could well be square dancing.

George and John gathered their rifles and ample ammunition, saddled up, and started back toward Happy Valley, the dog trotting alongside.[17] They rode south, toward Steens Mountain. They followed the route that Stilley Riddle, young husband of Sarah Smyth Riddle, followed as he led the entire Smyth clan to the homestead site that he picked for them five years earlier, unaware of the Paiute camp directly above. Unknown to George and John as they returned to George's ranch, that camp above was already busy with Paiutes arriving from the fish traps, who would soon be joined by a pair of Paiutes also named George and John.

The Bannocks on Steens Mountain had joined with one another into a fighting unit two weeks earlier. They had undertaken an immense gamble that pitted them against all whites and all uncooperative Indians. Their leader was now dead, but otherwise they had had few setbacks. Now this tightly knit group of warriors was camped with perhaps five hundred Paiutes, of whom about seventy—Oits's followers—were aligned with the Bannocks. The Bannock-Oits alliance was in control of the camp. The Paiutes' dread of Bannocks was now intensified by the Bannocks' superior numbers in weapons and warriors.

The Bannocks arrived at the camp with a focused agenda—to add the Paiutes to their ranks, preferably by choice; if not, by force. This issue was not negotiable for the Bannocks. Two or three hundred Indians had no chance of success against the whites. They needed many more, starting with the Paiutes. If they left Malheur with only a smattering of Paiutes, their chances of recruiting other tribes could evaporate.

Paiutes were as muddled and adrift as the Bannocks were united and focused. When Paiutes began leaving the Malheur Reservation for the Malheur River at noon on June 5, none of the leading chiefs was at the reservation, with the possible exception of Oits. Egan and Tanwahda were at the fish traps and had been there for days. Eagle Eye, a Weiser chief, had left the reservation on June 1 "going east" and on about June 11 joined the Bannocks and began depredations. Winnemucca and his son Natchez were on their way toward Malheur from McDermitt, but well short of halfway there.[18] Clearly there had been no planning or coordination. The sudden evacuation of the reservation had all the signs of a spontaneous reaction to an unforeseen and disturbing event.

Paiute families had limited experience in planning and coordinating with one another, even if they were aligned with the same chief. After the mass exodus from the Malheur Reservation on June 5 and 6, all families under all chiefs were suddenly, unexpectedly merged and migrating together to the Malheur fish traps. Not long after their arrival at the fish traps they were told that a meeting was planned with the Bannocks on Steens Mountain. Since they had fled from their reservation out of fear of Bannocks, there must have been apprehension over going to Steens to meet these very same Indians. Yet, Egan, Natchez, and the other Paiute leaders still believed that they could persuade the Bannocks to end their hostilities, for they were about to meet the Bannocks at Barren Valley for that very purpose. The Paiute leaders probably realized that convincing the Bannocks to end their war would be challenging and that success was by no means assured. On the other hand, risks of physical conflict with the Bannocks were likely to have been considered tolerable given the taboo against intratribal aggression.

At the Steens Mountain camp Paiutes were a swarm of independent family units with no structure for or experience in joint decision-making. The unified, well-armed warriors governing the camp therefore easily intimidated and managed the Paiutes. Peace-minded Paiutes were in no position to capitalize on their numbers by developing and communicating to the Bannocks a unified position. Once the Bannocks and Oits announced that the soldiers were preparing to attack and that all Indians would leave the Steens camp together, any remote chance of collective resistance to the Bannocks disappeared. Individual resistance would have been suicidal. With no practical alternative, the Paiutes who were opposed to the war nevertheless left Steens with the Bannocks.

Until that moment of departure from Steens, these Paiutes had been their own people choosing their own path for their own interests. They had nothing to do with the Bannocks' marauding on their way to the Steens Mountain camp—the killing of John Bascom at Glenns Ferry and the torturing of George McCutcheon, the stage driver who appeared to have escaped by mounting a horse that he had cut free of the coach harnesses, until the horse stumbled.[19]

It was only under the pressure of the Bannock-Oits alliance and the threat of the oncoming soldiers that the peace-seeking Paiutes acquiesced, joining the mass movement westward off the mountain. Most Paiutes had done nothing wrong and had no desire to fight the soldiers again. Many felt threatened more by the Bannocks than by the soldiers, yet they were riding alongside those they feared, in flight from those they did not. Somehow, through blameless acts done for worthy purposes, innocents were being stained with the blood of Bascom and McCutcheon.

CHAPTER 18

Silver Creek

On June 16 forces under General Howard approached Steens Mountain from the north, but by the time they reached the Indian encampment, seven hundred mounted Indians, along with another five hundred horses, had descended the mountain westward into sagebrush flatlands.[1] Some bent on mischief split from the group and burned ranches, killed the Chinese cook at Pete French's Ranch, and made off with ninety cavalry horses from Camp Harney.[2]

Oits's band descended from the Steens Mountain camp to Happy Valley, directly below. There the Indians discovered George Smyth's house and began piling sagebrush against it. A dog in the house began barking. Gunfire from upstairs felled Indians; others escaped. Then Oits's Indians returned to a side of the house with no windows. They piled sagebrush next to the house and ignited it, then trained their guns on the front door.

Once they finished their depredations, marauding Indians rejoined the main party. Moving west, an acre's expanse of horses, both mounted and free, rounded the south shore of Harney Lake, a dry, glaring bed of alkali, where vegetation ended and where, nineteen years earlier, Weyouwewa and Paulina had escaped from Henry D. Wallen's expedition with horses and rifles. From Harney Lake the Indian forces headed north into the valley of Silver Creek. A few miles upstream the canyon turned rocky; flowing water and forage grasses began to appear. Indians dismounted, made woven-grass shelters, slaughtered cattle, and assuaged their appetites. There had been little rest since the hasty departure from Steens Mountain, but the steady, relentless pace for over one hundred miles had earned time at Silver Creek to sleep, recover, and prepare for the next leg of the journey.

When the time of George and John Smyth's expected return came and went, John's brother Darius set out to look for them. As he approached Happy Valley in darkness, he could see that Indians had gathered horses from all the ranches. He drew close enough to hear the Indians talking to the horses but dared go no further. When he arrived back at Camp Harney with neither his father nor his brother nor any hard information, his brother John's wife and children became "frantic with grief."[3]

The following day Darius returned to Happy Valley. All appeared quiet. Rounding the bend leading to his father's house, he found it in ashes. He poked through the ruins until his fears were confirmed. He found a washtub in the debris. He carried the remains several hundred yards to the base of a hillside. He buried them. Then he began the ride back to Camp Harney, preparing what he would say to Candy, and how he would help her explain John's absence to her four young children.[4]

Long after the last voice in the Indian camp on Silver Creek trailed off into the inky void of a moonless night, several stars close to the eastern horizon disappeared, blocked by a slow-moving figure that came to a stop on a plateau overlooking the sprawling, makeshift community below. The figure was Rube Robbins, chief of the scouts working with Bernard. By starlight he selected several possible lines of attack and locations where troops could be secretly amassed in preparation for a charge. With battle strategies in mind he picked his way back down the rocky slope to his thirty-five scouts, who were now camped with Bernard and his four companies. He and Bernard formulated battle plans and issued orders. In the darkness Robbins led his scouts in a semicircle toward the upstream, north end of the Indians' camp to a point that he had picked out by starlight. Bernard stationed three companies at the downstream end, holding his fourth company in reserve.

At four thousand feet dawns are brisk in the high desert. All was quiet at first light in the Bannock-Paiute camp save for the piercing trill of a brown creeper, ubiquitous baby cries, and the soft music of Silver Creek. A few women were starting fires and tending to little ones.

A gunshot from upstream, followed by many more, brought the camp into turmoil. Parents such as Egan's adult son Honey clutched their infants, seeking cover. Warriors had no time and no reason to retrieve their horses. They jumped behind rocks or took cover in fortifications erected the night before, aimed their guns upstream, and were soon firing at Robbins and his scouts. As Robbins's command appeared, however, a bugle sounded from the opposite direction, followed by gunfire and shouts from Bernard's troops. Soon bluecoats were charging through the camp from both directions, firing six-shooters and carbines. Indians expecting bullets from upstream now had to find shelter from downstream fire as well. The downstream command under Bernard finished its charge through the camp, turned back, and charged again.

In the midst of the chaos Egan and his brother-in-law Charlie appeared on horseback. Descriptions of the battle mention no other mounted Indians. The fighting Indians' strategy was defensive, to use rocks or other objects as cover while firing at the soldiers. A mounted defender would present a conspicuous, unprotected target and lose accuracy firing while in motion.

Escape was on Egan's mind. He had told Winnemucca, Natchez, and Jerry that he was going to do so at the first opportunity.[5] He made an attempt on Steens Mountain, but Oits and his men forced him to retreat. The surprise attack at Silver Creek was an obvious opportunity. Bannocks were under siege by an enemy of unknown numbers. Fear of losing the battle, the war, and their lives had likely taken priority over guarding prisoners.[6]

An encounter developed between Egan and Robbins, firing at one another. Egan used the far side of his horse for a shield and fired back at Robbins, without effect. Robbins half stood in his stirrups and fired again, striking Egan's wrist and casting him to the dirt. As Egan tried to rise Robbins fired again, this time into Egan's chest. Another scout wounded Egan in the groin. Robbins's horse took a bullet and collapsed. Another soldier rescued Robbins. Two Indians dragged Egan away from the battle.[7]

The fighting was done. Vastly outnumbered, Bernard pulled his troops into a defensive position and sent for reinforcements. Indian women tended to Egan. In battle Paiutes carried wooden "plugs," an inch in diameter and an inch or two in length, to stop a hemorrhaging wound.[8] The women lashed willow splints to his wrist to immobilize the fracture, dressed and possibly plugged his chest and groin wounds, placed a pillow on the chest wound and strapped his splinted arm over the pillow and around his torso.[9] With Bernard's and Robbins's forces withdrawn, the Indians took care of their wounded, packed their horses, and continued north.

Two weeks later, on July 8, an army scout came upon a Paiute family—two adult men, one woman, and two children. They gave a description of the battle at Silver Creek that left little doubt that they had been present. They explained that Egan and Charlie were shot and severely wounded while trying to escape the Bannocks and join the soldiers. After the battle Egan and Charlie were again prisoners, they said, compelled to march with the Bannocks.[10]

This occurrence was reported to Captain Thompson at Camp McDermitt, possibly by the same Paiute family, possibly by other Paiutes. As recounted in the *Silver State*, the report was that Egan and several members of his band who were held prisoner by the Bannocks attempted to escape when Bernard was fighting the hostiles. They "got away from the Bannocks and tried to join the troops, but the latter mistaking them for hostiles, opened fire on them and compelled them to return to the hostiles."[11] If, as reported by the Paiute family, the Bannocks held Egan and his brother-in-law, Charlie, as captives after the Silver Creek skirmish, they did so in the belief that the encounter between Robbins and Egan was just as the Paiute family and the *Silver State* reported it—an attempt by Egan and Charlie to escape the Bannocks.

Just a week earlier Egan had capped off a decade of peacemaking by badgering the Bannocks against war so relentlessly that they imprisoned him. What the Bannocks stood for was anathema to Egan. It was entirely in character for him to do his best to escape from them. It would have been entirely out of character for him to fight in their cause.

Captain Thompson doubted that Egan was trying to join the U.S. troops. "It was just as easy for Egan and his Indians to get away if so disposed, as Naches and Jerry," Thompson said.[12] Thompson was unaware that the reason Egan remained with the Bannocks at Barren Valley when others escaped was Egan's determination—at considerable risk—to persuade the Bannocks to abandon their war.

General Howard reached the Silver Creek battleground after the fighting. His aide-de-camp, Erskine Wood, walked the area alone the next day under a fierce sun. One of the bodies caught his eye. He stared. It was motionless. But then it stirred. Sarah helped him resuscitate an elderly, blind, toothless Bannock woman, terribly dehydrated. After she recovered, Sarah and Mattie questioned her. Buffalo Horn was her nephew, she claimed, but would not answer questions. "If you do not tell us," Mattie pressed, "we will see why—you had better tell us." Now her tongue loosened. Oits had taken her nephew's position as leader of the Bannock-Paiute force, she said. The hostiles were on their way to the Umatilla Reservation because Umatillas had told Oits that they would help him fight the whites.[13]

CHAPTER 19

A Great Circle

The Nez Perce War ended with the surrender of Nez Perce chief Joseph in the fall of 1877, about eight months before the Bannock War began. As punishment, Joseph's band and his allies were sent to Indian Country (Oklahoma and environs), where disease took many. Howard's aide-de-camp and confidant, Erskine Wood, had met Chief Joseph at his surrender. The beginnings of a friendship had formed.

The following year, in the closing days of the Bannock War, Howard's strategy led him, Wood, and the rest of Howard's command through the Wallowa Valley. It was Wood's first visit to the land for which Joseph and the Nez Perce had fought so valiantly. He was taken with the beauty but also with the silence. Howard was on the verge of facing this year, with the Paiutes, much the same decisions that, consulting with Wood, he had faced with the Nez Perce—decisions that led to the melancholy Wallowa Valley, where the only remaining Nez Perce had no one to tend their graves.

From the battle at Silver Creek the Bannocks and Paiutes continued north over a rolling sagebrush desert punctuated with juniper. Precipitous, snaking canyons carved by the South Fork of the John Day River challenged both Indian and white forces. Constantly alert for clues to the Indians' intended route and destination, General Howard had begun even before the battle at Silver Creek to incubate a strategy for outwitting the Indians. He expected that they would go east "toward Salmon River country." After Silver Creek Howard refined his theory. "The indications," he felt, were that the enemy would cross the Snake River near the mouth of the

Grand Ronde River, an eastward flowing tributary that provides a gradual descent to the Snake.

As Howard was developing his strategy, he continued north, on the trail of the Bannock-Paiute force. Two weeks after Silver Creek, Howard joined Captain Bernard as he closed in on the Indians at Birch Creek. Sarah was with Howard as he watched the battle take shape. As Sarah described it, the Indians were "strongly posted on a rocky crest" with a pine forest at their backs. At the base of the rise seven companies of cavalry were poised with a Gatling gun. The Indian women and children, and the best horses were well out of the way, Howard noted, "seemingly toward the Grand Ronde. The flight is in that direction."[1] Sarah wrote that "all the officers and scouts said that they were making for the Grand Ronde, but I for one said, 'No, they will go back or through the Blue Mountains and Malheur Agency, and back to their own country.'"

At about 8:00 a.m. the bugle announced the charge on the Indians' elevated stance. Sarah "heard the chiefs singing as they ran up and down the front line as if it was only a play, and on our side was nothing but the reports of the great guns." She heard Oits cry out, "Come on, you white dogs,—what are you waiting there for?" The troops advanced "in a handsome manner, not a man falling out of the ranks." The Indians retreated uphill to a position with natural rocky defenses, but the soldiers soon gained that hill as well, forcing the tribesmen to retreat into the pines. After more charges and retreats, the soldiers rested, ending the battle.

In *Life among the Piutes*, Sarah wrote that five soldiers were wounded. She and Mattie cared for one of them, who died that night. She also made this seemingly bizarre observation: "Where was the killing? I sometimes think it was more play than anything else. If a white settler showed himself he was sure to get a hit from an Indian; but I don't think they ever tried to hit a soldier,—they liked them too well—and it certainly was remarkable that with all these splendid firearms, and the Gatling gun, and General Howard working at it, and the air full of bullets, and the ground strewn with cartridges, not an Indian fell that day."[2]

This comment betrays Sarah's inexperience and perhaps naïveté, for it is inconceivable that the Bannocks and Oits's band showed any trace of mercy to the soldiers. But Oits's band accounted for only ninety of the Paiutes. There were three to four hundred more, about one-third of whom were men of fighting age. Some were unarmed for lack of weapons. Of those who did have arms, Sarah's observation is plausible. In contrast to Rinehart and whites generally, Camp Harney soldiers had shown sympathy and occasional generosity to the Paiutes, who (except for Oits's band) had no enthusiasm for this war. They may well have put on a show of shooting at soldiers to avoid the wrath of their captors. There is one statistic that lends credibility to Sarah's comment. The total soldier fatalities in the war—two months of fighting against four hundred Indian warriors, two hundred of whom (the Bannocks) were regarded as the fiercest in the West—was a mere nine. Sarah's belief that any citizen who showed was sure to be hit is also supported by the numbers. Thirty-one citizens were killed.[3]

As Bernard's command pursued the Indians, Dr. Fitzgerald explored the battlefield. He came upon packs discarded by the Indians in their haste. He wrote to his wife, "I got you a fine beaded squaw robe, so you need not go to the expense of a new dress to go East in. This will just fit you." For their son Bert, he found a whip; for daughter Bess, "I got a whole lot of bead necklaces."[4]

After the Birch Creek skirmish General Howard led his command the remainder of the way to the Umatilla Reservation, where he reached the town of Cayuse on July 10. Stage drivers there told him that the "Snakes" had already left the vicinity of the reservation, heading east. Howard's suspicions were now confirmed. He saw "no other direction for them to take" but down the Grand Ronde and across the Snake. On July 11, after searching for and eventually locating a telegraph station whose lines had not been cut by Indians, he issued orders: Captain Egbert was to patrol western Idaho; Captain Evan Miles, augmented by Sanford's cavalry, was to continue pushing the Indians north.[5] Howard would now implement the plan that he had been fermenting since before Silver Creek. He and Bernard would make a great circle by steamboat up the Columbia eight miles to the mouth of the Snake, then up the Snake past Lewiston to the mouth of the Grand Ronde, a journey of three days. From the mouth of the Grand Ronde they would proceed overland. As the Indians made their expected flight down the valley of the Grand Ronde, believing that they were escaping from Howard, they would instead plunge into the ambush that he would set for them.[6]

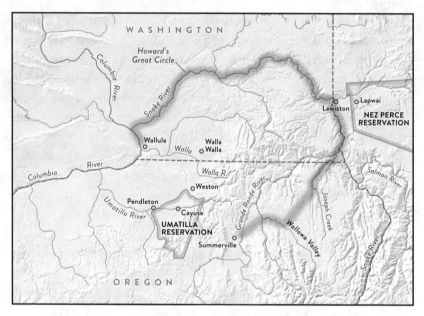

MAP 3. General Howard's great circle. Cartography by Erin Greb.

Later that day, before Howard and Bernard set out on their great circle, Howard met with Governors Chadwick of Oregon and Ferry of Washington Territory in Weston, one of the towns where he found the telegraph down. The governors asked Howard to reconsider his great circle. Once Howard and his command boarded a steamboat up the Columbia, the governors argued, Cayuse, Walla Walla, Pendleton, and the entire Umatilla Reservation would all be defenseless, exposed to the Indians whom Miles and Sanford were pressing directly into these population centers. Howard was unmoved.[7]

The great circle was a long shot. Howard was now perfectly positioned to protect the populated stretch between Pendleton and Cayuse. There was little risk in staying put to defend these towns. If the Indians attacked, he would be seen as a hero, at the right place at the right time. If the Indians turned east down the Grand Ronde Valley, as Howard expected them to do, while he was standing guard in the Pendleton-Cayuse area, the losses would be minimal—there were only occasional ranches on the Grand Ronde, and Howard could not be blamed for watching over population centers, as he was expected to do.

FIG. 11. General Oliver Otis Howard. Courtesy of the George J. Mitchell Department of Special Collections & Archives, Bowdoin College Library, Brunswick, Maine.

On the other hand, if Howard embarked on his great circle, the towns would be at risk, possibly altogether defenseless. If they were attacked, he would be pilloried, and properly so. The one remaining possibility was the one he was banking on—that he would launch his great circle plan, the Indians would descend the Grand Ronde, falling into his trap, and he would be celebrated for his uncanny prescience and his courage in rejecting the protests of those of ordinary intellect.

A strictly logical analysis pointed decidedly toward guarding the towns. That was not the choice Howard made, however. To understand Howard's decision to leave the Pendleton-Cayuse area, it may help to trace the path that led him there.

May 24, 1865, dawned clear and calm in Washington DC. Cedar waxwings and juncos infested dogwoods in full bloom. In front of the White House a modest grandstand adorned in the colors of the flag provided a dozen or more seats of honor on each side of Pennsylvania Avenue. It was the second day of "The Grand Review," celebrating the end of the war. After spectators endured seven hours of sultry heat watching the Army of the Potomac on May 23, expectations were low for the turnout on May 24. Yet the express train from New York had filled all seats and sold standing room for the last two days. As the 9:00 a.m. start time drew near, the crush of bodies lining both sides of the parade route gave the lie to the predictions. Today's march of the Army of Tennessee and the Army of Georgia had outdrawn yesterday's Army of the Potomac.

The scurrying of parade participants and watchers to their positions suddenly gave way to chaos when General Sherman appeared. His horse, decorated with a wreath of flowers and evergreen, had barely come to a stop before a mob encircled the general, hands reached up to shake his, children were raised to see the famous soldier eye to eye, and bouquets overwhelmed him. A reporter estimated that Sherman shook fifteen hundred hands before he put spurs to his horse to disentangle himself and take the lead of the column.

On his right a lesser known general was in full command of his mount with his one arm. Once the two generals reached the grandstand in front of the White House they took their seats with President Johnson, General Grant, and other leaders.[8]

In the final stages of the Civil War, while commanding Sherman's right flank in the March to the Sea and Carolinas Campaign, General Oliver Otis Howard had developed a friendship with his commander that was of no small aid to Howard in his next two decades. Indeed Sherman had already counseled Howard on the position that Howard had recently accepted. Edwin Stanton, secretary of war, had called Howard to his office. Plump, with a long, gray-fringed beard, Stanton had pushed a copy of the Freedmen's Bureau Act across the table to the erect, stern-featured soldier and explained that Lincoln wanted him to lead this new agency, charged with integrating former slaves into free society.[9]

As Howard later learned, the reason Lincoln chose him could be traced back to 1856, when he was stationed in Florida while his pregnant wife, Lizzie, was in Maine. After a Methodist revival, the "fullness of the glow of happiness" came into his heart, the "tugging and burning" left him, and the "choking sensation was gone." Christianity was with him for the remainder of his days. His was not a private faith; he did not mind being known as the Bible Chief. It was that reputation that drew Lincoln's attention and marked Howard for a position of such prominence.[10]

The Freedmen's Bureau could hardly have been closer to Howard's heart. He had lost his right arm in service of a noble cause for which scores of thousands had given their lives. It would be his task, indeed his honor, to help deliver to former slaves the fruits of the victory for which so many had given so much.

Reveling in his new position, he was seated with the president and Sherman, as sixty thousand troops of the Western Army, a fifteen-mile procession, passed before him.[11] It was a high point, possibly *the* high point, in his life to that date.

Sherman, however, foresaw what Howard did not. "I fear you have Hercules' task," he warned Howard. "It is not in your power to fulfill one tenth part of the expectations of those who formed the Bureau."[12] Opponents of the Bureau were encouraged and enabled by President Johnson, whose tepid support of Howard and his agency fooled few. Although Howard's integrity and competence in managing the Bureau are not open to serious question, his enthusiasm and high-mindedness occasionally crowded out circumspection and wariness. He became involved in a company that sold building blocks to a project funded by his bureau, approved the purchase of lumber from a relative, accepted a plot of land from a project connected with the Bureau, and used Bureau funds in ways that were well intended but of debatable legality. He probably neither sought nor received any personal gain from these acts, but he left himself vulnerable in his management of a highly visible and controversial agency.

The enemy emerged from the church he helped found in Washington DC. The minister's ill-disguised disapproval of Black members left Howard, head of the Bureau for the advancement of Blacks, few options. After the minister's departure, his fanatical son dedicated himself to avenging the "wrong" to his father. Howard was exonerated at the conclusion of two hearings lasting many weeks and generating considerable adverse publicity. The dismissal of all charges was gratifying to Howard, but did little to repair the damage to his reputation, bank account, or psyche. Still more attacks followed in the form of civil suits.[13]

Then, in 1874, an opportunity arose to escape the heat of Washington DC. Kientpoos's slaying of General Edward Canby at the Modoc peace conference led to an opportunity for Howard to take Canby's post. With his wife, Lizzie, their five children who were still living at home, his two aides, and their wives and children, he filled a railway car for a seven-day journey to San Francisco and then took a steamer up the coast, over the bar of the Columbia River, to Portland, Oregon.[14]

A year later, in preparing his first annual report to the secretary of war, Howard became acquainted with a controversy involving the Nez Perce under Chief Joseph, who claimed that his band was entitled to remain in the Wallowa Valley under a treaty that the United States said had been replaced by a later treaty. Howard's initial support for Joseph's position seemed to reflect the same values that motivated his work for African Americans in the Freedmen's Bureau.

As he was drawn deeper into the conflict with the Nez Perce, however, his egalitarian view of humankind had begun to wilt in the heat that he understood his beliefs had brought upon him. The prospect of forcibly removing settlers from Joseph's lands may have stirred concerns that he would generate the same kind of animosity that greeted his support for former slaves.

He responded with enthusiasm to a proposal to present the Nez Perce dispute to a commission, but with decidedly less enthusiasm to the knowledgeable Oregonians suggested as commissioners. Instead he asked Sherman for permission to return to Washington DC, then boarded a train before Sherman had time to say no.[15] Shortly after his arrival in the capital, he made a visit to the *New York Times.* The visit led to an article announcing that Howard was in town on a monumentally important mission to avoid a conflict that threatened a "general Indian war." Howard was organizing a commission, the story continued, that could prevent the war and save over ten million dollars.[16] Howard believed he would persuade Chief Joseph to move to the reservation, and by doing so draw attention to himself as a peacemaker, a friend of the Indian, and a skilled statesman who saved his country the millions that a lesser man would have squandered in fighting a war and alienating Native Americans.

Oregonian commissioners, however, did not fit into his plan. Instead, he recruited well-connected businessmen whose presence would assure that his success received its due in the eastern press, restoring him to his former prominence where the heart of the nation ticked.

Howard's plan progressed smoothly until he and the four commissioners began deliberations in Lapwai, Idaho, in the late fall of 1876. Joseph proved to be a savvy and nimble opponent. Unable to persuade Joseph to agree to move his people to a reservation, Howard pressed the commission to a recommendation that the Indians be removed by force if necessary. That winter the Interior Department adopted the recommendation.

In the spring of 1877 Howard returned to Lapwai to discuss implementation of the order. The friction that had developed in the commission meetings in the fall between Howard and Chief Toohoolhoolzote had not cooled and continued to focus on Toohoolhoolzote's "Dreamer" religion. As Chief Joseph recalled in an article several years later, Toohoolhoolzote insisted that the Great Spirit made part of the world for the Nez Perce: "I do not see where you get the authority to say that we shall not live where he placed us." According to Joseph, Howard responded to Toohoolhoolzote by losing his temper and telling him, "Shut up! I don't want to hear any more of such talk."[17] Howard claimed that he was not angry, listened "with no impatience," but did assume "a severity of tone."[18] Neither Howard's severity of tone nor his logic dented Toohoolhoolzote's conviction.

Throughout, the Nez Perce in attendance maintained their composure. Howard did not. He summoned a guard and imprisoned Toohoolhoolzote for five days.

Faced with a choice between a reservation and war, Joseph relented. The Nez Perce set about the staggering task of moving over five hundred shelters, two thousand horses, and a wealth of food supplies over a two-thousand-foot drop, all within Howard's arbitrary thirty-day deadline. Toohoolhoolzote had a different task. He was so outraged at his imprisonment that he urged the young warriors to fight. They secretly bought ammunition. When a young brave whose father had been killed by whites years earlier began killing, war broke out.[19] Now Howard's hope to be seen as a skilled statesman who needed only a veiled threat of force to overcome Joseph's resistance was gone. His hope of saving the nation ten million dollars was gone. His one remaining hope was to be seen as a great general. Fourteen hundred miles and many bloody battles later, that hope, too, was gone. He had won the war, but the victory brought him derision and scorn in the press.

Ten months after Joseph's surrender ended the Nez Perce War, Howard weighed his decision whether to guard Cayuse, Pendleton, and Walla Walla from the oncoming Bannocks and Paiutes, or attempt to surprise the Indians on the Grand Ronde. While there can be no certainty about his motives, it is safe to assume that he was confident he would win this war. But winning the Nez Perce War had done nothing for him. He may have come to the belief that, for the accolades he craved, he had to do something more than just block the Indians from the towns. He had to outwit the Indians. He had to win in style.

On the evening of July 11 Indians descended from the Blue Mountains to Cayuse and set fire to the Cayuse Hotel and other structures. With the reservation exposed and defenseless, with no working telegraph to summon help, Agent Cornoyer sent his swiftest rider with a message summoning Howard.[20] Before the messenger reached the Wallula dock, the steamer *Northwest*, glistening after scarcely more than a year of service, was churning upstream on the Columbia. Howard, Wood, Bernard, Dr. Fitzgerald, Sarah, Mattie, and the remainder of the command were beginning a three-day cruise in the cool morning air, oblivious of the destruction at Cayuse, where the embers of the hotel were still aglow.

In the last hour of daylight, as the *Northwest* fought the current of the Snake River, shadows were building, giving texture and shape to flat-lands that a few hours earlier had appeared to be a featureless, desiccated wasteland. Rising above the flats the Blue Mountains emerged from a complex of deeply eroded ravines. In the distance, beyond the break of the *Northwest*'s wake on the south shore, a swirl of dust approached. A shape began to emerge from the translucence, finally revealing itself as a horse and rider. The rapid collapse of the distance between rider and steamboat and the spurts of dust from hooves revealed the urgency of the mission. Soon the stern-wheel slowed and a dinghy was launched for the rider, who was taken aboard as his lathered horse cooled in the dusk.

As Howard read Cornoyer's plea for help, he was only a dozen miles from Wallula, all downstream. Cayuse was less than three hours away. Unable to write clearly with his left hand, Howard dictated his reply to Wood, stating that there were adequate forces in the area to deal with any emergency; the request for help was denied.

Howard and his command resumed their voyage upstream, completing the remaining 130 miles to Lewiston on July 14 and, later that day, reaching the mouth of the Grand Ronde. There was no sign of the Bannocks or Paiutes.

The following day a pack train led Howard's party up Joseph Creek into the lush grasses, undulating vales, and glaciated peaks of Wallowa Valley, which was at the heart of the prior year's Nez Perce War. Howard's conduct of the Bannock War and his treatment of the Paiutes in that war had their roots in and emerged from the war that preceded it. Through both wars Wood was much more than an aide-de-camp to Howard; he was a friend and confidant as well. Yet, as his dedication and loyalty to Howard grew, so did his misgivings about Howard's campaigns against the Nez Perce and Paiutes.

Erskine Wood's first assignment after graduating from West Point was to Camp Bidwell in northern California, bordering on the Paiute country of southeast Oregon. A captain at Bidwell put Wood in charge of record-keeping and report-writing, which left him enough leisure time that he was able to meet a Paiute family and camp and live with them. In addition to writing reports, Wood wrote copiously to Nannie Smith, his sweetheart in Washington DC, and submitted articles to *Harper's* and *Scribner's*, unsuccessfully.[21]

Late in the summer of 1875 Wood's Company H set out from Fort Bidwell, under orders to proceed three hundred miles north to The Dalles and to board a steamboat there to Fort Vancouver. The journey took Wood through Paiute country, which he spent his spare time exploring, dumbstruck that a land so utterly lacking in every traditional element of beauty—no soaring peaks or plunging chasms; no waters falling, tumbling, or even in visible motion; no dramatic or contrasting colors or anything besides gray and brown; no towering trees, or exquisitely patterned trees, or, for the most part, any trees at all—could seize him so and stir him to his depths. He came upon a flock of about thirty sandhill cranes whose raucous rattle seemed to suit the rawness of the landscape. Intrigued by the iridescent green, purple, and bronze feathers and the long, curved bill of a bird he could not identify—a white-faced ibis—he shot two for plumes for Nannie's summer hats. These Paiute lands inspired, years later, what many consider the most significant poetry and paintings of this prolific artist.[22]

Wood and his Company H continued north to The Dalles, where they boarded a steamboat for the final leg of their journey to Vancouver, opposite Portland on the Columbia River. Not long after reaching Vancouver, Wood made his perilous crossing of the Columbia River in a leaking boat and met General Howard for the first time.

As a result of an opportunity that Howard offered, Wood was traveling in Alaska when the Nez Perce War broke out. He joined Howard on June 27, 1877, just after the Battle of White Bird Canyon. His introduction to warfare was burying men with arms, cheeks, and heads gone, bellies swollen, faces blackened, amid a horrible stench. Less than a month later, Howard promoted him to aide-de-camp.[23]

Only eight months before the Bannock War began, Howard, with Wood's assistance, was navigating the aftermath of the Nez Perce War. It was not lost on Wood that throughout the Nez Perce War Chief Joseph, while traveling with women and children who outnumbered his warriors, had frequently outmaneuvered, outpaced, eluded, and outfought the soldiers. Wood knew as well that Joseph could have escaped to Canada, a day's ride away, but chose instead to go into captivity with his band. After the surrender Wood sketched Joseph's baby girl and the chief and listened through a translator to Joseph's expressions of grief over his dead brother and his torment over his missing eleven-year-old daughter. Joseph showed him a flesh wound on his back. Across the barriers of language, race, and war, a friendship was in the bud. The two traded saddles. Wood recorded Joseph's words of surrender, as translated. Perhaps it was the translator's intervention between the spoken and written word, as well as Wood's growing connection with the chief, that in Wood's mind freed him to refine the translator's language. Later Wood issued a press release attributing to Joseph the most famous words that Wood ever wrote: "From where the sun now stands, I will fight no more forever." They helped elevate Joseph to a prominence that enabled him to advocate for his people.[24]

In the closing weeks of the Bannock War, the final stretch of Howard's great circle ascended the valley of Joseph Creek into the Wallowa Valley, which, for the first summer in perhaps centuries, was devoid of Nez Perce Indians. It had been almost a year since Chief Joseph's surrender. The humanity and charisma of the man against whom Wood and Howard had spent months in battle were still percolating in young Wood's mind as, for the first time, he set foot in Joseph's country. Dazzled, Wood let his pen have its will, rhapsodizing over the "former home of Joseph, the Nez Perce Chief": "Jagged battlements and terraces, . . . deep canyons, rugged peaks and all the giant corrugations of mountain fret work . . . lost in drifting vapors and blue mistiness that wreathed the mountains and curtained the valley."[25]

As Howard's party progressed, Wood turned his attention to Sarah, asking her about Paiute customs. She described Paiute courting rituals, the "Feast of Wreaths" for young girls, and the frightening perception of whites that she had as a child. Sarah and Mattie discovered the graves of Nez Perce Indians, inspiring Wood to write in his personal journal that the graves were "spread with a wildflower quilt by the hand of Nature." His next sentence ended with the same term of finality that ended Wood's embellished version of Joseph's surrender: "Nature's hand must strew the flowers, for the people whose dead lie buried here have passed away from these scenes forever." Then: "Lofty snow capped mountains . . . seem to mourn over the inevitable fate of the Indians who claim this country as their own."[26]

Clearly touched by the tragic consequences of last summer's war and impressed by the prowess of the Nez Perce in battle and the honor and dignity of their leader, Wood danced not so deftly around the question of responsibility for this injustice. All of his writings of this era avoid any insinuation of wrongdoing or incompetence on the part of the army or Howard. Wood's implausible claim that the Nez Perce's fate was "inevitable" is the dutiful officer speaking, deflecting any perception of his comments as disloyal.

It required no great foresight to realize that the Paiute people against whom Howard was pitted in this Bannock War would soon be seeking to return to their homeland. Wood certainly understood the magnetism of their desert realm. He took from Paiute lands an inspiration as intimate, profound, and enduring as he had known from any other setting. A stanza in his poem, "Poet in the Desert," written years later, is reminiscent of his Wallowa diary entry mourning that the Nez Perce "have passed from these scenes forever." He wrote of the Paiutes:

Behold the signs of the Desert;
The stagnant water-hole, trampled with hoofs;
About it shine the white bones of those
Who came too late.
A whirling dust-pillar, waltz of Wind and Earth;
Glistening black walls of obsidian
Where the wild tribes fashioned their arrowheads.
The ground with fragments is strewn,
Just as they dropped them,
The strokes of the makers undimmed
Through the dumb and desperate years;
But the hunters have gone forever.

Wood was playing his part in engineering the destiny of the Paiutes, as the untended graves of the Nez Perce in the Wallowa Valley provided him a window into what that destiny would be.

The Nez Perce War had demonstrated to Howard and Wood the depth of the bond between an Indian people and their lands. The aftermath of that war had revealed the devastating effect of breaking that bond. As they completed the last miles of their great circle, they stepped into the final phase of the Bannock War, equipped by their experience with the Nez Perce to foresee how a military victory could erode, as well as build, the reputation of the victorious general; and how a military victory over Native Americans could be warped into a tool of degradation and oppression.

CHAPTER 20

Crania Absentia

Howard had become vulnerable again. Brushing aside the entreaties of the Oregon and Idaho governors and Agent Cornoyer, he had left the population centers without protection for nine days while marauding Indians were about. The *East Oregonian* was apoplectic: "What could have induced Howard to remove the troops after herding the Indians on us, we are unable to comprehend."[1] A military historian who was mostly complimentary of Howard thought that after his departure by steamboat up the Columbia River, "the hostiles had no opposition from joining the Umatillas and there was nothing to protect the citizens of Pendleton and Walla Walla from a murderous attack by the combined force of the Indians."[2]

On July 12, the day that Howard began his misbegotten great circle, Bannock-Paiute warriors were stealing down the drainage of Cottonwood Creek into the Umatilla Agency. Having had no response from the messenger sent in search of Howard, Agent Cornoyer sent another plea for help, this time to Captain Evan Miles, eighteen miles west at Pilot Rock. Miles promptly set out eastward toward Cayuse.[3] About eleven o'clock at night he reached Pendleton, where Cornoyer joined him for the remaining eleven miles back to the reservation. They arrived at dawn, July 13.

Indians descending that morning from the forests of the Blue Mountains toward Cayuse were surprised to see Miles's infantry having breakfast. The bluecoats quickly moved to defensive positions. The Indians came to a stop just out of range. The Battle of the Agency began with a desultory exchange of fire for half a day. That afternoon Miles suddenly charged, sending the Indians into a long retreat that effectively decided the war.[4]

The following day Umatillas, who had volunteered their services, set out in pursuit of the reeling Bannock-Paiutes. Without suffering a scratch, they killed thirteen and captured twenty-five women and children and sixty horses.[5] Among the dead were Egan's brother-in-law, Charlie, Egan's wife, Sally, and Egan himself. His son Honey and grandson Herbert survived, as did Annie Adams and her parents. In some accounts Egan's killer was Umapine (an Umatilla); in others Umatilla chief Homily; in still another Cayuse chief Five Crows. One version of the event is that Umatillas deceived Egan and those with him by feigning friendship and then attacking; another is that Egan was lured away to discuss an alliance with the Umatillas, who then killed him. The motive of the Umatillas was to demonstrate their loyalty to the soldiers; or, in another telling, to carry out a bargain with Captain Miles to produce Egan in exchange for amnesty for Umatillas who had joined the hostiles; or to avenge Egan's killing of Umapine's father.[6]

According to historian John Hailey, Colonel Robbins (who had shot Egan at Silver Creek) was ordered to locate those killed by the Umatillas. Doctor Fitzgerald accompanied Robbins. In early June Fitzgerald had crossed the Snake River with Captain Bernard in pursuit of Buffalo Horn and had remained with the forces under Howard throughout the war.[7] As an army physician, Fitzgerald was familiar with a memorandum from Surgeon General Joseph Barnes to field officers, asking that they collect for the Army Medical Museum (AMM) "1. Rare pathological specimens from animals, including monstrosities. 2. Typical crania of Indian tribes, specimens of their arms, dress, implements, rare articles of their diet, medicines, etc. 3. Specimens of poisonous insects and reptiles, and of their effects on animals."

A second memorandum from Barnes encouraged the contribution to the AMM of skull specimens to promote "the progress of anthropological science by obtaining measurements of a large number of skulls of the aboriginal races of North America." The skulls were to be measured for "ethnological classification . . . including craniology"—that is, for the same purpose that Morton collected skulls. Noting that medical officers had "already enriched the Mortonian and other magnificent craniological cabinets," Barnes expressed hope that they would show even greater zeal in collecting skulls for the Army Medical Museum.

Two weeks earlier, after visiting the Birch Creek battlefield, Fitzgerald had written to his wife that he had found a Paiute dress for her, among the other possessions that Paiutes had abandoned in their hasty retreat. Now, after he and Robbins returned from their visit to the last battlefield of the war, he wrote to her again about another relic of the conflict. He explained that he went "about a mile from camp on an errand for the Medical Museum. Yesterday morning, the Umatillas had a fight with the hostiles and killed 11 of them, one of them being the Piute Chief Egan. Well, I went out and got the latter's head and was back in camp in less than half an hour."[8] Robbins and Dr. Fitzgerald had found Egan's body with his arm bound up as a result of the shot fired by Robbins at Silver Creek.[9] After removing Egan's head, Dr. Fitzgerald evidently met with Sarah Winnemucca because she wrote to Natchez: "His scalp was taken, his deformed hand cut off and his head amputated for identification. Dr. Fitzgerald has the head in spirits."[10] It is likely that Fitzgerald told Sarah that the head was removed for identification, to avoid telling her that the actual reason was to use the skull to demonstrate Indian inferiority and to display it in a museum. If Dr. Fitzgerald put the head in spirits, it was to remove the flesh, not preserve it, for he sent only the skull to the Army Medical Museum.[11]

There were thirteen Paiute corpses at the site of the shootings. Robbins and Fitzgerald took only one skull and left the remaining dozen. Presumably it was not a matter of chance that the skull taken was that of the only chief among the dead. If the purpose of taking the skull was to compare it with the skulls of whites, why would Egan's skull be any more significant than the skull of any other Paiute?

Almost four months later Assistant Surgeon V. B. Hubbard went to the site where Egan was killed. Hubbard found Egan's headless body and, close by, the intact body of Egan's brother-in-law, Charlie, who had been at Egan's side at the battle at Silver Creek. Hubbard sawed off Charlie's head and sent it to the Army Medical Museum.[12] (A composite photograph of Charlie's skull with the skulls of five other Paiutes is in the archives of the Smithsonian Institution and has been intermittently displayed on various websites.)[13]

The Army Medical Museum was formed in 1862 to collect examples of Civil War battlefield pathology. In 1866 when the museum reopened in a new building, museum leaders feared that visitors would have little interest in the display of body parts ravaged by war. Yet in time it became one of the most popular tourist attractions in the capital, aided by the notoriety of its premises, the former Ford's Theater, site of Abraham Lincoln's assassination. Not at all reluctant to exploit the museum's location at the scene of a notorious murder known to virtually every potential visitor, the curator added an exhibit of the bones of the perpetrator, John Wilkes Booth.[14]

After the South's surrender at Appomattox slowed the flow of exhibits for the museum, Surgeon General Barnes reinvigorated the institution with his request to medical officers to collect Native American skulls. The result was a "furious 'mining' of American Indian cemeteries," according to one historian, which "became extremely competitive."[15] Among those who responded to Barnes's request was Acting Assistant Surgeon George Kober, who sent to the AMM "two Indian Crania (perfect) which I exhumed myself."[16] Kober elaborated: "Some of my leisure hours [in Nevada] were devoted to the exploration of [Paiute] Indian burial grounds, and the collection of crania and skeletons. These were usually found in rather shallow graves, covered with rocks, or in piles of rocks . . . The remains not infrequently were in a mummiform state, the soft parts having been completely desicated [sic] by the dryness of the atmosphere."[17]

Even more extreme was Assistant Surgeon George P. Hachenberg, who took "rascally pleasure" in craniology. He learned that relatives of a recently deceased Indian planned to keep watch over the body, but he "snatched his head, before he was cold in his grave" and before the kin set their guard. In one of his viler acts of skulduggery, he searched for days until he located and excavated the fresh grave of a beautiful young Indian woman who had been buried in a coffin. Hachenberg "was not disappointed in securing a fine specimen."[18] As a result of aggressive grave-robbing the AMM collected "a much larger series of American skulls than have ever been available for study."[19]

Euro-Americans have condemned as barbaric some Indians' practice of scalping their fallen enemies. Victors often displayed their scalps as badges of military prowess. Taking the skull of a defeated Indian, on the other hand, was defended as gathering evidence in aid of a scientific inquiry. The motives of those collecting skulls, however, were not always rigorously scientific. In *Bone Rooms*, Samuel Redman noted that skull collectors occasionally described "sentiments of excitement and feelings of danger. Gathering bones, as some people described it, was a nearly unparalleled adrenaline rush." It is not at all clear that these sensations differ from those experienced in the midst of a common burglary. Apparently the cause of the adrenaline rush was fear of violence from relatives of the deceased. "Ironically enough," Redman wrote, medical officers were "willing to risk life and limb to collect bodies or parts of the dead." Yet the risk may be exaggerated. Ann Fabian observed in *Skull Collectors* that "angry and horrified Indians tried to prevent the desecration of their graves," "but such activity often was carried out by military personnel against defeated tribal groups."[20] "Life and limb" were in all probability safe and sound for those, such as Dr. Fitzgerald, who removed Indian heads on battlefields that had been won and were controlled by soldiers. The taking of Indian heads was for these reasons not in any crisp or decisive way distinguished from scalping. And beheading is, of course, decidedly less gentle to the corpse.

The AMM maintained that the primary purpose of the collection was scientific. Heads were measured and volume calculated, so that skulls of different racial groups could be compared.[21] Scalps, on the other hand, were not measured or compared or studied for science. Like war medals, they were displayed on clothing, saddles, or structures to show a warrior's valor and success in battle.

To compare Indian and white skulls, of course, the museum had to have both. A few score skulls would not begin to suffice for either group because skull size varied so dramatically within and between groups. As the museum curator, Dr. Otis, explained, "the variations in the dimensions of crania of individuals of the same race and sex were so great that any generalizations of value could only be looked for in averages obtained by the examination of a large number of skulls."[22]

White skulls turned out to be more difficult to collect. According to Redman, "the number of American Indian and African American bodies that the museum acquired vastly outpaced the number of European American remains collected by the institution." The remains of whites that were collected, according to Redman, "often included . . . the fringes of society—criminals, the destitute, and those with unclaimed remains."[23] Those who did the collecting of whites' skulls did not snatch heads before they were "cold in their grave" or open the coffins of beautiful young women just buried. Rather, they limited their victims to the downtrodden, whose remains few cared about. As a result, the museum ended up with many Native and African American skulls, but apparently not enough white skulls to make a meaningful comparison. This deficiency may explain in part why, in a thorough study of the AMM, Elise Juzda found that "there is little evidence confirming the collection's explicit use in coming to conclusions of the racial standing of Native tribesmen."[24]

The "History of the United States Army Medical Museum, 1862–1917" contains only one entry that compares Natives to others. It states that "American Indians must be assigned a lower position in the human scale than has been believed heretofore."[25] No explanation of this conclusion is provided. Indeed Juzda found that "few studies were ever carried out on the skulls in the AMM's collection."[26] Craniologists seeking statistically significant evidence avoided the AMM's collection because it was unrepresentative and lacking in sufficient quantities and useful catalogs. The "sum total of the AMM's craniological research was unimpressive," Juzda concluded.[27]

In 1897 William Henry Holmes, a future leader of the Smithsonian, toured the Army Medical Museum. On his tour Holmes learned from museum curators that interest in comparative racial anatomy had withered. Many hundreds of skulls sat "unstudied, in wooden bone room cabinets."[28] Thousands of the relatives of those whose skulls languished in museum cabinets had endured the desecration of their loved one's remains to no good end. The AMM's failure to develop a thorough catalog of its collection, its failure to conduct any meaningful study of its collection, and its failure to attract any significant researchers stripped the scientific veneer from the museum's skull-collecting enterprise.

Egan's and Charlie's skulls, as well as the two thousand other Native skulls harvested by the AMM, did serve a purpose. Like John Wilkes Booth's bones, Native skulls intrigued the public, helping the museum to maintain its prominence and expand its constituency. But it was not just the museum's interests that the skulls served. Visitors learned from the "Army" in the name of the museum who had enabled them to observe these skulls in safety, feeling nothing beyond a shiver in the spine. The army's prowess was accentuated all the more if the skull was that of a chief, like Egan, drained of his savagery and exhibited for the world to see, not unlike a scalp dangling from a warrior's belt.

On one of the fragments of Egan's skull, the left parietal bone (the top and most of the back of the skull), was written in ink: "The extensive fracture of the cranium was the result of a single gun shot at close or short-range while the subject was in articulo mortis [at the moment of death]. JAF." The fragments were reassembled with wires, the lower jaw was attached to the cranium with a nail and wire, and other holes were drilled, "perhaps for mounting to a stand" to allow the skull to be exhibited to the public in the desired pose. Few members of the public knew, or had any way of knowing, the actual significance of the death that liberated this skull for "scientific" inquiry. The death certainly did not signify the army's military might or its dominance of dangerous nations. Egan had supported U.S. interests ever since his surrender at the end of the Snake War. At every turn he had been guiding the Paiutes on a path of peace and cooperation with Indian Affairs and the military, until whites' incompetent and in some cases malicious mismanagement of the Paiutes led to his death. There is no little irony in the U.S. attempt to show Indian inferiority through the skull of a man of such courage and principle whose friendship was squandered by myopic and blundering whites.

Under the law of Oregon at the time, decapitating the corpses of Egan and Charlie were crimes in an egregious category known as offenses against morality. The *minimum* punishment was three months in jail.[29] Yet it is not surprising that the military doctors paid no attention to this law. It was also unlawful to shoot an Indian, but in the words of Oregon Indian superintendent Joel Palmer, "no act of a white man against an Indian, however atrocious, can be followed by a conviction."[30] Major General H. W. Halleck concurred: "The civil courts will not punish a white man for killing an Indian."[31] In practice, then, only white corpses were protected from being defiled. Indians, both dead and alive, were fair game.

CHAPTER 21

Placing the Paiutes

After the battle at the Umatilla Agency, Paiutes and Bannocks fled toward their reservations, soldiers in pursuit. Many stopped short of their agency and went into hiding in fear of being taken prisoner. To overcome this reluctance, the military sent word by Indian couriers that, as later explained by General McDowell, "should they come in at military posts they would be protected, but should they remain away they would be treated as hostile."[1] As Indians arrived at Harney, McDermitt, and other posts, some as captives, most voluntarily, plans began to form on what to do with them. The pace of intake, however, outran the planning.

General Howard saw prisoners and punishment as measures of his success. Many prisoners and severe punishment were proof of a glorious victory over a numerous and vicious foe. In the last stages of the Bannock War, Howard was particularly sensitive about slights to his military prowess. Newspaper reports portrayed him as lenient with Indians and ineffective and timid in fighting them. The *Owyhee Avalanche*, for example, asked its readers: "Hist! Everybody keep still. General Howard is within 200 miles of the Indians. If no one makes a noise, he may slip up on them when he doesn't know it."[2] Later in the war the *Avalanche* excoriated Howard for his steamboat diversion to Lewiston and the Grand Ronde: "Upon his head must forever rest the blood of many of our best citizens."[3] He was also accused at about the same time of planning to forgive the hostile Indians and allow them to return to their reservations and receive their usual rations and other benefits as if there had been no war.[4]

On August 10, 1878, Howard sent a telegram to army headquarters denouncing these accusations as "wickedly false." He made sure that it was published in the *Idaho Statesman*, along with his insistence that "so far as it depended on him, the Indians should be punished."[5] In an apparent attempt to prove his rigor on the same day he proclaimed it, he then sent a second telegram to his superior, General McDowell, urging that six hundred Indian captives be moved "for punishment immediately to the Indian Territory . . . Shall we prepare them for this exodus?"[6]

General Irvin McDowell graduated from West Point sixteen years ahead of Howard, and began his career auspiciously with a victory at the Battle of Buena Vista in the Mexican War. His position on the staff of Commanding General Winfield Scott and his status as a military intellectual were promising signs, yet there were warning signs as well—a conspicuous paunch deprived him of the "look" of a capable field commander; a nervous condition could cause his speech to thicken and his face to flush; he tended to be sharp and abrupt with subordinates. At the onset of the Civil War he reluctantly yielded to pressure from General Scott to take command of the First Battle of Manassas against his West Point classmate, P. T. Beauregard. His conspicuous loss of this first major conflict of the war—a battle that the North expected to win—threatened his active-duty career, which effectively ended the following year with his loss of the second battle of Manassas.

In 1864 he was sent to San Francisco to head the Department of the Pacific, and at war's end he was recalled to the east. In 1876 he returned to San Francisco as commander of the Division of the Pacific. Among those who reported to him was another officer banished to the hinterlands of the west as a result of a checkered career, General Oliver Otis Howard.[7]

McDowell's testiness with subordinates sprang to life in response to Howard's proposal to send six hundred prisoners to the Indian Territory. McDowell's gritting teeth are almost audible in his instructions to Howard to specify the place where he wished to send the Indians and to give the number of Indians, their tribe, gender, and current location. In the next ten days more Paiutes surrendered, including Oits and sixty of his band, followed by another group of twenty-seven.[8]

On August 20 Howard alerted McDowell that another group of Indians would surrender soon and that he would send them from Camp Harney, Oregon, to Camp McDermitt, Nevada. McDowell responded, "Why is it necessary to send Indian prisoners from Harney to McDermitt? What is the object? What good expected?" After two days without response McDowell wrote: "Send no Piutes from their reservation to Camp McDermitt. The Indian Department has been urging the opposite course, namely to send the Indians from McDermitt to the Malheur."[9]

McDowell's telegram sounded to Howard to be perilously close to the leniency that his critics had predicted—simply returning the hostile Indians to their reservation, as if there had been no war. In his response to McDowell, Howard erupted: "Under no circumstances should the Piutes be allowed to return to Malheur Agency. The peace cannot be preserved there except by a large post. Such a course is rewarding crime. Please forward my earnest protest."[10]

McDowell shot back: "Your protest will neither be forwarded nor entertained." McDowell was particularly incensed that Howard proposed sending his prisoners to McDermitt, a small and distant fort. The prisoners belonged at Harney, which abutted the Malheur Reservation. "Your ordering them [prisoners] beyond the limits of your department, away from their reservation, to a small military post, was not called for by any reason that can be imagined," McDowell scolded. "Your remark about rewarding crime is utterly uncalled for, and suggests that you seem disposed to treat all Piutes as hostile, and punish the innocent for the sins of the guilty."[11]

The generals spun one another into a tizzy—McDowell had been annoyed by Howard dating back at least to the Nez Perce War, when McDowell would write sarcastic comments in the margins of Howard's telegrams before forwarding them to Sherman.[12] McDowell's actions incensed Howard because he feared that they threatened his public image. "The craving after newspaper applause overrides every other consideration," Howard's chief of staff in the Nez Perce War had observed.[13]

Distracted, the generals lost track of what they were about. The price for their blunders would be paid by the Paiutes. After further exchanges, McDowell finally realized that the reason Howard was planning to send this latest batch of prisoners to McDermitt was that he had sent many other prisoners there rather than to Harney, where McDowell thought they were going. Worse yet, Wilkins, the McDermitt commanding officer, had not realized that the arriving Indians were prisoners. "None of them were turned over to me as prisoners," he wrote to McDowell. "I have been simply issuing rations to them." In amazement Howard wrote to Wilkins, "Now you report no prisoners. Have you let them go?" Indeed he had.[14]

McDowell directed Wilkins to do his best to identify and recapture the Indians who had arrived as prisoners. Since Wilkins had not known that *any* had arrived as prisoners, it is no surprise that this effort accomplished nothing.

In the meantime McDowell ordered troops from Harney to proceed to McDermitt to take custody of the prisoners and return them to Harney. Among the Harney troops sent to McDermitt were Sarah Winnemucca and Corporal Lewis Hopkins, a slightly built soldier with a profuse handlebar moustache, later to become her husband.[15]

The inability to distinguish the free Indians at McDermitt from the accidentally released prisoners presented a dilemma. It was resolved with a shaky compromise. All the Indians at McDermitt (except for Winnemucca's band and Natchez) would be sent to Harney, divided in two groups. Leggins's band would go to Harney, but not as prisoners. From Harney they would be moved to the Malheur Reservation. The remaining Paiutes would go to Harney as prisoners, then sent on to a destination designated by Indian Affairs.[16]

Once Sarah arrived at McDermitt, she translated for the officers, explaining to the Paiutes that they needed to prepare for the journey to Harney. The Paiutes balked, sensing that "there is something wrong." The officers reassured them that there was nothing to fear; they would be sent to the Malheur Reservation. Sarah added, "You have not done anything. All the officers know that you have acted for the whites." Natchez told the Paiutes that the soldiers said that "you are to go back to the Malheur Agency." Chief Leggins then spoke up. If Rinehart was at Malheur, he said, "we shall die of hunger." At this the officers grew impatient and ordered the Paiutes to be ready in the morning.

Before the journey to Fort Harney began, Chief Winnemucca appointed Leggins chief of all Paiutes moving from McDermitt to Harney. When the Paiutes arrived at Harney, Leggins and his band were permitted to camp wherever they chose. The prisoners were confined and guarded. When prisoners escaped, soldiers enlisted Leggins's men to track them down.[17]

Few of the prisoners were strangers to Harney. After the Snake War, most had suffered in hunger there for five years, afraid to separate themselves from the soldiers for fear of whites stirring up trouble that General Crook would blame on the Paiutes. The suffering at Harney ended with the opening of the Malheur Reservation and the arrival of Samuel Parrish, whose dedication to the Paiutes brought two years of decent living conditions and honest, supportive leadership. Rinehart's arrival brought another reversal of fortune—a bully for an agent, cuts in federal funds, and the invasion of the Bannocks. Whether the Paiutes' declining fortunes would continue or change for the better would depend in large measure on the approaching deliberations between the War and Interior Departments.

After his harsh exchanges with McDowell, Howard may have welcomed Wood's announcement that he was engaged to be married on November 26, 1878, in Washington DC. Howard promptly arranged for Wood to replace him in discussions at the capital over the placement of the Paiutes. About October 1 Wood set sail from Portland for San Francisco, where he boarded a train that delivered him to the capital in time for an October 19 meeting with General McDowell and Secretary of the Interior Carl Schurz.[18]

Like so much of the Bannock War and its aftermath, this meeting was haunted by the preceding year's Nez Perce War. On this exact date in 1877 the *Chicago Daily Tribune* published the article that, after the Nez Perce War, Howard had held in his hand as he approached Wood, shattered, pale-faced, "his empty sleeve jerking and waving on one side and the newspaper waving on the other."[19] Proud of his victory over the Nez Perce, Howard had been unprepared for the *Tribune*'s accusations that Howard's overbearing demands had caused an unnecessary war; that Chief Joseph had outmaneuvered and outwitted him; and that his underling, Nelson Miles, had won the war. Wood spent many of the ensuing months watching the anguish take its toll on Howard, as he and the general struggled to salvage Howard's public image and his stature in the army.[20]

Wood was keenly aware as he sat with Schurz and McDowell on October 19, 1878, that Howard expected him to seek a decision that would cast a favorable light, preferably a heroic light, on his victory over the Paiutes and Bannocks. The more Indians imprisoned after the war (whether they deserved imprisonment or not), the graver the threat that Howard would be credited with subduing. Wood knew this. He also knew that the luster of Howard's victory would be dulled by messy details about Bannocks confiscating Paiute weapons and holding Paiute leaders hostage as terrified Paiutes fled from the Bannocks.

In his telegram exchange with Howard over the disposition of the Paiutes, McDowell had chided him for seeking to punish the innocent for the crimes of the guilty. As the October 19 meeting began, McDowell picked up where the telegrams had left off. He "boldly placed himself as the friend of the Indian," Wood wrote to Howard. McDowell said that he would "never approve" Howard's proposal to place the Paiutes on the Lummi Reservation on the northern coast of Washington. McDowell then "touched on the Harney question." Camp Harney had to be kept strong, he said, as long as the Malheur Agency was in existence.[21]

This was Wood's cue. At age twenty-six he was seated with the commander of the Division of the Pacific and the secretary of the interior. They were waiting for *him* to inform *them*. For he had lived the war at Howard's side. He had read every telegram, letter, and memo to and from Howard. He had circled and traversed the entire region of the war, all the while serving as Howard's closest confidant.

In the last two summers, however, Wood's attention had often strayed from troop movements, logistics, casualty counts, and battle strategies. The natural beauty of Joseph's Wallowa Valley had moved him. The poignancy of the beauty made all the more troubling the separation of the Nez Perce from their valley. In his private journal Wood wrote that the mountains "seem to mourn" the fate of the Indians. Nez Perce graves were "left to the solitude of the mountains." Flowers on those graves were frail forms of beauty "dr[awn] from death."[22]

As Wood sat with Schurz and McDowell, the fate of a different tribe was hanging in the balance. Wood had traveled much of the Malheur region during the war, but knew it most intimately from his 1875 journey from Fort McDermitt to The Dalles, when the land held him spellbound and he shot two white-faced ibis for their feathers. He was still coming to grips with his role in separating Joseph's people from the Wallowa Valley as he faced the question now before him of removing the Paiutes from their homeland, the Malheur high desert, which may have already had

Wood in the grasp that in later years produced the whimsical delight of his poem, "Sagebrush":

O I am sick for the sagebrush,
The great, gray sagebrush plain;
And I would give the heart of me
To ride through the sage again.
To feel it scratch my stirrup,
To smell it after rain.
I would give my very heart-blood
For that bitter breath again.
To ride toward the purple hills;
Wind through a tossing mane;
Christ! for a horse between my legs
And the sagebrush once again.

Few soldiers could sense as Wood could the strength of the bond between the Paiutes and the Malheur region. Yet the power of the emotions that had coursed through him just three years earlier as he rode the Paiute domain of juniper and milkvetch, ibis and rail, alkali and lichen was now drowned in the headiness of this moment in the halls of power.

Since the Paiutes had "gone en masse to the hostiles," Wood said, it would be a good plan to remove them to the Lummi Reservation; Camp Harney could then be closed. Wood's words worked wonders on McDowell, for closing Camp Harney would save him the expenses of that remote outpost. At once his vow to "never approve" sending the Paiutes to Lummi melted away.[23]

As the conduit for all communications with Howard during the war, Wood was aware of the Bannocks' coercion of the peaceful Paiutes. From Sarah he heard what Egan had said when the Bannocks arrived on Steens Mountain: "We are at peace. Why should you bring the soldiers upon us? You have made war and now you come among my people to bring war on them. My people will be killed." Wood was sufficiently impressed that he recorded the statement in his private journal.[24]

Wood's private wartime journal of personal observations and thoughts was separate from his official journal of troop movements, locations, and communications. The two journals reflected two chambers of his mind, sealed off from one another. As he met with McDowell and Schurz, the private chamber was quieted, allowing him to say that the Paiutes had "gone en masse to the hostiles." The statement was misleading, but it brought results. Howard got the punishment of the Paiutes that he sought; McDowell was able to close a remote fort that was expensive to maintain. Wood had brought about a decision that would please Howard. Only the Paiutes lost—all Malheurs were saddled with blame for the war, their reservation was put in jeopardy, and many innocents were punished.[25]

Yet the Erskine Wood who wrote his private journal could not have been comfortable with the Erskine Wood who declared that the Paiutes had "gone en masse to the hostiles." His private journal oozes a growing disquiet over the fate of the Indians against whom he was pitted by his duty of loyalty to Howard and the army.[26]

The conclusion reached in the October 19 meeting was not entirely without benefit to the Paiutes, for the Lummi Reservation held promise as a healthy and peaceful home. The reservation was located on a peninsula in Bellingham Bay, eighty miles north of Seattle. The Indian agent at Lummi wrote in his 1879 and 1880 reports that the land at Lummi "is unsurpassed by any in the Territory." While the government took pains to locate reservations in places unlikely to appeal to settlers, Lummi was an exception. Poor soil in other parts of the Tulalip Agency was unproductive, but farming at Lummi "amply repays" the Indians' efforts, he reported. Schools were orderly and well run. No serious crimes occurred. Many Lummi residents had "pleasant homes" and "live as bountifully as the white settlers in the immediate vicinity."[27] The conclusion of the October 19 meeting, however, was only a recommendation. The final authority rested with Commissioner Hayt and Secretary Schurz.

On Sunday, November 24, 1878, Wood sat in his mother's bedroom in the family home in Baltimore, tending to her every request as she struggled to shake her illness in time for the wedding. In every spare moment he dashed off another few words in the letter that he was composing to Howard. It was a bit more than a month since the army made its recommendation to remove the Paiutes to Lummi. Wood wrote: "I am so whirled about, so tormented with things to do, things to be done over, things to remember, that I am growing thin. Like Shakespeare's lover. I have forgotten to shave and to comb my hair and if I wore long stockings doubtless my hose would be ungartered and about my heels."

In his breaks from writing Wood may have cleaned dishes, brewed tea, and then picked up his pen again:

> Everything that I succeeded in accomplishing has been undone by the commissioner [of Indian Affairs, Ezra Hayt] on the ground of expediency and economy . . . The resolve is now that [Paiute] prisoners . . . shall be lumped on the Yakima [Reservation]. . . . I am to be married day after tomorrow and will kiss the bride for you myself . . . Day after tomorrow at 6 PM. My! It kind of takes one's breath.
>
> Credit me General for knowing a more absurd and incendiary move could not be made than to crowd these discontented and incongruous savages on a reservation already overcrowded and unfit for its residents.

Wood wrote that he had invited himself to Sherman's house and in Sherman's parlor had characterized Commissioner Hayt's decision as "the most foolish course conceivable." He then described Sherman's response: "They don't care. Shan't interfere. I shan't say a word. They are mad and jealous of us [i.e., the army] at the Interior [Department] anyway and they are a damned bad lot down there. Won't have anything to do with them. Only lie about us and blame us. They are damned dishonest."

Wood assured Howard that after the parlor meeting with Sherman he had received Howard's telegram. He took the telegram to Sherman's office and tried again. He described the result to Howard: "And he said no no no. Telegraph Howard from me that I can't do it. Just say I won't do anything at all. Won't say a word. Tell him to turn the Indians over to the nearest agent."[28]

On November 28, two days after Wood's wedding, a telegram reached General Howard in Vancouver. It was Thanksgiving, a day that, to most Americans, represents harmony between Indians and settlers. The telegram confirmed that Hayt had successfully scuttled the War Department's plans to place Paiutes on the lush and productive lands of the Lummi Agency. In Howard's words, he was instructed "to remove the Bannock and Piute prisoners (then under guard at Fort Harney) a distance of about 350 miles to the Yakama Reservation. I was to detain from them as prisoners a number of the worst. The winter was already upon us before the execution of the order could be accomplished."[29]

Wood's work in Washington was now done. He and his bride soon boarded a westbound train to cross the continent again, carrying a basket of gourmet foods, a gift from friends. By only about a month they missed Chief Joseph's visit to the capital, where, in a speech at Lincoln Hall, he said, "I have asked some of the Great White Chiefs where they get their authority to say to the Indian that he shall stay in one place, while he sees white men going where they please." It was the same question that Toohoolhoolzote asked General Howard in the spring of 1877, just before war broke out. In the year and a half that had elapsed since then, Joseph had received no better answer to the question than (according to Joseph) Howard gave to Toohoolhoolzote: "Shut up."[30]

Now that the Paiute prisoners had been told that they were to stay in one place, the Yakama Reservation, preparations were underway to march there from Fort Harney. At first light on the last day of 1878 leafless willows lining the banks of Rattlesnake Creek in Fort Harney began shedding fragile sheaths of snow accumulated during the night. Occasional breaths of wind freed the willows of snow within the next few hours. Four-horse wagons began to arrive and park outside of the fort. By dusk thirty-nine wagons and an ambulance were in place as 160 horses and forty-six ponies grazed on frozen bunchgrass.[31]

On the following morning, New Year's Day, soldiers stacked next to each wagon the goods it was to carry—boxes and bags of cornmeal, flour, beans, rice, coffee, beef, pork and bacon, bags of grain for horses, blankets, tents, water buckets, axes, shovels, medical supplies, tools for wagon repair, and more. The civilians packed their wagons as Captain W. H. Winters watched over the process, questioning his officers over the sufficiency of supplies, inventory tracking, and security. By last light wagons were loaded, each of the five officers had reviewed assignments for his nineteen or twenty men, harnesses and saddles had been checked, wheels lubricated, and passenger assignments made to each wagon. Fort Harney quieted for the night, ready for the march to begin. Blankets, clothing, and subsistence were known to be at the Malheur Agency, fifty-five miles away, but they were left behind.[32]

FIG. 12. Camp Harney, 1872. National Archives.

Early on January 2, 1879, thirty-nine farmhands, laborers, ranchers, clerks, and settlers hitched their horses. Sarah Winnemucca directed 222 Paiute women and children to wagons. Among the women were B. E. Susan, Chinaman's First Wife, Waterbelly's Widow, Auntie Thacker, Weather's Mother, and Sallie. Among the women who needed Sarah's help were Becky, who was nearing the end of her pregnancy, and Mattie, Sarah's sister-in-law, who had been injured in a fall from her horse. Several weeks earlier five women had escaped at night. At the soldiers' request Sarah and Mattie had joined the effort to capture them. In the darkness Mattie had been unprepared for her horse's sudden swerve. She had lost her grip and landed frightfully. When Sarah reached her, Mattie had been bleeding from the mouth and apparently dying.[33] She survived, but continued to suffer.

Behind the wagons sixty-nine Paiute men took their places, including Frank Winnemucca, Dr. Johnson, Lee Winnemucca, Chinaman, Bear Skin, Left Handed, Leggins, Blind, Uncle Sam, and three who were named after well-known persons, Sam Parrish, Linville, and Paulina. They were clad in blue military coats and chained together in pairs. Sarah helped an elderly man, We'ga'you, to a seat in a wagon.[34]

Not long after the procession began, a heavily loaded wagon approached from the opposite direction. Winters spoke to the driver. When he learned that the shipment was beef and flour for the Malheur Reservation, he asked that some be issued for his Malheur Indians. The driver declined and resumed his journey to the empty Malheur Reservation.[35]

As Captain Winters led the Paiute prisoners north toward the Yakama Reservation, Leggins and his band waited at their camp just outside of Fort Harney to be taken to the adjacent Malheur Reservation. On January 6 a cavalry command finally appeared, but Leggins probably sensed something was amiss when the troops formed a circle around his camp. Major Cochran dismounted and explained to Leggins that his band was not going to the Malheur Reservation as had been promised. Instead they were to be escorted to Canyon City, where they would join Captain Winters's party for the remainder of their journey to the Yakama Reservation. Unlike the prisoners in Winters's party, however, Leggins's band would ride their own horses and retain their guns.

At the outset of the war Leggins had the choice to align with the soldiers or with the hostile Indians. The one he chose would be his friend, he thought. The other would be his enemy. He chose the soldiers. Ever loyal, Leggins complied with the army's requests that he name those who were most active in the war and that he hunt down escaping prisoners after the war, thereby making enemies of the Paiute prisoners.[36] Unlike Leggins, the army was loyal only as long as loyalty was convenient. When it finished using Leggins, it broke its promise to place him on the Malheur Reservation and instead imprisoned him at the Yakama Reservation with those he had alienated in service of the army. Now Leggins and his band were surrounded by enemies.[37]

Captain Winters had halted his march at Canyon City amid heavy snow to await Leggins. On the last evening at this location, the elderly We'ga'you was left in a wagon for reasons never explained. In the morning the citizen contractor who owned the wagon pushed We'ga'you's frozen corpse to the ground, jostled the reins, and picked up his awaiting passengers.[38]

Shortly thereafter Becky gave birth, but the baby was dead by morning. Its grave was dug in snow because the ground was frozen. Becky was barely alive as the march resumed. She died that night. Her body was left by the road. Before the march was done four other children were dead.[39]

The procession continued for two hundred miles to the Columbia River, then crossed by ferry at The Dalles. With the prisoners now depleted by weeks of daily exhaustion in bitter cold, they began an ascent of almost three thousand feet over a distance of about one hundred miles of mostly treeless terrain, exposed to the wind, through deepening snow.

CHAPTER 22

A Big Talk

The winter march of Paiute prisoners was bound for the Yakama Reservation, which was in the charge of James H. Wilbur. Like all agents, Wilbur reported to the commissioner of Indian affairs, who reported to the secretary of the interior, Carl Schurz. In his 1878 annual report, Schurz declared Wilbur "the most successful agent in the service." It was no accident that Wilbur had risen above all other Indian agents. His indefatigable commitment showed in his reservation, with a school, an Indian police force, and decent houses, some with individual plots and farming equipment. He took pride in the steam sawmill, the shingle mill, and the planing mill, all built without expense to the government, with fees from grazing leases.

Duty-bound, disciplined, Wilbur had little patience for the disorderly or the disorganized. He was therefore incensed to learn that 543 Indians had been sent to his reservation a month ago, without notice to him, and had now arrived with provisions for only one more day. Struggling for words to vent his outrage, but without disrespect, he wrote to Commissioner Hayt that the surprise arrival of 543 Indians was "a marvel of marvels."[1] He also scrawled a telegram to Hayt: "Five hundred and forty-three Snake and Piute Indians arrived without official notice of their coming. In a destitute condition nearly naked something must be done immediately to feed and clothe them."[2] As he wrote later, "They [the Paiutes] were turned over in the most destitute condition of any Indians I have ever known in this, or any other country. Some of them are quite literally naked."[3] He refused to take custody of them for eight days while the Yakamas built

174

a shelter. Just after the Paiutes moved under the shelter a storm struck, leaving three feet of snow over the course of a week.

Conditions in the shelter were squalid. Sarah Winnemucca wrote that it was the kind of shelter used for stock animals, that the snow was waist deep, that there was no wood for a fire, and that they suffered from the cold.[4] The shelter was 150 by 17 feet, allowing each occupant a space equal to one foot by five feet.[5] Wilbur estimated that twenty died within a short time after their arrival.

In 1846 Wilbur and his wife, Lucretia, had sailed from New York for Oregon, where he began his Methodist mission work. After fourteen years in Methodist positions, chiefly teaching and administration, he took a job in 1860 at the Yakama Indian Agency. Quarrels with his superior and with believers of other faiths led to a suspension in 1862. Apparently more troubles followed, but in 1864 he traveled across the continent and persuaded President Lincoln to appoint him agent for the Yakama Reservation.

Acclaim for Wilbur came from many quarters: "As far as the quality of agents selected by the Missionary Society is concerned, Wilbur was out-standing, and one of the Society's happier choices";[6] "Father Wilbur was a remarkable man of powerful physique, an indomitable will and as utterly fearless as it was possible for a man to be, of a genial, kind-hearted, generous nature, he was as sternly just and firm as a New England Puritan. . . . He feared God only";[7] "During his administration the Yakama Indians made greater progress than any other Indian tribes in the United States."[8] He was not a wealthy man, but he made a generous bequest to Willamette University, a Methodist school.[9] Wilbur was not the type who thought himself above physical labor. A colleague wrote: "He goes with the Indi-ans to the mountains, camps with them, and with ax, saw and gad, assists and shows how to cut and haul sawlogs; with his carpenter, and assists in building houses and barns for the Indians; with the farmer and instructs the Indians in cultivating, sowing, planting, harvesting and thrashing the crops. . . . He visits the sick and dying and comforts the afflicted."[10]

Among believers of every persuasion, there are many whose faith arrives only after doubt and vacillation, and even then it is not always strong enough to deflect troubling questions and uncertainty. Wilbur was not such a person. Doubts, vacillation, and uncertainty never blurred the boundaries of his unswerving path through life. Believing that Indians were "destitute of moral character," he thought that the only way to inspire virtue in them was "by the plain, open, unequivocal manifestation of virtue on my own part . . . I find the result of my labors a perfect justification of my theory."[11]

He appointed Sarah as a teacher and interpreter and praised her teaching as "noble" and her work as his interpreter as "*essential service.*" Sarah's belief in Methodism, which may have seized her at the very moment she learned that Wilbur was a Methodist, did her no harm in Wilbur's eyes.[12] She pleased him further by teaching Paiute women to cut fabric and make garments.[13]

As Wilbur's Paiute translator, however, Sarah was the conduit for communications between Wilbur and her people. She therefore knew that Paiute claims that Yakamas stole their blankets and military coats were much too persistent to justify Wilbur's refusal to credit any of them. Wilbur's consistent acceptance of the word of the Yakamas over that of the Paiutes served only to encourage the thievery. After Wilbur repeatedly dismissed the complaints of Leggins's band that Yakamas stole their horses, Sarah wrote, he "kindly told us he did not want to be troubled by us about our horses."[14] Similarly Yakama schoolchildren discovered that they could bully Paiute children without repercussions. Wilbur further fueled the friction between the two tribes by using Yakamas to chase down the many Paiutes who attempted to escape. Through her translating duties Sarah also learned that material issued to Paiutes for clothing was inadequate and that Paiutes died off so rapidly that Wilbur would no longer allow them to be buried in the reservation graveyard.[15]

Rather than maintaining order by requiring all Natives to comply with the same rules, Wilbur exploited intertribal frictions, condoning and facilitating the Yakamas' domination and abuse of the Paiutes. By doing so he was able to strengthen his hold over both effortlessly, and at no cost beyond the dignity, living conditions, and health of the Paiutes.

As tensions increased between Wilbur and Sarah, Mattie's agony from the fall from her horse finally ended. "Oh, how she did suffer before she died!" Sarah wrote. Sarah's pain was not just for Mattie, but also for her own loss of a friend, possibly closer than any other. Sarah's brother Lee and Chief Leggins had refused to speak with her after Leggins was forced to join the prisoners at Yakama. Her two brief, failed marriages had long since ended. Her freedom to leave and enter Camp Harney and Yakama, where all other Paiutes were prisoners, did little to endear her to those who had no such freedom.[16] While the Paiutes recognized, and sometimes called upon, her remarkable verbal talents, they did not see her as one of them. As Sarah's life unfolds in her book, *Life among the Piutes*, few were closer to her than Mattie. Yet, despite Sarah's estrangement, the Paiute people remained the center of her universe. From *Life among the Piutes* it is evident that she measured herself and the life she led by what she did or failed to do for her fellow Paiutes.

As she came to realize that her people were profoundly unhappy at Yakama and that conditions were unlikely to improve, she began to formulate a plan to restore the Paiutes to Malheur, their homeland, and to win for them the terms she had sought in her eloquent request to Major Henry Douglas eight years earlier. Her plan would not lack for audacity.

While these events were in progress at Yakama, Rinehart had been attempting to attract Indians to his empty reservation. The Malheur population had grown steadily under Parrish, but declined when Rinehart replaced him. A dropping population does not reflect well on the agent; Rinehart had particular reason for concern because his strained relationship with the Paiutes was no secret.

In an effort to rebuild his population, Rinehart had attempted to recruit Chiefs Winnemucca and Ochoho and their followers. In his meetings with Winnemucca in April 1877 and again the following April, the chief's polite interest did not disguise his indifference to Malheur or his passion for a new reservation on the upper Owyhee River in Idaho. Chief Ochoho was even more resistant than Winnemucca. In the fall of 1877 Rinehart's subagent, William Turner, returned from a visit with Ochoho convinced that he would not move to a reservation except at gunpoint.[17]

Polite persuasion had failed, but Rinehart had a deep arsenal. He wrote to Commissioner Hayt accusing Camp Bidwell in California of the "indiscriminate" feeding of Ochoho's band and Camp McDermitt in Nevada of doing the same for Winnemucca's followers, in violation of a War

Department order. Both camps should be abandoned, he urged, because
their only function was "to watch and feed these vagabond Indians who
have strayed from agencies to avoid the little labor required of them."
Disbanding the camps would relieve the settlers "of the dreaded presence
of straggling Indians." He claimed that Indians at Fort McDermitt engaged
in "brothel dances." They knew that they could not get subsistence at
the Malheur Reservation without work, he argued, while they could get
all they wanted at McDermitt and Bidwell by "the prostitution of their
women."[18] All of these Indians, Rinehart made clear, belonged at Malheur.

General McDowell asked officers at the two camps to respond to
Rinehart's allegations. On the subject of subsistence, the denials by the
commanding officers were not entirely convincing. In response to Rinehart's
"vagabond" charges, however, the officers vigorously defended the Paiutes
as industrious workers, valued by the white communities. The McDermitt
commander bristled at Rinehart's allegations of prostitution and "brothel
dances." These assertions were based on information "grossly and I believe
intentionally misunderstood by the agent of the Malheur Reservation."[19]
Rinehart was probably disappointed, but not surprised, to learn in May
1878 that his diatribe failed to cause the camps to be abandoned or the
Native people to move to Malheur.

After the war Rinehart resumed his efforts to recruit Winnemucca,
Ochoho, and their bands to Malheur. Grant's Peace Policy had lost much
of its momentum, but its leading tenet, that Indians belong on reservations,
was still the position of Indian Affairs and therefore still the marching
orders of Commissioner Hayt. Rinehart had an ally in Hayt.

In February 1879 Rinehart wrote to Hayt that a postal contractor
had informed him that the Paiutes at Fort McDermitt wanted to move
to the Malheur Reservation. In April 1879 Hayt responded, instructing
Rinehart to plant crops for arriving Indians and to have the McDermitt
Paiutes come to Malheur.[20] Rinehart leapt into action and was soon at
McDermitt, where one hundred Paiutes and five chiefs turned out to hear
his pitch and Winnemucca's response. But Winnemucca refused to budge
while Leggins, his subchief, was confined at Yakama. His refusal had the
desired result, for Rinehart returned to Malheur and took up Leggins's
cause.[21] He wrote to Hayt a detailed account of Leggins's efforts to save
the Crowleys and Scott from the Bannocks at the June 11, 1878, encounter

in Barren Valley. However, Hayt would have none of it.[22] Rinehart made one more trip to McDermitt in June 1879, but the initial promise of this effort had collapsed by July.

Again gentle persuasion had failed. It was certainly not coincidental that shortly thereafter a petition dated September 4, 1879, arrived at General McDowell's office in San Francisco. The petitioners stated that they resided in the Quinn River Valley, where Fort McDermitt lies. The valley had become "too thickly settled," according to the petition. Paiute Indians "stampede our cattle, destroy our fences, turn their stock on our meadows . . . and annoy us in many vexatious ways." The word *vexatious* in a cattlemen's petition was a clue. Another was the request in the petition for the "immediate removal of these Indians from this Valley to some Agency."[23]

General McDowell put Captain Corliss at McDermitt in charge of responding to the petition. Corliss issued a notice calling on the petitioners to provide details of the Indian actions complained of. He interviewed many of the petitioners. Several withdrew their names. Some said they had signed to avoid offending the neighbor who asked for his support. Others said the Indians had never troubled them. Only two responded to Corliss's request for specific allegations. Corliss dispatched soldiers to investigate these claims and found them groundless. He concluded that the petition had "no foundation on substantial facts" but was "inspired by some person or persons who desire the removal of the Indians as a source of revenue."[24]

In the meantime Commissioner Hayt, furious that Paiutes had refused to go to reservations, instructed Rinehart to prepare the commanding officers at Forts Bidwell and McDermitt to remove the Indians from both posts to the Malheur Reservation.[25] Rinehart surely knew that, after his letter to General McDowell accusing both posts of feeding Indians in return for sexual favors from Indian women, neither fort commander would give him the time of day. He sent Jack Scott in his stead. It is likely that Scott had already been to McDermitt to drum up support for the petition against the Paiutes. In any case Rinehart gave Scott a letter authorizing him to act on his behalf and dispatched him to McDermitt.

This was not the first collusion between Rinehart and Scott. A local historian described Scott as "a peculiar character" who delivered cord wood and hay to Fort Harney from 1875 to 1880.[26] Before the war, in May 1878, John S. Devine, the first resident of Harney Valley and one of its wealthiest cattlemen, delivered to Rinehart a proposed lease of about five hundred square miles of the Malheur Reservation at $200 per year. Within hours of Devine's visit, according to Rinehart's records, Jack Scott delivered to Rinehart $100 "to secure the execution of a proposed lease" for the exact same five hundred square miles that Devine had proposed to lease, but at $1,500 yearly, paid in advance. Rinehart sent both proposed leases to the commissioner of Indian affairs, advocating Scott's lease and requesting a "speedy reply."[27]

It is not likely that $1,500 rent, paid in advance, was within Scott's means on his earnings as a delivery driver. It is equally unlikely that Scott discovered the Devine lease proposal on his own, within a few hours after Devine had delivered it to Rinehart. Rinehart had seen an opportunity. Whether his plan was crooked or merely shady, he was plotting to exploit inside information in a way that was unlikely to do Devine any good and Rinehart any harm, provided that he had a minion to front for him. That was Jack Scott.

During the war Rinehart had also used Scott as the source for his claim that in Barren Valley whites were killed (they were not), Egan wanted to fight (he did not), and Egan said he was going to war to get more supplies and to spare his people from working (highly doubtful contentions).

It was against this background that Rinehart again enlisted Jack Scott in his postwar campaign to force Winnemucca to the Malheur Reservation. Armed with Rinehart's letter, Scott arrived at Fort McDermitt in the fall of 1879 and lurked about for days, warning Indians of their impending move to Malheur, threatening that he could bring two or three companies of soldiers if needed, and looking for evidence that the Indians were drawing rations at the fort. The Indians alerted Natchez Winnemucca, who decided that there should be a "big talk." He arranged to use a courtroom about seventy-five miles south of McDermitt at the Humboldt County seat, the town of Winnemucca, named about a decade earlier after Chief Winnemucca, or perhaps after his family.[28]

Natchez invited Jack Scott and the editor of the *Silver State*, and circulated word among the Paiutes.[29] The "big talk" was well attended. Natchez began by asking Scott for his authority to speak for the government.

Scott produced Rinehart's letter and claimed that he had full authority to inform the Indians that they were required to move to the Malheur Reservation.[30] Then Paiutes were given an opportunity to speak. Captain Jim said, "I and my people live at peace with the whites, and we do not want to go to Malheur." "I have a house," he added, "a stove, plenty to eat and wear, and if the Indian Agent will go with me to my house, I will board him free for a year."

Buena Vista John said that he was raised on the Humboldt River, which flows through Winnemucca. "I have four good wives; you, my friend [meaning Scott], have none. I will give you one. I live with the whites, and get along without trouble; you, my friend had better go home. When we cannot live where we were born, we will send for you."

Captain Charley was next. "There is always trouble among Indians at reservations," Charley said. "The Indians at Malheur were starving when the Bannocks went there a year ago. That is why they went on the war path. . . . If we do wrong, put us in jail and punish us as you do white men, but do not put us on reservations to starve."

The last two speakers were Winnemucca and Natchez. In their remarks lie the end of the story of June 11, 1878, events in Barren Valley. "My friend," Winnemucca addressed Scott, "you remember last summer, when the Bannocks surrounded us, we went to save you, but you went away from us. I wanted to ride behind you, but you would not let me. When my horse gave out, I said, 'Take me on.' You said you could not wait for me and went off and left me. We saved your life, but you would not help us. Leggins' party saved you, but you sent him to Yakama. . . . You bring Leggins and my boy, Lee [back from Yakama] then come and talk to us."

Finally, Natchez stood. "I saw you when surrounded by hostile Bannocks and Oitz' band . . . I saw Oitz take your hair in his hand when water ran out of your eyes.[31] I saved your life, but you would not help me. I heard you read paper two ways, and we can not trust you. . . . My people will not go with you. You let them alone. They live in peace here. You come to my camp and I'll board you for nothing." (Natchez's statement shows that newspaper reports that Egan lifted Scott by the hair and threatened him were just another example of Egan being blamed for Oits's misdeeds.)

When the speaking was done, a vote was taken. The result was unanimous. They would stay in Nevada.[32]

CHAPTER 23

Doing Right by the Paiutes

Sarah's rescue of her father had been widely reported, including in this front-page headline in the *New York Times*: "A Brave Indian Squaw Sarah, Daughter of the Piute Head Chief, Penetrates to the Hostiles' Camp and Rescues Her Father and Brothers."[1] "Princess Sarah" had a name. By the time her pay arrived for her work for Howard, she had a plan to end her people's confinement at Yakama. She rented Platt's Hall in downtown San Francisco, a capacious three-story structure that hosted orchestras, senators, governors, and generals, talks by Oscar Wilde, and performances of every variety. Her first appearance was November 26, 1879, the day before Thanksgiving. The stage scenery represented a forest. Her cousin Jerry, Chief Dave, and one other from Winnemucca sat at the back of the stage. Sarah wore a headdress of eagle feathers set in a scarlet crown, bright red stockings, a short skirt, and a buckskin shirt trimmed with beads and long buckskin strips. About her neck was a necklace that had been given to her brother Natchez in recognition of his daring rescue of the Crowleys and Jack Scott.[2]

Jack Scott was at Platt's Hall that evening, fresh from his failed attempt to intimidate the Paiutes at Winnemucca into moving to Malheur. He was on another mission for Rinehart, this time to persuade members of Sarah's audience that she was a liar. According to Sarah, once she was on stage and got word of Scott's devilry, she challenged him to stand on the stage and deny her statements. (His response is not recorded.)[3]

As Sarah began her talk, her unselfconscious manner put the audience at ease.[4] Her primary target was Rinehart, whom she accused of lying, abusing, ill-treating, and cheating her people; of driving Paiute men into

FIG. 13. Platt's Hall, San Francisco, where Sarah Winnemucca spoke in November and December 1879. Pacific Coast Architecture Database, 2656.

the arms of the Bannocks because they would rather die in war than be starved to death by such a man. She described white atrocities but admitted that the Paiutes who fought in the Bannock War should be punished. There were many empty seats, but the audience enjoyed the performance, as did a critic who wrote, "The lecture was a literary gem."[5]

She spoke again on the day after Thanksgiving, but hit her stride on December 4, again at Platt's Hall. This time there were few empty seats. Sarah's outfit was the same, other than a change in jewelry. She began by describing the warmth and kindnesses of Agent Samuel Parrish and his sister-in-law, who taught Indian children to spell two-syllable words within five months. Her description of the fundamental decency of the Parrishes made Rinehart's cruelty and duplicity all the more vivid.

With the audience in her grasp, Sarah intensified the emotion. The Chinese, she said, "sometimes do fearful things, and commit horrible murders, but you search for those men [and] . . . punish them. You don't attack all the Chinese who are with you. No, you let them live with you."

Then she reached her high point: "You take all the natives of the earth to your bosom but the poor Indian, who is born of the soil of your land and who has lived for generations on the lands which the good God has given to them, and you say he must be exterminated." Without waiting for the applause to fade, Sarah repeated her statement once, then again, with a rising passion that drove the applause to even greater heights.

Continuing a theme that she had begun almost a decade earlier in her letter to Major Henry Douglass at Camp McDermitt, Sarah inveighed, "We want you to try us for four years, and if at the end of that time we don't learn, or don't work, or don't become good citizens, then you can do what you please." Cheers filled the hall.[6]

Sarah's complaints to government officials had produced nothing but backlash. But her speeches drew a different reaction. This young, marginally educated woman of a remote Indian tribe knew the difference to a public official between reading a complaint in a letter and reading it in a newspaper; she knew how to use that difference to her advantage.

In the midst of her lectures Sarah sent to Secretary of the Interior Schurz a detailed description of Rinehart's abusive conduct and a petition asking that Rinehart be replaced by Samuel Parrish.[7] A special agent of the Interior Department, J. M. Haworth, responded. He met Sarah, Winnemucca, Natchez, Jerry Long, and others in Winnemucca in late December 1879. The meeting led to an invitation to Washington DC for four, including Winnemucca, Sarah, and Natchez.

In mid-January 1880 Haworth accompanied the Paiute delegation by train to Washington DC and showed them into the Tremont House Hotel. They were one among a half-dozen Native delegations in the city at that time, one of which was Chief Ouray of the Utes and his wife, who had just arrived from Utah. A reporter came to the Tremont to interview the Ourays but was quickly charmed and lured away by Sarah, whom the reporter declared a "confirmed coquette." She told the reporter that she found Washington DC superior to San Francisco, Chicago, and St. Louis. The reporter found Winnemucca a "wrinkled old specimen," and Natchez monosyllabic. Captain Jim "squatted on the floor, nodded his approval and grunted out of pleasure." Sarah, in contrast, was dressed in the latest style and "in intellect, grace and knowledge of the world," the story concluded, "will compare favorably with many belles of Pennsylvania Avenue."[8]

The following morning Haworth showed the Paiutes into Carl Schurz's office. Once the pleasantries were behind them, Schurz said to Sarah, "I want you to tell me from the first beginning of the Bannock War."[9] As he listened to Sarah's account of her rescue of her father, he surely relived an episode of his youth.

When Schurz was even younger than Sarah as she sat before him, he had joined with a professor, Gottfried Kinkel, in the leadership of a democratic movement in Prussia, inspired by the French Revolution. In time Schurz and Kinkel had taken up arms against the autocratic Prussian regime. As a revolutionary soldier, Schurz had demanded the overthrow of the Prussian government.

Now, as secretary of the interior, *he* was the government. Those sitting before him asked not for the reins of power, although their cause might have been more worthy than the cause of the rebellion in which he had fought. They asked only that their people be released from captivity and returned to a reservation comprising a fraction of what had once been theirs.

The revolution in which Schurz and Kinkel fought came to grief when the fortress the revolutionaries occupied fell to a siege. Schurz fled through a sewer and escaped to France, but Kinkel was captured, convicted of treason, and sentenced to life in prison, spinning wool every day. Schurz later slipped back into Germany. With funds raised by Kinkel's wife he bought a top hat, kid gloves, a starched collar, silk neckband, and fashionable cane, calculating that those hunting down revolutionaries would pay no attention to a tasteless dandy. He spent months putting a plan in place. On the appointed night he paid off a prison guard and met Kinkel at the bottom of a rope from the prison roof, not yet feeling the fire in his palms. Unlike Sarah's and Winnemucca's headlong, dusty flight to Howard's post, Bannocks in hot pursuit, Schurz and Kinkel stepped into the carriage of a wealthy farmer. He drove his horses so hard that one collapsed and died. A well-to-do shipowner provided the last leg of the journey, aboard a schooner with a cargo of wheat for Newcastle. Schurz then had to manage their journey to London with an English vocabulary limited to words like *cherry* and *beefsteak*. Schurz's magnificent rescue attracted wide attention and helped launch his career in America.[10]

Schurz was now conversing with a woman—in a tongue native to neither—who was in his office on the strength of her impulsive, spur-of-the-moment rescue that was in some ways more daring than his carefully orchestrated effort, funded and assisted by a wide network. When Sarah completed her tale, Schurz directed Haworth to take them "everywhere to see everything," then to bring them back to his office the next day. Haworth did as he was told. He also kept the Indians on a tight leash, heading off any chance for Sarah to speak with the press.

Carl Schurz had arrived in America in 1852 at age twenty-three and, along with many other German immigrants, settled in Wisconsin. An urbane, gifted orator, he gained prominence by campaigning tirelessly for the Republican Party, for which President Lincoln rewarded him with an ambassadorship. He served in the Civil War and then as a United States senator for Missouri until President Rutherford B. Hayes decided to put Schurz's reform ideas to work in the Interior Department. When Commissioner of Indian Affairs John Q. Smith resigned, Schurz replaced him with Ezra Hayt, who had earlier served on the Board of Indian Commissioners.

Schurz had no experience with Indians as he took control of the Interior Department, but he soon endorsed the existing policy of removing Indians to large central reservations, remote from white communities. By the time Sarah's petition arrived, late in 1879, Schurz had made a trip to western states to study the Indian problem and meet with Indian leaders. This journey and a second trip the following year changed his mind about reservations. In November 1880 he announced a new policy allowing Indians to remain on their native lands. Although that change in policy was still ten months away when Schurz met the Winnemuccas in January 1880, he may well have had misgivings about removing Indians from their native lands at the time Sarah asked that the Paiutes be returned to theirs.[11]

There was another matter on Schurz's mind at the time of the Winnemuccas' visit. Commissioner Hayt had been accused of dropping charges of misconduct against an Arizona Indian agent in return for a silver mine. Hayt denied the allegations, noting that the mine had not been transferred to him but instead to one Edward Knapp, who, Hayt claimed, was only an acquaintance.[12] Just over a week before he met the Winnemuccas Schurz had given an interview to the *New York Times* on the investigation. The *Times* reported that Schurz described Hayt as "a man of means, to whom the salary was no object."[13]

When the Winnemuccas arrived at Schurz's office on the morning of the twenty-fourth, he began by asking Sarah not to lecture in Washington; it would not be right on a trip requested and paid for by the government. "The government is going to do right by your people now," he said. He then handed her a letter stating, "Pi-Utes, heretofore entitled to live on the Malheur Reservation, their primeval home, are to have lands [on the reservation] allotted to them in severalty."[14] Schurz had not only freed the Malheur Paiutes from their Yakama prison and allowed them to return to Malheur, he had granted Sarah's request that each family be allotted its own tract of land.[15]

On January 29, five days after he had handed this letter to the Winnemuccas, Schurz made public the results of the investigation of Commissioner Hayt. It showed that Edward Knapp, Hayt's acquaintance who took title to the silver mine, was actually Edward Knapp *Hayt*, the commissioner's son. Schurz fired Hayt that day.[16]

Did Schurz know of Hayt's corruption when he decided in favor of the Winnemuccas? Schurz's well-publicized mission for Indian Affairs had been to weed out corruption. Now his handpicked commissioner, whom Schurz had defended as "a man of means, to whom the salary was no object," had crassly misused his office, making Schurz appear naive and ineffective.[17] Whether Schurz was originally inclined to grant the Winnemuccas' request, once he discovered Hayt's misdeed it would have taken a steely discipline to uphold Hayt's decisions against the honest, courageous Paiute woman beseeching permission for her people to return to their native lands.

Oregon Paiutes had endured the whites overrunning their lands and eroding and depleting the sources of their nourishment. They had suffered a catastrophic war in which hundreds of their people perished. Their successful life on a reservation under Agent Parrish had suddenly become a life of starvation and oppression under Rinehart. Most had been manipulated into a war that they wanted no part of, then imprisoned for the crimes of others.

History does not repeat itself, Mark Twain supposedly said, but it does rhyme. For the second time the reservation designed for Paiutes, on Paiute lands, was assured to Paiutes. With the wind in their wings from Schurz's letter, the Paiutes appeared to have a way ahead to a respectable, comfortable place in the American community.

CHAPTER 24

Backlash

Before Sarah completed her return to Yakama, she wrote to Secretary Schurz asking for subsistence for her people until they could be removed to the Malheur Reservation. Acting Commissioner Brooks replied that he could not grant her request, but that there was "a large quantity of subsistence supplies" at the Malheur Reservation; therefore "it will be in their interest to remove [to Malheur] at as early a day as possible."[1]

On May 8, 1880, Sarah arrived back at Yakama, Secretary Schurz's letter firmly in her grasp. Wilbur appeared to be glad to see her, but made no mention of the letter. She expected him to know about it because Schurz told her that Wilbur would receive a copy. The letter was also quite public; it was published in the *New York Times*, for example.[2] But after four days passed without a word about it from Wilbur, Sarah finally showed it to him. He read it with obvious disapproval. He offered to pay Sarah $50 and recommend that she be hired as an interpreter if she kept the letter confidential. She was noncommittal.[3]

Several days later a group of Paiutes sent for Sarah. She and her brother Lee, whose anger at Sarah was moderating, went to the group. Chief Leggins rose to his feet. Tears rolling off his cheeks, he said that Sarah "sold us to Father Wilbur . . . She first sold us to the soldiers and had us brought here, and now she has sold us to this bad man to starve us." This brought Lee to his feet. "For shame," he said, "why don't you ask before you talk?" Sarah then read the letter aloud. The Paiutes erupted in jubilation.[4]

The Paiutes tried to talk to Wilbur about their journey back to Malheur, but he refused to meet. Finally he summoned Sarah. You have put "the devil into your people's head," he scolded her. She retorted that if he was truly a Christian, he would "see that my poor, broken-hearted people get home. Hell is full of just such Christians as you are."[5]

Earlier Wilbur had written that it would be "childish" to return the Paiutes to Malheur. After seeing Schurz's January 24, 1880, letter, he wrote to the commissioner, "From all my years of experience among Indians and my knowledge of frontier character, I protest against any measures looking to the return of the Piutes to Malheur."[6] Just over a week later he wrote again, this time to advise that he had received letters from "prominent citizens of Eastern Oregon" and from General Howard "declaring that from the state of feeling in Eastern Oregon, the contemplated return of the Piutes would be the signal for bloodshed and murder." For that reason, he said, he would not allow the Paiutes to leave unless he was ordered to do so.[7]

The "prominent citizens" who predicted bloodshed if the Paiutes returned were not disinterested observers. In his classic study of cattle and cattlemen in the Oregon Country, J. Orin Oliphant observed that by the beginning of the 1870s, the intermountain country in the Pacific Northwest had become pretty generally a cattleman's country. Virtually anyone who might be considered "prominent" was a stockman. As available grazing land grew scarce, many cattlemen began "to cast greedy eyes" on Indian reservations. It was "on the Malheur Reservation that stockmen made the most flagrant and persistent encroachments."[8] These intruders were the very "prominent stockmen of southeastern Oregon" who were forecasting "bloodshed and murder" if the Paiutes returned.[9] This violence, Wilbur claimed, would arise from "the state of feeling in Eastern Oregon," not from the state of feeling among Paiutes at Yakama. Wilbur showed no reluctance to side with the cattlemen, whom he expected to commit crimes of "bloodshed and murder," and against their expected victims, who asked only to return to the land of their ancestors to which they were legally entitled, without being bloodied or murdered.

As resistance mounted to Secretary Schurz's January 24 letter allowing all Paiutes at Yakama to return to the Malheur Reservation, Natchez Winnemucca initiated a related effort to liberate Yakama Paiutes. Natchez's plan arose out of Mattie's merciful passing on May 29, 1880, after months of suffering from the fall from her horse while in pursuit of escaping Paiutes.

As a result of her death, her husband Lee Winnemucca and their children were released from Yakama and allowed to return to McDermitt. There he told Natchez that the Indians at McDermitt at war's end, principally from the bands of Oits and Leggins, had "been selected . . . indiscriminately from the friendly and hostile members of his tribe."[10]

Lee's account prompted Natchez to ask General McDowell's permission to travel to Yakama to identify the innocents. Captain Bernard conveyed Natchez's request to McDowell: "Natchez states that they know all who participated in the Bannock War, and will have nothing to do with any of them, but *want only those taken away by mistake*."[11]

The military had made at least two commitments to Indians after the fighting stopped. Leggins and his band were induced to accompany soldiers from McDermitt to Malheur on the representation that they were not prisoners and would not be incarcerated, but instead taken to the Malheur Reservation. The second commitment, made by McDowell personally and conveyed by Indian couriers, was that all who turned themselves in at Army posts would be protected; those who did not would be treated as hostile.

The Army kept neither commitment. It lost track of which Indians at McDermitt were prisoners and which were free, and so it confined all at Yakama. It sent Leggins's band to Yakama as well, despite the promise to Leggins that his band would go to Malheur. Once they reached Yakama, Wilbur considered them all to be prisoners.

Natchez's message to McDowell presented an opportunity for the Army to fulfill at least some of its commitments to the Paiutes. Instead of accepting Natchez's offer, however, McDowell sent Arthur Chapman, an interpreter, to take innocent Paiutes back to Oregon.

When Chapman arrived at Yakama in late October 1881, Wilbur, alarmed, sent a telegram to the Commissioner seeking instructions "immediately."[12] On the same day Wilbur wrote to the Commissioner, lamenting Schurz's January 24 letter freeing the Paiutes at a time when "they knew they had forfeited their reservation." "No greater folly than [Schurz's January 24 letter] is conceivable," Wilbur argued, for the Paiutes' return to Malheur would be a "raid of pillage" among settlers who have determined "to exterminate them."[13]

Four days later Wilbur pressed his case further, urging the Commissioner that "what the Piutes might accomplish here is illustrated by Oitz and his band, who have definitely concluded to accept this as their future home and gone to work like men." If Leggins and Paddy and other malcontents could be removed, he continued, "the remainder would accept the situation and follow the example of Oitz and his band."[14]

Just as Chapman was on the verge of leading the Paiutes out of Yakima, freedom seemingly within their grasp, the Commissioner's response to Wilbur arrived, forbidding the Paiutes to move.[15] Wilbur had won. Nothing in his writings suggests that he had any information about commitments made to Paiutes during and in connection with the war. Ignorant of and incurious about the facts, enchanted by his own unfounded polemics, Wilbur sabotaged the plans that would have remedied many wrongs and prevented many others.

Wilbur claimed that the Paiutes wanted to live at Yakama rather than Malheur. "In spite of all the efforts of Sarah Winnemucca," he wrote to Schurz, a "large proportion of the Piutes—all who acknowledge the leadership of Oitz—have determined to remain here. They are steadily at work and earnest in their efforts to become self-supporting. . . . But for the unfortunate return of Sarah Winnemucca, all the Piutes would be in the same condition."[16]

In fact Oits's leadership was limited to his band of ninety.[17] Near the end of the war, some Paiutes said that they hoped the soldiers would hang Oits. "If they don't, we shall kill him ourselves," they said, according to Sarah, "for he is to blame for all." At the Yakama Reservation, in a general Paiute meeting after Sarah returned with Schurz's letter, Paddy said to Oits, "You were first on your horse when the Bannocks came. You got us all into trouble, and only for you we had been in our own country. You are the cause of all our suffering." No one disagreed. Oits simply wept.[18] The man who Wilbur thought was the Paiutes' primary leader was instead a virtual outcast, still followed by his small faction but barely tolerated by the rest.

A study of the performance of Methodist agencies under President Grant's Peace Policy found that the work of Methodists was "largely a failure. It did little to improve the service or the condition of Indians. It did much to perpetuate sectarianism and intolerance and bigotry in America."[19] Wilbur had no small role in the failings of his religion. An example is described in an adulatory article portraying Wilbur's scorn of the Indian "dreamer" religion and his use of his immense strength and physical stature (six feet four and over three hundred pounds) to enter a crowded room of Indians.[20] The article admires his Christian thuggery: he "pitched headlong, this way and that," clearing a path to the leader, whom Wilbur "seized . . . by the nape of his neck and literally yanked . . . out of the house head foremost, handcuffed . . . , picking him up bodily, and then pitched him into his hack."[21]

General Howard matched Wilbur in his dedication to keeping the Paiutes confined at Yakama. He repeatedly raised his voice in support of vigorous and prolonged punishment of the Paiutes, often citing white hostility to the Indians as a reason to banish them.[22] The "hostility" of whites, however, was aroused by Indians who fought against whites. It was not aroused by the hundreds of Paiutes who did not fight in the war.[23] Had imprisonment been imposed only on the guilty, the whites would have been more likely to have directed their hostility against those who earned it. The merging of the innocent and guilty at Yakama eliminated any chance of preserving the distinction between the two. As an advocate for punishing all Paiutes rather than just the guilty, Howard was a leading architect of the whites' indiscriminate "hostility" against all Paiutes, which he then invoked to prolong the unjust confinement of the innocents.

Wilbur's attack on Sarah paled next to Rinehart's. On January 14, 1880, ten days before Schurz met with the Winnemuccas, a letter signed by nine individuals was sent to Representative T. H. Brents of Oregon in Washington DC. The letter began by proclaiming that William Rinehart "always maintained, and yet maintains the confidence of this community for honesty, integrity and reliable business qualities." The remainder of the letter, and its many attachments, is devoted to defaming Sarah Winnemucca. A skilled writer with a broad vocabulary, Rinehart could not resist words such as *licentious, contumacious, profligate,* and *lascivious,* even in a letter that he was hoping would appear to have been written by ranchers and cattlemen.

Among the many accusations against Sarah were that she was "a notorious liar and malicious schemer," of "adulterous and drunken habits," and that she took her prostitution pay in whiskey.[24] Those who signed the letter were Rinehart's relatives and employees as well as cattlemen eager to please a man who controlled so much prime pasturage.[25]

Rinehart could not resist adding that Sarah had been fired from her job as translator. Of course Rinehart was the one who had fired her, for reporting his abuse of Indians to soldiers. But he had fabricated a more presentable reason—that she had encouraged disobedience of a regulation providing rations only to Indians who worked. Now, however, he had a different need—to create the impression that she was a loose woman. Encouraging Indians not to work was not the kind of "looseness" that Rinehart had in mind. Substituting one false reason for another, he now claimed she was fired "by reason of her known and notorious lewd and lascivious habits."[26]

These reactions to Schurz's letter came about during an unsettled time at Indian Affairs. In August 1880 E. M. Marble was appointed acting commissioner of Indian Affairs. He was the third commissioner since January 1880. Commissioner Hayt left in that month after his corrupt acquisition of a silver mine was discovered; his successor left in July for health reasons.[27] In the next several months Acting Commissioner Marble pondered his decision on the questions provoked by Schurz's January 24 letter to the Winnemuccas.

If Marble was casting about for guidance, he need not have looked farther than the highest official in the administration, President Rutherford Hayes, who was in the midst of the first presidential visit to Oregon as Marble was preparing his decision. On October 2, 1880, at an Indian school just west of Portland, Hayes gave a speech that was printed on the front page of the *New York Times*. Warning against "race prejudice," Hayes said, "This country was once theirs. They owned it as much as you own your farms." He urged that we "should do our best to improve their physical, mental, and moral condition. We should prepare them to become part of the great, American family."[28] President Hayes's objectives were well served by Schurz's January 24 letter, which declared that the Paiutes' imprisonment would end, that individual Paiutes would receive fee simple ownership of their native land, and that government aid would be provided to assist in starting their farms and promoting their civilization.

Hayes, however, was within a few months of the end of his term and had pledged not to seek another. The Paiutes' future was in Marble's hands.

CHAPTER 25

Untethered from Truth

A "self-constituted delegation, consisting of the chief, Winnemucca, and other members of his band, visited the city." This sentence began Acting Commissioner Marble's explanation of his resolution of the issues raised by Secretary Schurz's January 24 letter. In fact the delegation was constituted by Schurz's assistant, Haworth, not by the Winnemuccas.[1] Marble's error on a matter of no apparent importance seems inadvertent, until it is viewed in context.

The report continues that the delegation (that is, the Winnemuccas) made an "agreement to remove to Malheur," and to bring Chiefs "Ochoho . . . and Weiser" and their followers to Malheur as well. In fact no "agreement" had been made. The outcome of the meeting was Schurz's letter, which said nothing about an agreement. Moreover, Winnemucca and Ochoho had for years steadfastly refused to go to Malheur. It is not credible that Winnemucca would speak for Ochoho, much less promise that Ochoho would do what that chief had repeatedly and adamantly refused to do.[2]

Winnemucca had declined to go to Malheur before the Bannock War. After the war Leggins, his subchief, was taken to Malheur with the promise that he would remain there, but the promise was broken and he was taken instead to Yakama and imprisoned there without cause. Having learned that the whites imprisoned Leggins at Yakama after promising that he could remain at Malheur, Winnemucca was not so foolish as to be taken in by the same ruse.[3]

As for Marble's claim that Winnemucca promised that Chief Weiser would come to Malheur, there was no such chief and no such promise.

195

Marble claimed that Schurz's January 24 letter did not apply to these Paiutes sent to Yakama. But the letter says that it applies to "those of the Piutes who, in consequence of the Bannock War, went to the Yakama reservation." It could not be clearer.

Marble argued that the letter was not meant to benefit the bands of four chiefs (Weyouwewa, Oits, Ponee, and Egan), but instead those of three chiefs (Winnemucca, Ochoho, and Weiser). The three chiefs, Marble claimed, "properly belonged at Malheur." Since those three bands failed to move to Malheur, Marble continued, Indian Affairs had no alternative to closing the reservation.

This argument is also indefensible. The reservation was created because in 1869 the four chiefs had refused to move to the Klamath Reservation, insisting on their right under the Huntington agreement to a reservation "in their own country." The Indians who "properly belonged at Malheur" were the successors to the four chiefs. The remaining Paiutes were welcome at Malheur, but, as later found by the United States Court of Claims, "Winnemucca's band, O-Che-Ho's and Chock-Tote's bands did not at any time claim the Malheur country, or any part of it, as their own, and had no attachment to it or desire to live there."[4] As stated by Rinehart, "This is not their home."[5] There was no basis for Marble's claim that these Indians "properly belonged at Malheur." The Indians who "properly belonged at Malheur" were those whom Marble barred from Malheur.

Marble claimed that on January 24 Winnemucca had promised to come to Malheur, causing the government to order supplies for Malheur that went to waste because the Indians broke their promise. In fact the government ordered supplies for Malheur, then forcibly removed the Paiutes, assuring that the supplies intended for them would arrive after they were gone.[6]

The law establishing Oregon as a territory provided that Indians retained aboriginal title—that is, the right to occupy their lands—unless they gave up that right with the consent of the United States.[7] This was not an obscure requirement. Six federal statutes containing essentially the same terms had been enacted since 1790.[8] Neither of the two nineteenth-century Paiute treaties with the United States gave up this ancestral land. While the reservation could be eliminated at the stroke of a pen, the Paiutes' right of occupancy of the land could not. As later ruled by the Indian Claims

Commission, the Paiutes "never ceded nor relinquished their original Indian title to said lands."[9]

It was perhaps because of this right that Marble did not leave the Paiutes with nothing. They would never have the land that comprised the Malheur Reservation, but that land would be sold and the proceeds from the sale would "be invested for the benefit of the Indians," Marble declared.

The following year Commissioner Hiram Price considered another challenge to the Paiutes' interest in the value of the land that had been the Malheur Reservation. The challenge was in the form of a memorial by the Oregon legislature to Congress requesting that the Malheur Reservation "be restored to the public domain." The memorial urged that since 1878 no Indians had returned to the reservation; it falsely claimed that Paiutes at Yakama "refuse to return to the Malheur Reservation." Keeping the lands for Indians, it asserted, "was a great detriment to the settlers and business of Eastern Oregon."[10]

Price responded decisively. The Paiutes who had lived on the reservation were scarcely able to support themselves. The reservation, therefore, would be sold only under a plan that provided "substantial return" to the Indians, for they "will need assistance in the future in their efforts at self-support."[11] Paiutes had lost their land, but by law they were entitled to be paid for it, Commissioner Price assured.

CHAPTER 26

Gold and Cattle

During the 1860s cattlemen in the Willamette Valley lacked sufficient markets for their growing herds. Pasturage grew scarce as herds expanded. In southeast Oregon, on the other hand, there was ample, prime pastureland. Indeed many considered it the natural habitat of a cow. One reason was white sage. Cattle have little interest in white sage in the summer and fall, but the first frost renders it irresistibly succulent. Since little white sage is consumed in the summer and fall, there is a plentiful supply in winter, the most difficult season to keep cattle fed and healthy. Because of white sage, an impression took hold that cattle in southeast Oregon could roam safely the year round, "while stockmen smoked pipes, fondled their poker chips, and worried little, if at all."[1]

There was no reason to raise cows in a place without an accessible market for beef. In 1860, however, gold strikes in Idaho led to expanding mining communities within convenient reach of southeast Oregon pasturage. As the demand for beef grew, Willamette Valley cattlemen began to move herds to the intermountain region.[2] In 1868 the industry began to flourish when the Central Pacific Railroad extended its service north to Winnemucca, Nevada. The four-hundred-mile cattle drive from southeast Oregon to Winnemucca opened a vast network of new markets to Oregon cattlemen.

Arriving in Harney Valley in 1869, John S. Devine, the first permanent settler, formed a partnership with W. B. Todhunter that accumulated land and cattle at a rapid pace. Pete French, partner and son-in-law of Hugh Glenn, the "wheat king" of California, started a ranch just north of Steens

Mountain. A man of humble origins and limited education, French was operating two ranches by 1879. His ranches covered a combined area of roughly three thousand square miles, held not by title but "by right of undisturbed possession," meaning that anyone who tried to make a claim in this area would receive a visit from French's people and then promptly decide to move on.[3]

These men did not look with favor on President Grant's 1872 decision to exclude whites from almost 1.5 million acres of southeastern Oregon and set it aside for a people who did not understand the cattle business, were not citizens, and paid no taxes. Todhunter and Devine, French and Glenn, and other prominent cattle businesses began grazing their stock on reservation lands with increasing boldness, which reached new heights after Paiutes were exiled to Yakama in 1879.[4]

At about this time the partnership of Miller and Lux appeared on the scene. When Henry Miller and Charles Lux first met in San Francisco in 1854 and heard one another's accents, they probably suspected that they had led similar lives. Indeed they had. They grew up within one hundred miles of one another in southwest Germany, moved to New York City and worked as butchers, relocated to San Francisco within the first two years of the gold rush, briefly took jobs as butchers, then opened their own shops. Only then did they first meet. In 1858 they formed a partnership, solidified by marriages into the same well-to-do family. Yet the two had nothing else in common. "There is no similarity between Lux and myself," Miller assured, "not in sympathy nor in views nor nothing."

In 1878 in Kern County, California, about seven hundred miles south of the Malheur Reservation, an illness broke out in a Miller and Lux herd. They lost thousands of cattle to the disease, a splenic fever that causes the spleen to double in size. It tends to occur in regions with hot climates and without cold winters. In 1879 splenic fever broke out in another of their herds. Whatever their many differences, Miller and Lux had no difficulty agreeing to look north for a place to raise cattle where the winters were cold.[5]

Miller and Lux acquired land in the Malheur Reservation eventually totaling at least eleven thousand acres. When Todhunter and Devine failed to set aside sufficient feed as insurance for drought years, Todhunter was forced to sell. Miller and Lux bought his land and his forty-three

FIG. 14. Cattle grazing along Malheur River, near the location of the former Malheur Agency. Author photo.

thousand head of beef cattle for a million dollars, becoming "the largest cattle company in American history."[6]

Commissioner Price's firm dismissal of the Oregon legislature's memorial seeking the former Malheur land did little to dampen appetites for that land. Rinehart's efforts to fend off the trespassers had little effect. A leading Idaho newspaper asked, "Is [Rinehart] afraid the cattle will eat up all the grass? . . . The cattle that happen to roam over the Malheur reservation do no more harm than the wild goats on our mountain peaks." The U.S. district attorney in Portland refused Rinehart's request to prosecute those who grazed their cattle on the reservation. "The grass was growing and if not fed down would fall down and rot," he told Rinehart.[7]

Then in 1882 the lands that had been selected in fulfillment of a U.S. obligation to create a reservation for Paiutes "in their own country", that had been set aside for the "sole benefit" of the Paiutes, and that "these Indians will need in the future in their efforts at self-support," were confiscated by Commissioner Price. The sole reason offered for the confiscation was the "most urgent and persistent appeals on the part of the people of Oregon."[8] The small portion not returned to the public domain was slated to be sold for the benefit of the Paiutes. But that was not done. By executive order of May 21, 1883, all the remaining lands, except a tract of 320 acres, were restored to the public domain. Seven years later the 320-acre tract was also restored to the public domain, completing the total confiscation of all lands of the Paiutes.[9]

The Paiutes had a right of occupancy of their territory that they had not yielded by treaty or otherwise. In a few short years the Paiutes' land, rich with forage year round, their only asset, was overrun with cattle that corralled the miners' dust and swirled it into the already bulging pockets of a handful of the nation's wealthiest cattlemen. The Paiutes were left with nothing.

According to Howard

When the last bullet of the Bannock War came to rest, there was no letup in the war of words over the blame for the war's losses. The *East Oregonian* cried out the pain and rage of its readers: "not only have our citizens been killed," but our "whole country has been devastated." Entire neighborhoods, according to the story, fled in panic, leaving crops to Indians and marauders who followed in the wake of the army. Returning settlers would be faced with "beggary and starvation." Every Indian, "whether friend or foe, caught off the Reservation, will bite the dust, and all here will say amen to it."[1]

A man by the name of Blackwell is a reminder that not all settlers fit the *East Oregonian*'s facile stereotype. Blackwell came upon a Paiute woman left in a fort by Howard's troops. The woman had been "shot across the loins, scalped and entirely helpless . . . a wide flap of skin, cut loose in scalping, fell forward over her eyes." Her tongue was swollen for lack of water. Blackwell clipped the flap of skin with sheep shears, dressed her wounds, and fed and cared for her for ten weeks until she could again ride and was ready to return to her people.[2]

The role of Oits's band in the war was virtually identical to that of its Bannock allies. The remaining Paiutes had no role in the origin of the war, which had been fully joined before the hostile Bannocks arrived at Barren Valley and Steens Mountain. Nor did those two encounters have any real potential to end the war, given the Bannocks' resolve to maintain their grip on the Paiutes and to continue the hostilities. The chief question at issue at Barren Valley and Steens Mountain was whether the conflict would remain a two-party affair (Bannocks-Oits alliance versus United States) or expand to absorb the remaining Malheur Paiutes.

The truth about the war was important to Paiutes, for much of the fighting had been in their country. Mourning and outraged settlers were, or would become, neighbors of the Paiutes. The public perception of the war would determine whether settlers and their descendants considered Paiutes to have been the Bannocks' allies or their victims. But the Paiutes had little influence over how their role in the war was described in print. To those who had such influence, truth and facts were not always priorities. The complex circumstances under which the Paiutes became entangled in the war played into the hands of those who sought to obfuscate and distort.

Among the sources of information about the war were the writings of General Howard. The economic setback that Howard suffered in defending claims arising out of his work for the Freedmen's Bureau left him financially strapped in his later years. He took up writing about his military career to supplement his income. In books he published in 1907 and in 1908, Howard described Egan's role in the Bannock War. Since then virtually every history of the war appears to have adopted Howard's position. None has questioned it. Yet Howard's description is like a piece of a jigsaw puzzle dropped into the wrong box.

In his 1907 book, *My Life*, Howard wrote that Egan "had been very reluctant at first to join the Bannocks, but under threats and persuasions he concluded to take Oytes, the Dreamer, as his counselor, and become the military head of all the tribes represented. In former years Egan had successfully fought General Crook and other officers, and had won quite a reputation for heroic valor."[3]

Howard's 1908 book, *Indian Chiefs*, written for young readers, claimed that Egan "held out against war as long as he could get a hearing . . . but after long reflection and the saving of the lives of several of his friends, whites and red men, Egan at last agreed to be their war-chief. He commanded in several battles, but was never very successful."[4] The war was started by Bannocks (after considerable provocation), but Howard's assertion that Egan led the Bannock-Paiute warriors shifted primary responsibility for the war from Bannocks to Paiutes.

Among the first to write about the war after Howard was George

Brimlow, who declared that "Egan at last consented to be their war chief," citing Howard.[5] J. F. Santee also cited Howard, stating, "After much persuasion, Egan consented to lead in the war against the whites."[6] After Brimlow and Santee, most historians apparently considered Egan's leadership role to be an accepted fact requiring no citation. According to Merrill Beal and Merle Wells, "the dominant leader was a Umatilla named Egan, who decided to fight."[7] Robert Utley wrote that, at Steens Mountain, the Bannocks "united with Egan, Oytes, and the Malheur Paiutes. . . . Egan, the Paiute war chief, reluctantly agreed to take the place of the fallen Buffalo Horn as hostile leader."[8] Similar views were expressed by Steward and Wheeler-Voegelin (Egan "became one of the leaders in the Bannock war" and "the Indians left the Reservation to join the Bannocks in warfare"),[9] Sally Zanjani (Egan "accepted the position of Buffalo Horn's replacement as war chief of the hostiles"),[10] Brigham D. Madsen ("Chief Egan, convinced that his people wanted war, took over the leadership from Oytes and united with the Bannock to become the principal leader of the combined Indian forces"),[11] Robert Hamburger ("with Chief Winnemucca muzzled and Chief Egan tempted by Oytes's arguments, the Paiutes were drawn into the rebellion"),[12] Parsons ("command of the allied forces of Snakes and Piutes devolved upon Egan"),[13] and Trenholm and Carley ("contrary to his better judgment," Egan decided to fight to get "more supplies" from the Great Father and to persuade the Great Father not "to make his people work").[14] There does not appear to be any historian who disagrees.[15]

Yet, Howard's statement, so influential with later historians, is contradicted: "He [Oits] may truly be said to have been the leading Indian of the hostile Piute and primarily the cause of the troubles of that tribe." These are Howard's own words, from a letter dated December 20, 1878, when the events of the war were fresh in his memory. In the same letter he stated that Oits "led the party who brought Eagan back to the hostile camp, when that Chief attempted to escape," and that Oits's second in command was Hatch, "a devoted adherent to the teachings of Oitz."[16] These statements, made near the time of the events, are more reliable than Howard's writings thirty years later. Howard's 1878 opinion of Oits's leadership role was confirmed by Buffalo Horn's aunt, who traveled with the Bannocks after they left Steens Mountain and who was therefore in a position to observe who was in command. She told Sarah that "Oytes had taken her nephew's place as chief over the Bannocks."[17] Lee Winnemucca told Sarah, when the two met on Steens Mountain, that Oits "is their chief now, since Buffalo Horn is killed."[18] Steward and Wheeler-Voegelin concur that "Oytes [took] over the Bannocks of Buffalo Horn."[19] Further confirmation lies in Rinehart's April 1878 statement that Oits "is now the principal disturbing element and is generally to be found at the bottom of all our petty troubles." Should Oits's misconduct continue, Rinehart added, he would "ask authority for [Oits's] permanent removal to some distant reservation."[20]

Howard was writing to support himself. He knew more about Egan than about Oits because he had interviewed Egan's niece and adopted daughter, Mattie, during the Bannock War. In the absence of any other explanation of Howard's switch from Oits to Egan, it is not easy to dismiss the possibility that, with Egan as chief, he had a more compelling story with greater appeal to young readers. Mattie was the source for much of his information and a central character in *Indian Chiefs*. Early in the chapter on Mattie, Howard described his own experience of listening to her: "She talked with a pretty musical tone, each sentence sounding sometimes like a song, and sometimes her sentences were like poetry." With Egan, Mattie's uncle and adoptive father, as the Paiute chief, Howard had a more integrated, tightly knit, and appealing tale than he would have had with Oits as chief.[21]

Although, like Egan, Oits was a Paiute leader, he represented a small, militaristic faction. Egan was their primary chief. His actions and words were seen as their actions and words. Howard's 1908 claim that "Egan at last agreed to be their war-chief" therefore tainted all Malheur Paiutes with the blood, misery, and poverty inflicted by the war.

Howard's 1908 claim that Egan was "war-chief" is untrustworthy for a host of other reasons besides his own contradictory statement written just after the war. Howard's 1907 and 1908 writings about the Bannock War are unreliable. In *My Life* he accused the Paiutes of inventing a false grievance as an excuse for going to war. They "took advantage of a grievance," that is, the removal of Samuel Parrish as their agent. It was not a genuine grievance, Howard claimed, because "I would have helped them remedy that, if they had asked."[22] But a year later, in his next book, Howard admitted, "I was written to and besought to stop the change if

I possibly could."[23] He had claimed that he would help if they asked, but they *did* ask and he did not help. Howard had therefore known that the grievance was genuine at the time he claimed it was not.

Howard also lauded the "extraordinary expense [that] was incurred for their [Paiutes'] protection and comfort" on their journey to the Yakama Reservation. But Rinehart knew the truth, that "no provision had been made for the comfort or safe-keeping of these prisoners."[24] The "protection and comfort" of the journey was such that on their arrival they were, according to the Yakama physician, "without exception the most miserable lot of human beings I ever saw," and, according to Wilbur, in "the most destitute condition of any Indians I have ever known in this, or any other country."[25] Howard knew full well the extent of the Paiutes' suffering from this journey because he met the procession at The Dalles and saw for himself that, in his words, "much suffering has resulted from cold and snows."[26] After the Paiutes reached Yakama, Wilbur wrote to Howard that they were "in a most destitute and suffering condition—quite a number I think about twenty young & old died."[27]

Howard also declared, "It would have been a reward to misconduct to have given them [Paiutes] back the reservation which they had robbed and deserted when they went to war."[28] As for the robbery, Rinehart investigated it. At the time of the investigation Howard expressed hope "that Major Stewart might be able to find some of the reservation Indians hiding away in that vicinity [where the thefts occurred]."[29] But after nine months Rinehart found no evidence implicating the Paiutes. The thefts were committed instead by Howard's troops, one of whom was convicted, as Howard surely knew when he blamed the Paiutes.[30]

Howard had a second reason that, in his view, justified taking the Paiutes' reservation from them—the fact that they "deserted [it] when they went to war." This argument would be persuasive if substantially all Malheur Paiutes had voluntarily gone to war. In fact Paiutes were disarmed, threatened, and coerced by the Bannocks. For hundreds of Paiutes, Howard's claim that they "went to war" is not tenable. The Indian Claims Commission found years later that the United States violated Paiute rights in their land, "in forcibly removing them [Paiutes] from said lands to the Yakima Reservation."[31]

Howard's errors in his writings about the war are not random. Each error disfavors the Paiutes, as does his claim that Egan led the joint Indian forces. Each makes the Paiutes appear undeserving and, therefore, his victory over them just.

This chapter of Howard's book ends with the Paiutes returning to their homeland, which had "always been the hunting and fishing ground of their people . . . to beat their tom-toms and dance and dream in their old haunts."[32] Howard's rumination has earmarks of a tale spawned by Morton and the phrenologists, foretelling the passing of the Indian people. It is not unlike a passage in one such tale that appeared on the front page of the *Oregon Statesman*: "The forest was their home; hunting and fishing, and dancing, and fighting, constituted their chief employment, and their life was rather that of a talking animal, than of a thinking intelligence."[33]

Howard's claims in his 1907 and 1908 books that Egan led the Bannock-Paiute forces were influential given his position as commander of U.S. forces in that war. It is not surprising that so many writers and historians accepted his word. Yet his claims ignore inconvenient evidence and, in Howard's quest to portray himself as a heroic, even-keeled commander, ride roughshod over the truth.[34]

CHAPTER 28

A Yale Ho-Chunk

In his January 24, 1880, letter to the Winnemuccas, Secretary Schurz had freed the Paiutes from Yakama and promised them individual plots within the Malheur Reservation as well as government assistance in starting their farms and in "promoting their civilization."[1] Wilbur's deceit caused Schurz to change his mind and leave the Paiutes imprisoned at Yakama. Wilbur retired late in 1882. The following spring Paiutes fled Yakama to locations in Oregon, Nevada, Idaho, and California. Steward and Wheeler-Voegelin estimated that fewer than twenty-five percent went to reservations.[2] The largest group attempted to return to the Malheur Reservation but it had been dissolved. Although the Paiutes had Indian title to the land that had been the Malheur Reservation, they were in no position to know their property rights under U.S. law. The most promising avenue to such information for most Native Americans was their reservation agent, but the Paiutes' agent had been a source of deception, not fact. To gain for himself the appearance of innocence, he had deployed a constellation of falsehoods giving his Indian charges the appearance of the guilt that he feared would otherwise be his.

Unaware of their rights, the Paiutes, in the words of their chief, Johnny Capp, "did not dare go to Malheur Reservation." He explained: "White people were on the reservation. . . . It seems we were always on the white peoples' land. Whenever they did not like us we had to move." "When we had our land," Chief Capp said, "we went hunting and fishing, we had plenty meat and fish to eat, had the furs to keep us warm."[3] But now, barred by whites from the land that had always been theirs and that by law still was, Paiutes could no longer sustain themselves on traditional food sources.

Largely ignored by the government that had taken their land, deprived of all dependable means of support, the Burns Paiutes slid helplessly into poverty. The knowledge, the work ethic, the organizational skills, and the discipline that had sustained them for centuries could not make life's necessities out of nothing. The Paiutes did their best to adapt, struggling to find work and performing well the few opportunities that came their way as farmhands, sheepshearers, "cat skinners" at Hines's logging operations, and mill workers at Hines Lumber. Some women were hired by whites to do housework and manual labor. Some also tanned deer hides and made leather gloves for sale.[4]

In 1898 a special agent, William Casson, arrived in Burns to allot land to the Paiutes under the 1887 Dawes Act. The purpose of the law was to end the paternalistic role of the federal government as the "Great Father" of the Natives and transform them into independent Americans, soon to merge into the general populace. To bring about these changes the Dawes Act provided for a national school system, Indian citizenship, and 160-acre allotments.

Casson's land allotments were described in a short history of Burns by James Donegan, an attorney and leading citizen. Donegan's views of the Indian wars did not fit the frontiersman stereotype. "The white man disregarded the Indians' rights and title to the land," Donegan wrote, "with the result that it cost millions of dollars in money and thousands of lives before the Indian land question was finally settled. In my mind the position of the Indian was absolutely sound. As a socialist he believed in the common use of the land, and when the government sought to confine him on limited reservations of poor land, and without due compensation for the land that was taken he revolted and did what you and I would have done, fought in defense of his birthright."[5] Donegan's views were not formed in an ivory tower. His wife, née Margaret Smyth, the first white born in Harney Valley, had lost her father and grandfather in the Bannock War when Oits's band set fire to her grandfather's home.

Turning to the land allotments, Donegan wrote that Casson formed a commission with two others to select the allotments. "To their everlasting credit," he continued, "they allotted to the Indians the best lands that were available." But all of the good land had already been snapped up by large cattle companies and small settlers, leaving the Paiutes, according to Donegan, "160 acres of land on which a jack rabbit could not make a living."[6]

FIG. 15. James and Margaret Smyth Donegan, 1899. Courtesy of Western History Room, Harney County Library.

After allotting land to tribesmen, Indian Affairs expected that, as envisioned by the Dawes Act, the role of the government would diminish as the Indians grew increasingly independent. Yet the allotments for the Paiutes were arid, alkaline land that would grow only rabbitbrush, salt grass, brittle bladder fern, and the like. Also, allotments were provided only to the 105 Paiutes who were able to show that they were descendants from a band of one of the chiefs who signed the 1868 Huntington treaty. The remaining Paiutes lived instead at the Burns dump.

Although the implementation of the Dawes Act did little if anything to make up for the hundreds of thousands of acres taken from the Paiutes, the federal government expected the Paiutes to be independent, for that was the purpose of the act. As explained by the assistant commissioner of Indian affairs, "The fund situation . . . precludes the possibility of giving these Indians any great amount of financial assistance. Scattered Indians, such as those at Burns, who have no particular claim upon the government

FIG. 16. Old Camp, 1915, Annie Adams on right. Photograph by Agnes Sayer. Courtesy of University of Oregon Special Collections.

and who have not been the recipients of any great amount of assistance in the past must necessarily work out their own salvation to a large extent, and must be cared for as far as possible by local and state authorities rather than by the Service."[7]

Chief Capps did not exaggerate in saying that "the Government had abandoned us entirely."[8] As Donegan put it, "after dispossessing the Indians of all their land," the federal government felt that it paid its "full debt to the Indians by giving him 160 acres" of worthless land. Until about 1924, therefore, it "rested on [its] oars and the Indian received no aid or assistance from the Government."[9]

In 1924 the Baker Diocese of the Catholic Church appointed Father Peter Heuel to the Holy Family Parish, which included Burns. Feisty, bordering on pugnacious, Heuel had had troubles, ending in shoving matches with a parishioner who, through it all, remained friends with Heuel. In any case, meekness was not in Father Heuel's makeup.[10]

When Heuel discovered how poor these Indians were, he washed the men with his own hands, cleaned and salved their sores, and hired women to do the same for the rest. He performed marriage ceremonies for the couples. When he encountered victims of government neglect, he typed their stories and mailed them to the commissioner of Indian affairs and other officials. His precisely phrased letters, supported by sworn affidavits, equally precise, helped expose the neglect and misconduct of the Indian Affairs teacher and contract doctor at Burns.

Short on finesse and long on belligerence, Heuel offended many who had earned his outrage, but also some who had not. Opposition to Heuel first arose when he invited Paiutes into his church. He did not help his cause by accusing Edward Hines, a wealthy Catholic and principal of Hines Lumber Company, of robbing the Paiutes by purchasing logging rights on their former reservation. Pressured by Hines, the church relieved Heuel of his parish. Unbowed, Heuel continued to befriend the Paiutes and do battle for them.

After Heuel was brushed off, ignored, and insulted, he fought back until he penetrated the federal bureaucratic morass to Lynn Frazier, chair of the Senate Committee on Indian Affairs. Frazier asked Commissioner Rhoads to look into Heuel's complaints. Rhoads sent Henry Roe Cloud, a Ho-Chunk born on the banks of the Missouri River on the Winnebago Reservation in Nebraska in the mid-1880s. He attended an Indian boarding school where all Indian languages were forbidden and where his most vivid memory was turning a washing machine for two years. With the encouragement of a Presbyterian pastor, he eventually gained admission to a college preparatory school and then to Yale. By the time of his arrival in Burns in August 1932 he had been ordained a Presbyterian minister with two degrees from Yale and had served for four years in preparing the Meriam Report, a highly regarded and "remarkably thorough" study of Indian administration informed by staff visits to ninety-five reservations, agencies, hospitals, and schools.[11]

At Burns Roe Cloud interviewed many witnesses and prepared a detailed, comprehensive report on the Burns Paiutes. Father Loeser, who succeeded Heuel, told Roe Cloud that, "All these Indians are good workers. They are ambitious." He added, "Put them [Paiutes] above the white people in morals. They don't steal . . . . I think they are better than whites." But he conceded, "There is no chance for work. There is a lot of prejudice among the whites. The whites get the jobs."

When Heuel took Loeser to the city dump where the Paiutes lived, Loeser saw Paiutes eating the entrails of jackrabbits. "I've never seen Indians as bad off as these," he reported to Roe Cloud. They ate so regularly out of garbage cans that some restaurant workers wrapped their garbage for them. Most lived in the Burns dump. The tiny houses built to sell to them in 1924 could not accommodate beds in most cases. They slept on the floor, but there was no foundation and no insulation. Burns winters are frigid. They could not afford fuel for warmth and could not gather wood without traveling long distances. Malnourished and cold, the Paiutes lost much of their resistance to disease. The Indian Affairs contract doctor, who was reportedly a member of the Ku Klux Klan, orchestrated changes in the ownership of the local hospital that resulted in the exclusion of the Paiutes. Trachoma, an eye disease, raged among the Paiutes, blinding some. Tuberculosis and other diseases beset them. "When they get sick, they die quickly," Loeser observed.[12]

Only the poorest of the poor—the bottom ten to fifteen percent—received rations. Yet the superintendent of the Warm Springs Agency, which included Burns, protested to the commissioner of Indian affairs that there was "too much paternalism towards the Indians at Burns." He charged, "They continually demand more and more, and seem to make less effort to provide themselves a living by their own efforts."[13]

From his investigation Roe Cloud found that the Paiutes had been oppressed so profoundly that they could no longer help themselves. They were "vermin infested, liable at all times to typhus fever, living in filthy rags, contracting trachoma and tuberculosis, going blind and dying." "The main cause" of their condition, Roe Cloud wrote, "is, first, the loss of their reservation." While a number of events contributed to that loss, the culminating and decisive factor was Wilbur's false narrative about the Paiutes at his reservation, tricking Commissioner Trowbridge and Secretary Schurz into reversing Schurz's decision to return the Paiutes to Malheur.

Calling on his broad knowledge of the condition of Natives throughout the nation from his work on the Meriam Report, Roe Cloud concluded, "These Paiute Indians at Burns are the most destitute we have in the United States."[14]

CHAPTER 29

White Whim, Paiute Penury

The Paiutes' decline started when whites arrived in their lands. Yet whites arrived in the lands of all Native Americans. How did these Paiutes become the most deprived, undernourished, poor, and diseased? Were they inferior to other Indians? Did they lack resolve? Were they just unlucky?

Part of the answer begins centuries ago, when the distribution of edible plants and animals in the high desert defined Paiute food-gathering units (or kin-cliques), which in turn defined the shape and structure of Paiute society. Efficient food gathering required small groups in most circumstances. The relentless demands of fueling the body in desiccated, infertile lands, so sparsely vegetated, required kin-cliques to spend most of March through October in places where edible plants, roots, and seeds were ready for harvest. Planning the food-gathering route of a family unit was a complex undertaking. A richly productive plant one year could be barren the next because of a dry spell during a critical phase for that plant. Last year's abundant resource might be picked clean by a different family this year. Seeking the remote and the isolated helped assure the best harvest, but atomized the Paiute population, separating the family units from one another for most of the year. The isolation of kin-cliques for the greater portion of every year required them to make nearly every important decision on their own. Their autonomy left no meaningful function to be performed by a larger entity. Hence no such larger entity existed. Out of necessity, then, the leadership of a family unit was limited to persons in the unit, for it would not do to have a leader who was almost never present.

Since family leaders answered to no one, they were free to manage their family as they wished, to welcome and exclude as they chose.[1] A family unit's complete independence meant, of course, that other family units were equally independent; none had much influence over any family unit other than its own. Each was in a sense a mini-tribe, gathering and making all of life's necessities on its own, under its own internal rules and customs, led by its own "chief." Each mini-tribe could enjoy relationships with those in other mini-tribes in winter and occasionally during the rest of the year. Rarely was there a need to correct or discipline individuals outside of one's own family unit because it was easier to simply avoid them. This was a sensible arrangement when kin-cliques were truly independent of one another.

After the arrival of whites, however, that independence began to wane; larger groups, each under a single chief, gradually began to form. In the 1850s as war chiefs emerged, multiple family units became aligned under each chief. There was nothing permanent or binding in these allegiances. They could be severed at any time. Still, with the development of war chiefs, cooperation and dependence began to migrate across the boundaries separating kin-cliques. Stock taken in raids was shared. Multiple family units joined in military efforts, both defensive and offensive.

After the Snake War Paiutes progressed further toward a unified community. When the Paiutes surrendered in June 1868, settlers began moving onto Paiute lands. Paiute access to traditional sources of foods diminished, while danger from unprovoked shootings increased as whites spread over southeast Oregon. Many Paiutes gathered near Fort Harney for the protection and occasional meals provided by soldiers. Smaller groups gathered at or near the Klamath Reservation, Warm Springs, and Fort Warner.

Kin-cliques drifted even further from their original function when Paiutes moved onto the Malheur Reservation in 1873. For the first time hundreds of Northwest Paiutes gathered in a relatively stable, year-round community. Rations issued three or four times per month to each family unit became the main source of nourishment except during summer. Food acquisition, which in the past had driven family units apart from one another, now brought them together from October until May. (From May until October many still gathered roots and seeds and hunted and fished.) Paiutes from many families now occupied the same lands under the same agent; they worked together on agricultural projects; they shared the same agency physician, they took rations together; their children attended school together; and adults received agricultural instruction together. Since these benefit programs were organized and administered by the federal government, there was no need for Paiutes to change their leadership structure. Families therefore remained autonomous, although the reasons for that autonomy were largely gone.[2]

Before 1850 Paiute families controlled their own fate. The quality and quantity of their clothing, weapons, shelters, and food reserves were determined by their own industry, ingenuity, persistence, and luck, and were not affected significantly by the actions of other families. One family's dispute with another tribe rarely ensnared other families because they were typically scattered to places unknown. Each family's relations with other tribes were, therefore, largely in that family's hands.

By 1873, when the Paiutes moved to the Malheur Reservation, these circumstances had shifted markedly. Although families were still independent and free from any central authority, their lives and therefore their destinies had become thoroughly entwined. Many needs of Paiute families were now filled from a single source, the federal government. The concentration of all Malheurs on a single reservation gave the appearance of a single, united entity, magnifying the risk that the misdeeds of an aberrant faction would be attributed to the Malheurs generally and that the central source of benefits for all would be jeopardized by the acts of a few. Malheurs were at the mercy of minor factions, yet without the central authority and organizational structure to control them. The Malheurs were for these reasons ill equipped to manage Oits and his followers in the run-up to the Bannock War in 1878.

Oits had been a periodic cancer on Oregon Paiutes for a quarter of a century, apparently without remorse. Agent Parrish held him in check during his tenure, and Oits's cousin Weyouwewa may have done so as well until his death in 1873. Yet Oits's episodes of good behavior did not signal any change in the dark side of his character. He had plotted to kill both Agent Parrish and Agent Linville. He had refused to work for Parrish, at least at the beginning, and had instead taken his people to trade with the "bad" Columbia River Indians. He claimed to have sickened fellow Paiutes and threatened to sicken them more. Sarah related that one winter when many became ill and died, Oits claimed to be the agent of the illness and demanded payment or they would all die. All paid, yet more deaths ensued.[3] Sarah, her father, and Egan all feared his claimed shaman powers, at least on occasion.[4]

Yet Oits was a more complicated character than these events suggest. After Parrish confronted him, he became friends with Parrish and began farming. He joined Sarah and Egan in meeting with soldiers about Parrish leaving and to complain about Rinehart.[5] There were times when Sarah and Egan, and even Winnemucca, considered him a colleague.

But when Oits stirred up trouble, there was no central authority or procedure for managing him. Unrestrained, unrepentant, probably half-believing that he was not an ordinary mortal, Oits was woven into the fabric of the Malheurs even though he rarely let pass an opportunity for personal gain at the expense of fellow tribesmen.

In the Bannock War, Oits and his band were firmly allied with the Bannocks. Oits led the party that prevented Egan's escape from the Steens Mountain camp; he took charge of the combined Bannock-Paiutes force. Oits was instrumental in the Bannocks' domination of the Paiutes in the lead-up to the Bannock War. "He may truly be said," Howard concluded, "to have been the leading Indian of the hostile Piute and primarily the cause of the troubles of that tribe."[6]

Yet it is hard to fault the Paiutes for failing to manage Oits. The period of 1850–78 was a time of unprecedented challenge and turmoil for the Paiutes. They adapted to white aggression by developing war chiefs and fighting bands. Oits was an important war chief in this new militarism. But after the Snake War snuffed out the Paiute military, these tribesmen were in no position to be restructuring internal tribal relations, for they had been robbed of many of their sources of nutrition, and knew that any attempts to hunt or gather that brought them into conflict with whites could incur the wrath of the dreaded General Crook. They were fragmented and starving until their move to the Malheur Reservation in 1873 brought all families under the authority of the Indian agent.

According to Sarah, after the Bannock War Paddy Caps confronted Oits in a group Paiute meeting, stating, "You were first on your horse when the Bannocks came. You got us all into trouble, and only for you we had been in our own country."[7] Paddy Caps's final condemnation of Oits,

"You are the cause of all our suffering," is overly harsh, for there were other causes at work.[8] For centuries before Europeans arrived, Paiutes learned to extract life's necessities from the arid and unforgiving Great Basin. After whites arrived and occupied the best lands of the Great Basin, Paiutes learned the art of guerilla warfare, which served them well until General Crook's campaign and the Snake War. With hundreds of their people dead at the end of that war, Paiutes took up the shovel and hoe at Malheur and demonstrated that they could learn to cultivate the soil, until congressional cuts and Rinehart's tyranny put an end to farming. They endured the Bannocks' coercion and the soldiers' bullets in the Bannock War, the trail of tears to Yakama, the taunting and derision of the Yakamas, and Wilbur's condescension and intolerance.

At each stage of their reckoning with the whites, Paiutes faced tangible, visible enemies and challenges. Deception, however, was a weapon of a different, insidious character. It was in a language that few Paiutes understood. Its existence was usually unknown to the Paiutes. It was "like the wind, powerful enough to knock you down but invisible."[9] The destructive capability of these deceptions was rooted in the positions of trust held by the deceivers. The government's capability of fulfilling its policies on indigenous people and meeting its obligations to those peoples depended on the honesty of its agents. The degree of trust vested in these officials was magnified by the isolated locations where their service was necessarily performed. The difficulty of overseeing such work and detecting misdeeds heightened the responsibility of the position and, hence, the capacity to do harm.

An Indian agent's charges were the original owners of the continent. Through no choice of their own, they had become surrounded by a social, political, and economic system foreign to them, conducted in a language equally foreign. Providing guidance to Natives in navigating that system is the minimum obligation of any people of common decency displacing aboriginals from their land.[10] It was the duty of Indian agents to provide that guidance. They "were often the only means by which the Indian side of a question was made known to the men in authority."[11] A study of Indian agents observed, "Frequently the agents became the champions of the Indians."[12]

The arrival of warring Bannocks at Malheur in June 1878 entangled the

Malheur Paiutes in controversies that could not be understood without knowing the Paiutes' side of the story. They had no one to assist them in explaining these events to white authorities because their agent, who should have been helping to communicate their circumstances, was instead falsely indicting Egan and thereby all Malheurs. They were defenseless against Rinehart's campaign of disinformation.

Rinehart's deception of army leadership and the commissioner, the manipulated statement he secured from the blacksmith's wife, and his communications to the press—all gained credibility and authority from Rinehart's stature as the government-appointed protector of these Native peoples. His apparent knowledge of the state of affairs at Malheur lent his reports a credibility that was difficult to challenge, for the truth was not obvious. Rinehart's deception saddled Egan and the Paiutes with responsibility for a war which Egan opposed, which most Paiutes sought to escape, and from which an agent of integrity might have saved them.

Effective and enduring as it was, Rinehart's duplicity did not spell the Paiutes' inevitable doom, for the imprisonment of the Paiutes at Yakama in January 1879 for their role in the Bannock War was not the final word. A year later in his January 24 letter Secretary Schurz declared them free to return to the Malheur Reservation.

After Wilbur first learned of Schurz's January 24 letter, he erupted, "I protest against any measures looking to the return of the Piutes to Malheur." Instead, he urged, they should be permanently located at Yakama, and the Malheur Reservation abandoned.[13] As Wilbur continued to lobby to retain the Paiutes, Schurz was in the midst of a fundamental change, which he announced on November 1, 1880, rejecting as "mistaken policy" the practice of removing Indians from their native lands and placing them on distant reservations. It is vastly better, he declared, to "respect their home attachments, to leave them upon the lands they occupied."[14] Since Schurz now favored leaving Indians on their home territory, there must have been something specific to the Paiutes' situation to cause him to keep them separate from theirs.

The specifics came from Wilbur. Schurz and Commissioner Trowbridge in Washington DC were dependent on Wilbur's honesty and integrity for an accurate account of the Paiutes' circumstances. Wilbur betrayed their trust. He told them that "many [Paiutes] have declared their intention to remain [at Yakama] under any circumstances." His successor, Robert H. Milroy, like Wilbur, a Methodist, admired Wilbur's accomplishments, and had nothing to gain by criticizing Wilbur. Yet Milroy's reports to the commissioner revealed what Wilbur had hidden for so long. "It is impossible to overcome [the Paiutes'] determination never to regard this Reservation as their home," Milroy wrote. The Indian Claims Commission agreed. Many years later it found, "From the time of their arrival at Yakima Reservation in February, 1879, the majority of the Snake or Piute Indians were discontented there and insisted on being allowed to return to the Malheur Reservation . . . They were regarded as intruders by the Yakima Indians. . . . The Piutes felt that they were ill-treated and were determined never to regard Yakima as their permanent home."[15] The words of Milroy and of the Indian Claims Commission were confirmed by the actions of the Paiutes themselves, who, according to a flattering biography of Wilbur, made "continued attempts . . . to leave the Yakima Reservation and find their way home. Time and again he [Wilbur] sent police after them."[16] In his last report Wilbur admitted that two hundred Paiutes had escaped, but added, "Nearly all the fugitives were overtaken, and returned to their camps."[17] All the while that Paiutes were repeatedly fleeing Wilbur's reservation, he was, from one side of his mouth, lying to Washington that the Paiutes were content and, from the other, congratulating himself for "the plain, open, unequivocal manifestation of virtue on my own part."[18]

Wilbur told Schurz and Trowbridge that the Yakamas "manifest every interest in the welfare of the Piutes" and "spare no pains to encourage and instruct them," that the Paiute children "are making astonishing progress in their studies," and that the Paiutes showed "marked improvement." Yet Milroy reported to the commissioner that the Yakamas "regard and treat the Piutes as inferiors," there has never been "any social intercourse" between the two, young Yakamas "regard the Piutes as fair game, and miss no opportunity to show their contempt." He continued that the "utmost vigilance is constantly required to prevent the Piute children from being positively abused by the Yakamas" and Paiutes "have made absolutely no progress in civilization, or towards self-support."[19]

Wilbur also claimed that Sarah had deceived her people by asserting that Wilbur was stealing from them and that if they returned to Malheur numerous benefits would be theirs. Yet the Indian Claims Commission and Milroy both found that the Paiutes were vigorously opposed to living at Yakama from the very outset. Sarah had no reason to persuade her people to leave a place from which they were constantly seeking to escape—a place where they "were never contented."[20]

Deceived by Wilbur, Trowbridge and Schurz reversed Schurz's earlier decision to release the Paiutes from Yakama and to allow them to return to Malheur. Without Malheur, Paiutes had no other option than Yakama, which was no option at all. Reservation life included important benefits. To the Paiutes, however, the Yakama Reservation came at an intolerable price, their dignity, for they understood long before Martin Luther King said so that "it is better to suffer in dignity than to accept segregation in humiliation."[21]

Much was revealed when Milroy replaced Wilbur following his retirement. The Paiutes continued their escape attempts after he was gone, but now no one pursued them. Before long all were gone (except for Oits's and Paddy's bands, which feared that they would be arrested and prosecuted at Burns). Wilbur's rants at the Paiutes for "[taking] up the hatchet" and "reeking with the blood of murdered wives and children" apparently mattered only to Wilbur, for once he was gone, no one cared whether the Paiutes stayed at Yakama. Indeed the Bannock prisoners of war had long ago been released to their reservations even though they were primarily responsible for the war. Having no Wilbur personally invested in holding them captive, the Bannocks had been free for three years by the time that the Paiutes made their final escape.[22] It is hard to avoid the conclusion that most of the Paiutes' four years of imprisonment at Yakama, as well as the suffering that followed, was the work of a dishonest religious zealot, deaf to the interests of the people he was duty-bound to protect.

Twelve years earlier Sarah had asked for "a permanent home on [our] own native soil," "allotted to us as our own," the "advantages of learning," and protection against encroaching whites. After listening to Sarah's account of the Bannock War, including her rescue of her father, Secretary Schurz granted Sarah's requests. What Schurz had given, Sarah had predicted, would open the way for Paiutes to become thrifty and law-abiding members of the community.[23] Wilbur, however, eliminated that opportunity, depriving the Paiutes of what they deserved so that he could gain what he did not deserve. "Leave your mark," Wilbur once said, "so that those who come after will know you have passed this way."[24] Wilbur brought spiritual and material benefit to some. Wilbur's mark on the Paiutes, however, left them in a condition that the U.S. Court of Claims described as "abject," "destitute," and "deplorable."[25]

Conclusion

Of the Malheur Paiutes, only a minority of perhaps twenty percent favored the war. Still, Harney Valley residents could not be faulted for believing that their wartime losses were as much the work of Paiutes as of Bannocks since Oits's band did kill and plunder in Harney Valley.[1] From some newspaper accounts it was evident that a cold war of sorts divided the Indians, but the dominant theme of the press was that Paiutes conspired to meet the Bannocks at Steens Mountain, the two tribes launched the war together, and Chief Egan led the hostile force, composed mostly of Paiutes. It was Paiutes, therefore, who bore the brunt of the blame in the minds of white settlers mourning their dead and trying to feed their families as their crops, barns, and houses lay in ashes. If those Indians were hungry, cold, sick, and friendless, perhaps it was not random chance but an intelligent force that delivered to them exactly what they dealt to Harney Valley settlers—or so some may have thought.

Much of the story, however, was hidden from Harney Valley residents and, indeed, from officials in Indian Affairs and the Department of the Interior. Agent Rinehart's false narrative about Egan planning and leading the war was parroted in Northwest newspapers, which continued to portray Egan as war chief throughout the war. The myth of Egan as warmonger laid the foundation for the claims of broad-based Paiute participation in the war, which led to imprisonment of all Paiutes for a war that only a small fraction supported.

Among Native American histories, the narrative of Paiutes in the Oregon Country stands apart in two respects in particular. First, the subhuman condition into which Paiutes were subjugated was (at least as of the 1930s) unparalleled, in the opinion of one whose nationwide experience qualified him to judge. Second, the war that was the Paiutes' undoing was erroneously, and apparently unanimously, blamed on them for over 140 years. The two are not unrelated, for the government officials' falsehoods about the Paiutes' role in the war became the foundation for the false history as well as the cause of the Paiutes' imprisonment, the loss of their reservation, the loss of their opportunity to return to Malheur, and the loss of their land and governmental support.

By traditional measures the Snake War (five hundred Paiute deaths) was far more deadly than the Bannock War (eighty Paiute deaths).[2] The Snake War left ghastly battlefields dense with the bodies of Paiute families. Yet the true human cost of the Bannock War may have been the greater of the two. The Snake War survivors eventually landed on a generous reservation with a committed and supportive agent, a school, teachers, medical resources, and more. Once the Paiutes settled on the Malheur Reservation, there were genuine hopes and opportunities.

The Bannock War, however, shattered those hopes and opportunities. The human toll of the Bannock War was measured not in those felled by enemy bullets, but in young parents overwhelmed by relentless obstacles to giving their children basic nutrition, health, and education; in toddlers and tweens robbed by hunger and disease of the exhilaration of discovering toads, stars, and song; in teens resentful that they had to find their meals in garbage containers, while young whites buying radios, theater tickets, and ice cream spent sums that would feed an Indian family for months; in communities drained of their creativity, spontaneity, and prosperity by the perpetual burden of fighting off malnutrition, trachoma, and tuberculosis. The Bannock War and its aftermath left the Paiutes bereft of reservation, land, benefits, and good will, and, as a consequence, any chance to escape the poverty and disease that continued to afflict the Paiutes into the 1930s and beyond. Every child born into that community during that era became, to one degree or another, a victim of the Bannock War and its 140-year-long myths.

If there is truth to the aphorism "Those who cannot remember the past are condemned to repeat it," the same must be true of a past concealed and therefore never known at all.[3] The Paiutes' poverty and suffering were open and obvious, but the cause, hidden by dishonest officials, was not. The oppression visited on the Paiutes is crime enough, but concealing the Indians agents' offenses tarnished the Paiutes with the illusion that they were the architects of their own misery. With the curtain now pulled back to reveal what government officials hid so long ago, the full, jarring injustice to the Paiutes in the wake of the Bannock War is exposed, too late for any justice to be done for the generations that have come and gone since the war's end.

The unthinkable wrongs suffered by the Paiutes were the result not of a white plot to single out this people but of white indifference to the people they displaced in their greed for land. A new rising tide of that indifference was inspired by the pseudoscientific claims of the Fowlers and Morton that Natives are different from and inferior to whites. The new racial theories became the elixir that allowed those robbing Natives of their only access to life's necessities to disavow truth, to unlink cause from effect, and to accept without question dubious claims of Native guilt.

Is the Paiutes' chronicle unique? Or the tip of an iceberg? How much do we really know about Natives who, like these Paiutes, have been in the public spotlight only intermittently? If the narrative of these Paiutes is typical, what passes for the history of this nation's treatment of such peoples may conceal and distort the past rather than reveal it, nourishing unfounded condemnation of indigenous peoples and equally unfounded adulation of their conquerors.

Epilogue

After the Roe Cloud Report

Paiutes made "a phenomenal comeback" between 1937 and 1947, according to a feature article in the *Sunday Oregonian*.[1] It began when the federal government opened twenty-five larger, insulated houses for the Paiutes on an 800-acre tract that came to be known as "New Camp." By 1940, thanks to a new form of treatment, trachoma was eliminated at New Camp; by 1945 tuberculosis was gone as well. That year S. L. Harryman took charge of the Indian village and its education functions. Harryman was a welcome change from Clinton Talley, the Bureau's teacher at Burns, who pretended not to know Paiutes when he encountered them in public. Harryman proudly led and publicized a multitude of events bringing Paiutes into the Burns community.[2] But in 1947 the Burns subagency of Warm Springs closed and Harryman's position was eliminated.

Yet progress, always late, always slow, always short of the mark, persisted. In 1956 the Indian Claims Commission upheld the Paiutes' claim, begun by Father Heuel, that their land was unlawfully taken, ruling that these Paiutes "were actually deprived of their Indian possessory and occupancy rights or title to these lands in January, 1879, when they were removed from their lands and placed on the Yakima Reservation."[3] Yet it was another thirteen years before the amount of the recovery and the persons entitled to it had been determined; in the end the amount per person was a pittance, $743.20. Of greater importance was the adoption of a tribal constitution and bylaws, allowing the tribe to receive government grants and contracts and on October 13, 1972, federal recognition of the Burns Paiute as an independent tribe.

Charles Erskine Scott Wood

When General Howard returned to West Point in 1881 to serve as super-intendent, Wood accompanied him. While he was there, he finagled an opportunity to study law at Columbia University. In 1884, equipped to launch a new career, Wood finally brought his uneasy relationship with the army to a close. He, Nannie, and their children, Erskine and Nan, moved to Portland, where three more children arrived and Wood practiced maritime and corporate law with considerable success for the next thirty-four years. He was a larger-than-life figure in Portland, championing progressive causes, speaking at gatherings of every sort, promoting the arts, socializing with John Steinbeck, Charlie Chaplin, Langston Hughes, Mark Twain, and Ansel Adams, among others. Writing and painting filled much of his time away from law; he contributed regularly to literary journals. Wood hosted Chief Joseph at his home in 1888 and twice sent his son Erskine to summer with Joseph on the Colville Reservation. When the Oregon State Bar refused to admit a Black attorney, he resigned.

Wood returned again and again to the land of Weyouwewa, Oits, Egan, and Sarah; of Steens Mountain, Alvord Desert, and Malheur and Harney Lakes; of sage hen and rail, alkali and greasewood. In 1910 he met a young poet and suffragist, Sara Bard Field Ehrgott, thirty years his junior, married to a Baptist minister. She saw promise in his poetry inspired by Paiute coun-try. Their five-year collaboration produced a single lengthy poem, *Poet in the Desert*, and an enduring romance. Later he wrote two further distinct ver-sions of the poem. It was the work for which he wished to be remembered. In 1918, after establishing a trust for his family, he moved to California with Sara. The *Oregon Encyclopedia* sums up Wood: "Soldier, lawyer, poet, painter, raconteur, bon vivant, politician, free spirit, and Renaissance man, Wood might also be the most interesting man in Oregon history."[4]

William Rinehart

In 1914, four years before his death, Rinehart gave a talk to the Military Order of the Loyal Legion in Tacoma, Washington. In 1931 his talk was published in the *Washington Historical Quarterly*. Near the end of his talk Rinehart read a quotation that, he said, was an editorial. He did not identify the publication in which it appeared. The following are excerpts from the editorial:

We were glad to welcome our old friend Major Rinehart, this morning. We have wintered and summered with him in the land of Tan-wa-dah, Egan, Oits and We-ow-we-wa. We think we know him. Few men know better the lay of the land along the trail of the receding Red man east of the Cascade Range. There he had taken pot-luck and dried crickets with the Piutes. . . . He has fasted with the Diggers in winter and feasted on Kouse and desiccated grasshoppers with the Cayuses in summer. Alone he has crossed the trackless desert, guided only by his pocket compass and the snow-peaks a hundred miles away. Sleeping with nothing but his courage within and the friendly stars over him. Like the Indian, he can ride without curb or snaffle and can tell the hour of night by the Great Bear in the heavens. . . . He has heard the defiant war-song of the Bannocks, the sad mourning of the Shoshones and the prayers of the Nez Perces; the incantations of the Wiesers, the love-songs of their maidens, the legends of their war-chiefs—all have mingled in his dreams with the scalp-dances and stick-games of their painted warriors. Come again, good brother!

The author of the editorial is not named, but among the hints is "scalp-dances," in the second to last sentence.

Sarah Winnemucca

In 1882 Sarah's autobiography was published. *Life among the Piutes: Their Wrongs and Claims* was the first book written by a Native American woman. With the help of Elizabeth Peabody, a wealthy philanthropist, Sarah gave over three hundred lectures in the Northeast in 1883 and 1884. In September 1884 she opened a school for Paiute children at the Pyramid Lake Reservation in Nevada, but with no government support the school closed five years later. She died on October 16, 1891, in Montana. The cause of her death and the location of her grave are unknown. A statue of Sarah Winnemucca stands in the U.S. Capitol Visitor Center, a gift of the state of Nevada.

Peter Heuel

In 1945, on one of his trips to Washington DC on behalf of the Paiutes, Peter Heuel died, probably alone. The diocese records contain no notation of the date of his death. His name was removed from the official list of priests who have served in the diocese.[5] However, he left something richer and more enduring than an entry on the official list of priests. His protests led to the Roe Cloud investigation and the eventual removal of the teacher, Talley, and the doctor, Smith. He began the lawsuit that determined that the Paiutes had been unlawfully deprived of their land rights. But his true legacy is in the hearts of the Paiute people. Others had supported the Paiutes—William Rector in some degree, Lindsay Applegate, and Samuel Parrish. But Peter Heuel was in a class of his own, having devoted his last two decades to them as he became increasingly isolated from the white community. After his death his church disowned him. He has no grave in the town that was his chosen home. (He was apparently buried in Cincinnati.)

The oral traditions of the Paiutes preserve his part in their history, which is probably close to the words of Father Loeser, Heuel's successor: "He fed them oatmeal, got them to bathe in Lysol. Petitioned the Government for homes for them. Singlehanded he got them homes and schools. He put salve on them, took them to nonreservation school. He begged all over the United States and got at one time $1000 worth. He would go to shoe stores and buy shoes out of style. Same with dresses, etc. . . . Everybody said he was crazy. . . . He's a fighter. . . . Everything they have out there is due to him."[6]

Fred Townsend

On a brisk November day in 2018 Fred Townsend took a visitor from out of town to the Paiute graveyard in Burns, where Townsend's mother, Rena Adams Beers, had been buried that January. Slender and agile, Townsend looked a decade or more younger than his eighty-one years. A photograph of Rena Beers holding Townsend at the toddler stage shows her as a strong woman with a warm smile. The hair of the child in her arms is perfectly parted. His white socks and white shirt are as bright as the light reflecting off his shoes. In videos of Beers in her last years taken by a reporter for the *Oregonian*, she was as trim and well-spoken as her son.

During much of Townsend's youth his parents lived out of town where his father was able to find work. Townsend frequently stayed with his grandmother, Annie Adams. They cleared weeds and cleaned chicken coops in return for dinner. She would also pound deer hides to soften the leather and make gloves to sell. She worked chokecherries into patties, dried them, and used them in puddings for her grandson. In her later years

FIG. 17. Old Camp, Burns, Oregon, about 1928. *From left:* Nellie Adams Jimmie,
Father Peter Heuel, Ethel Jimmie, Rena Adams Beers (Fred Townsend's mother),
Jack Adams, Josephine Jimmie, Annie Adams. Courtesy of University of Oregon
Special Collections.

Adams's daughter, Rena, Townsend's mother, started her own business making and selling cradleboards. She made them in the traditional way, with traditional materials. Townsend helped her. He had little patience with Indians who claimed that there was no way to make money in Burns.

At age four Annie Adams was at the Bannock War Battle of Silver Creek, in which Egan was wounded. After the war she and her parents were imprisoned, first at the Yakama Reservation and then at Camp Boise. Adams gave birth to Rena in 1918. They lived in Old Camp, just outside of Burns. In 1937, the year that Adams acquired one of the houses at New Camp in Burns, Rena gave birth to Fred.

Beers gave a number of interviews, some on video, in her last years. Her early life was very difficult, she said, but avoided giving details. In one video interview a grandson drew out a few of the specifics—that the people in Burns did not like Indians; they saw Indians as dirty, inferior; they would not admit them to the movie theater.

Fred liked to talk about the opportunities he enjoyed and the pleasures of his life—golfing for half a century, regular walking, and weight lifting. Throughout his schooling he "never had a problem." He enjoyed school, he recalled: "Kids were innocent; kids were different." Left unsaid was how the kids changed as they reached adulthood and lost their innocence.

The cemetery was modest. Grave markers were not obvious. However, Rena Beers's grave was festooned with colorful memorabilia. Nearby was the memorial for Egan and Charlie, a thick concrete platform supporting a cairn of flat, rust-colored rocks, cemented in place, about four feet in height. It marked the location where their skulls were buried. There appears little danger that Egan's or Charlie's remains will be disturbed again. There was no explanation of the significance of the memorial. It was for those who already knew.

After the graveyard, Townsend made another stop. He pulled his truck to the curb in front of a small house, painted a dark gray, bordering on black. It appeared to be unoccupied. A bare lightbulb was visible in the covered entryway. On either side of the front door was a single window framed in white. Fragments of boards, gravel, and brush were strewn about the yard. "This was Peter Heuel's house," Townsend said. Heuel had been dead for seventy-three years. Townsend was just eight when Heuel went off to Washington DC for the last time. But to Townsend, the trip to his mother's grave and Egan's memorial would not have been complete without a stop at the house owned many decades ago by the priest who put justice for the Paiutes above the demands of his own parishioners and above his standing in his church and his community; and who, in return for his many sacrifices, was taken into the hearts of the people closest to his own.

"Two Were White"

On a bright fall afternoon in 2018, Carol Smyth Sawyer led a visitor through a wheat field to a small, fenced enclosure. The route to the enclosure was roughly the route that Darius Smyth took 140 years earlier, carrying the tub of the charred bones of his father and brother, which he then buried on this hillside. Within the enclosure were a number of modest headstones and a cube-shaped cinderblock enclosure about four feet in each dimension. (See preamble, xxiii.)

On the cinderblock structure was a metal plaque reading in part:

IN MEMORY OF PIONEERS

GEORGE SMYTH   Died 1878
    and wife

Margaret Dent Smyth   Died 1895
    and their son

JOHN SMYTH   Died 1878

The Smyth family graveyard is an hour from Sawyer's home in Burns. She had not had an opportunity to visit the graveyard in years and was visibly pleased to see it again.

Sawyer's parents bought a building in Burns when she was in grade school and opened a grocery store, Smyth's Market. Her father used to deliver groceries to Paiute customers. She heard other customers questioning her father about selling and delivering to these Indians. Her father, a good businessman, would make light of the comments, but he told her that he would rather sell to the Paiutes than a number of his white customers. The Paiutes paid their bills. There were some Paiute break-ins to the store, but they never took anything but beer. There was a big tree behind the store. When she was six or seven her mother would warn her not to go near the tree. There are Paiutes there, her mother would say,

FIG. 18. Memorial in Smyth family cemetery. Author photo.

and they are all drunk. But she claims that she learned no resentment and held no resentment.

The deaths of her distant relatives 140 years ago have not filtered into her life or her family's in any tangible sense. There is an unmistakable separation between the races in Burns—both social and geographical. How much of that distance is a legacy of the Bannock War, as opposed to the separation of races that would occur in any town, is probably unknowable. The real legacy of the Bannock War is the decades of economic distress into which it thrust the Paiutes, with the inevitable repercussions for health, education, and housing.

After high school Sawyer left eastern Oregon on a scholarship to Willamette University in Salem, Oregon. Even with the scholarship, however, the University of Oregon cost less, so she transferred to Eugene for her last three years. She lived in western Oregon working as a nurse, finding a good man, and raising with him a good share of children. When Smyth's Market became too much for her aging parents, Sawyer and her husband returned to Burns, cared for her parents, and ran the store. She enjoyed living again in the town where she was raised. She started an organization to celebrate diversity in Harney County. She put on performances by Basques, Scots, and Paiutes, among others. For years she has headed the Harney County Special Olympics. She directs three choirs in Burns and was voted Harney County Senior of the Year for 2019. She cared for her parents in their final years and now cares for her husband, who is blind and on oxygen. She has neither the time nor the disposition for resentment or ill will.

"Two Were Paiute"

Nancy Egan held the hand of her ninety-seven-year-old grandfather Hubert Egan as he sat in a wheelchair, neatly dressed in a white shirt, jacket, and a brimmed cap. A blanket with geometric patterns covered his lap and legs against the chill of a drizzly morning in Burns in early May 1999. Nancy had driven her grandfather 325 miles from Owyhee, Nevada, to Burns for the burial ceremony. Hubert's father, Herbert, and his grandfather Honey were both with Egan during the Bannock War when Herbert was a baby and Honey a young man.

Hubert's eyes were closed much of the time, but opened as his grand-daughter leaned close and spoke in Paiute, "Here's cedar in front of you." She removed his cap. He reached out and pulled the purifying smoke toward him to take in the blessings from earlier generations, until the kettle of smoke was passed to the next person. The final moment was approaching of a ceremony that had begun the previous day in two large teepees and that continued in prayer and song the night through.

A federal law enacted in 1990 required that museums in possession of Indian remains offer to return them to descendants (the Native American Graves Protection and Repatriation Act). Descendants of Paiute chief Egan had convened to choose a representative to speak for the family in the process of repatriating the remains of Egan and Charlie. The family elected Nancy. She had fulfilled the requirements of the law, and the National Museum of Natural History had arranged for the museums in possession of the skulls of Egan and Charlie to place them in the custody of her grandfather, Hubert Egan, a great-grandson and the oldest living descendant of Chief Egan.

In response to her application, Nancy had also received a lengthy report that gives the impression that it addresses matters of great moment. Its four-page glossary defines terms such as *button osteoma, antimeres,* and *perimortem.* The report states: "Assessments made in this report are based on information contained in the NMNH's computerized anthropology collections database (INQUIRE), SI accession records, NMNH anthropology ledger books, Physical Anthropology Division catalog cards, transmittal lists and correspondence sent to the Army Medical Museum (AMM), by the original collectors, and other primary historical documentation."

Despite the detailed description of Egan's skull, nothing in the report explains why the skulls were taken in the first place, what was done with them, or what benefits were derived from the exercise. It is an elaborate description of procedures followed, measurements taken, observations recorded, inferences drawn, all for no discernible purpose.

There *was* a reason that Dr. John Fitzgerald and Dr. V. B. Hubbard sawed off Egan's and Charlie's skulls 121 years earlier, but it was not revealed to the Egan family. As explained in the House Report of the Repatriation Act: "In 1868, the Surgeon General issued an order to all army field officers to send him Indian skeletons. This was done so that studies could be performed to determine whether the Indian was inferior to the white man due to the size of the Indian's cranium."[7]

The surgeon general, the Army Medical Museum, and the museums that later took the skull collections invested time and capital on this project, collecting, inventorying, measuring, describing, and displaying about three thousand Indian skulls. All of this labor and expense was inspired by Morton's *Crania Americana* and its degradation of Native Americans in the guise of science. The museums gave up Egan's and Charlie's skulls, as required by the statute, but in their communications to the Egans showed no sign of disavowing the cause for which the skulls were collected. If Egan's and Charlie's skulls had been in the museum for some different purpose, one would expect that purpose to be identified. The impression left is that the Indian skulls retained by the museums represent a continuation of the original program under which they were collected, that is, for the purpose of showing Indian inferiority.

Nancy Egan and her grandfather watched as two cedar boxes containing the skulls of Chief Egan and Charlie were placed into the graves and buried. *They were good men, family men.* (See preamble, xxiii.)

"We are finished," she said. She has the gentle voice of one who does not need to vie for attention. There is a presence about her.

A Smithsonian Museum case officer attended the ceremony. Afterward

FIG. 19. Memorial for Egan and Charlie at Burns Paiute graveyard. Author photo.

she said to a reporter, "This is where he should have always been."[8] It was a sentiment that cried out to be spoken. Yet nothing of the sort was expressed to Nancy. Nothing of the sort appeared in the cold, clinical documents sent to the family.

From her grandfather Nancy had learned that Egan was a spiritual leader as well as a chief, and that spiritual leadership is not learned but comes from the creator. Nancy identifies with Chief Egan's spirituality. A year after the repatriation ceremony she returned to Burns. On her way she sensed that she had to stop for a bottle of water but did not know why. At the cemetery she took a rake from the trunk of her car. The moment she picked up the tool, however, a gentle, warm, comforting breeze washed over her. Now she knew that she was there to say a prayer. She knew to pick up the water bottle and to sprinkle it on the grave as she said a prayer. A large eagle appeared. It circled, four times, then headed west. She felt an immense burden lift from her as, after 121 years, Egan had finally been freed.[9]

NOTES

AUTHOR'S NOTE

1. Hallowell, "The Impact of the American Indian on American Culture," 207.

INTRODUCTION

1. Crook, *His Autobiography*, 142–43.
2. Limerick, *Something in the Soil*, 34; Hopkins, *Life among the Piutes*, 172.
3. Brimlow, *Bannock Indian War*, 214.
4. Sartre, *Literature and Existentialism*, quoted in Bartlett, *Bartlett's Familiar Quotations*, 743.
5. For example, "Indian Rows," *Humboldt Register*, March 19, 1875, 3; "The Princess Sarah," *Silver State*, January 5, 1880, 3; "Sarah Winnemucca Arrested for Sending a Challenge," *Sacramento Daily Record-Union*, February 19, 1880, 3. All three reproduced in Carpenter and Sorisio, *Newspaper Warrior*, 139–40, 217–18, 232.
6. *Daily Alta California*, November 26 and 28 and December 4 and 24, 1879; "The Piute Princess," *Silver State*, November 28, 1879.
7. James Wilbur to Commissioner, May 31, 1880, National Archives M 574, roll 74, special file 268, Bureau of Indian Affairs; Wilbur to Commissioner of Indian Affairs, July 21, 1879, M 574, roll 74, special file 268, Bureau of Indian Affairs, National Archives; Wilbur to Commissioner of Indian Affairs, May 22, 1880, H.R. Exec. Doc. No. 1, 46th Cong., 3rd Sess. (1880).

1. PAIUTE-WHITE ENCOUNTERS

1. Elliott, "Peter Skene Ogden," 231, 245; Ogden and Elliott, "The Peter Skene Ogden Journals," 344–46, 349–51, 353; Steward and Wheeler-Voegelin, *Northern Paiute Indians*, 185 (Ogden "provides the earliest historical source on the 'Snakes' of the John Day River").
2. Information about William Failing is drawn from excerpts of his diary published under the title, "Tale of Terror," *Oregonian*, February 19, 1897, and from letters written to him and found by a descendant in a family barn in Boring, Oregon.

3. Ludlow, *Heart of the Continent*, 494.

4. "Letter from The Dalles," *Oregon Statesman*, March 17, 1862, 1.

5. Ludlow, *Heart of the Continent*, 498.

6. "Tale of Terror," *Oregonian*, February 19, 1897.

7. Ray et al., "Tribal Distribution," 399.

8. Lockley and Barry, "Autobiography of William Henry Rector," 63–64; Hines, *An Illustrated History of the State of Oregon*, 613–14; ARCIA 1861, 155.

9. Wiart and Oppenheimer, "Largest Known Historical Eruption in Africa," 291.

10. Caldbick, "Rains, Heavy Snow, and Unprecedented Cold."

11. Miller, "The Great Willamette River Flood of 1861," 183, 205.

12. Wells, "Notes on the Winter of 1861–1862," 76–81; Shaver, *An Illustrated History of Central Oregon*, 116–17.

13. *Washington Statesman*, February 22, 1862.

14. Shaver, *An Illustrated History of Central Oregon*, 116; Mass, *The Weather of the Pacific Northwest*, 51; Wells, "Notes on the Winter of 1861–1862," 76.

15. Reed, *Report of the Adjutant General of the State of Oregon for the Years 1865–6*, 11. See also Victor, "The First Oregon Cavalry," 130.

16. "Removal of U.S. Troops," *Oregon Statesman*, July 22, 1861, 2.

17. *Oregon Statesman*, July 22, 1861, 2. John Drake, an officer in the volunteer cavalry, wrote: "Impediments were thrown in the way of organizing the regiment whenever it could be done secretly. There were a good many people in Oregon at that day in secret, and some of them in open, sympathy with the rebellion. Many of them were influential people and they made their influence felt." Drake, "The Oregon Cavalry," 393.

18. Woodward, *The Rise and Early History of Political Parties in Oregon*, 10, quoted in O'Donnell, *An Arrow in the Earth*, 76.

19. Drake, "The Oregon Cavalry," 396.

20. Jewell, "Doing Nothing with a Vengeance," 603–16. The firsthand account in Jewell's article punctured the romanticized image of the volunteer popular in some quarters at the time. For instance, Frances Fuller Victor wrote that "the men who composed it [the volunteer service] pledged themselves at the beginning to temperance and pure living. If any violated their pledge it was never reported." Victor, "The First Oregon Cavalry," 134.

21. Edwards, "Oregon Regiments in the Civil War Years: Duty and the Indian Frontier," 32.

22. After leaving Failing, Eddy returned to Watertown, enlisted, fought in the battles of the Wilderness and Spotsylvania, and was promoted to first lieutenant in time for the Battle of the Crater. The North tunneled under the South's position and detonated a mass of explosives, an event for which the North was prepared fully and the South not at all. The North quickly squandered its advantage, however,

by marching its soldiers into the crater left by the explosion, where they became mired in mud and one another, easy targets for rebel sharpshooters smart enough to stay on the rim. Eddy's regiment of 2,800 was the first into the crater. He was one of his regiment's six hundred survivors.

23. Although the Paiute scout and the features of the trail are hypothetical, the features are all genuine to Paiutes of that era. Stewart, "The Northern Paiute Bands," 127; Fowler and Liljeblad, "Northern Paiute," 435–65; Couture, Ricks, and Housley, "Foraging Behavior," 150–58; Wheat, *Survival Arts of the Primitive Paiutes*, 9; Scott, *Karnee*, 20–21.

24. The story of the Otter Bar miners is from "A Tale of Terror," *Oregonian*, February 19, 1897.

25. Temperatures for that winter were recorded in The Dalles by Judge W. C. McLaughlin and later published in Shaver, *An Illustrated History of Central Oregon*, 116–17.

26. The expedition began with twenty-three. Soon after Wood and Eddy turned back a group of nine miners from California happened upon and joined the Woodward-Lewis group, bringing the total to thirty.

27. American Indian Society of Delaware Forum, "Burns-Paiute Tribe," September 24, 2007, http://udaisd.proboards.com/thread/3323/burns-paiute-tribe; interview with Wilson Wewa, Paiute historian at Warm Springs.

28. Fowler and Liljeblad, "Northern Paiute," 454–55; Knack and Stewart, *As Long as the River Shall Run*, 13–14 and note 12.

29. Lamb, "Linguistic Prehistory in the Great Basin," 96, 99; Sutton, "Warfare and Expansion" 77; Madsen, "Dating Paiute-Shoshoni Expansion," 82–85 (dating of Paiute-Shoshone pottery supports the linguistic evidence); Knack and Stewart, *As Long as the River Shall Run*, 364–65.

30. Hunn, *Nch'i-Wana*, 66.

31. "Masiker's Reminiscences," *The Dalles Optimist*, August 5, 1927, Lulu Crandall Collection, The Dalles City Library, v. 75.

2. BEFORE WHITES

1. Wilson, *Seeking Refuge*, 24, 28, 29, 59–60. See also Johnson, "Staging and Wintering Areas of Snow Geese Nesting," 86.

2. Wheat, *Survival Arts of the Primitive Paiutes*, 47–53.

3. Wheat, *Survival Arts of the Primitive Paiutes*, 9.

4. Wheat, *Survival Arts of the Primitive Paiutes*, 11.

5. Couture, Ricks, and Housley, "Foraging Behavior," 155.

6. Couture, Ricks, and Housley, "Foraging Behavior," 153.

7. Knack and Stewart, *As Long as the River Shall Run*, 17. At Surprise Valley in Northern California, "starvation was frequent," especially in late winter. Kelly, "Ethnography of the Surprise Valley Paiute," 75.

8. Steward and Wheeler-Voegelin, *Northern Paiute Indians*, 28.

9. Fowler and Liljeblad, "Northern Paiute," 446.

10. Fowler and Liljeblad, "Northern Paiute," 450; Knack and Stewart, *As Long as the River Shall Run*, 22; Steward and Wheeler-Voegelin, *Northern Paiute Indians*, 27–28.

11. Steward and Wheeler-Voegelin, *Northern Paiute Indians*, 27–28, 39, 42, 46.

12. Fowler and Liljeblad, "Northern Paiute," 436, 443, 447, 450–51.

13. In the fall when rabbits were fat from summer vegetation and had grown thick fur for winter, each man contributed his rabbit net to a collective net that stretched in a wide arc. A rabbit shaman then directed a circle of men closing in around the net opening, driving rabbits into the trap. The men removed the pelts, while the women sun-dried any meat that was not eaten. The pelts were woven into square blankets to be worn over the shoulders and used for covers at night. Depending on the location there were also collective mud hen hunts and cricket hunts. Steward and Wheeler-Voegelin, *Northern Paiute Indians*, 31, 40. In many locations aside from Oregon, where the tree does not grow, pine nuts were harvested by large groups.

14. Ray et al., "Tribal Distribution," 398–99; Ramsey, *Coyote Was Going There*, 227–29.

15. Steward and Wheeler-Voegelin, *Northern Paiute Indians*, 6.

16. Madsen, *The Bannock of Idaho*, 15, 24–26, 143.

17. E. V. Eggleston to E. H. Ludington, February 12, 1872, Office of Indian Affairs, Letters Received, Oregon Superintendency, roll 617, frames 12–14.

18. Steward and Wheeler-Voegelin, *Northern Paiute Indians*, 203–4.

19. Nancy Egan, directly descended from Chief Egan, preferred that the anglicized form be used in this book.

20. Howard, *Famous Indian Chiefs*, 260–63. Presumably Howard learned of Chief Shenkah from Mattie. The Egan family lists Shenkah as an ancestor. The August 14, 1877, and August 1, 1878, annual reports of the Malheur Agency show that Egan was raised in the Weiser Valley. ARCIA 1877, 174; ARCIA 1878, 116. See also Steward and Wheeler-Voegelin, *Northern Paiute Indians*, 299.

3. WHOLLY AND COMPLETELY DIFFERENT

1. An observer in 1843 saw "the bones of [Chief Chenamus's] people . . . scattered upon the rock and hills, and their dwelling places are their graves. The bones of hundreds, perhaps thousands, lay heaped promiscuously together. And every isolated rock that rises out of the Columbia is covered with the canoes of the dead." Johnson and Winter, "Route across the Rocky Mountains," 178–79.

2. French, *The Golden Land*, 15; Steward and Wheeler-Voegelin, *Northern Paiute Indians*, 174.

3. Scott, "Pioneer Stimulus of Gold," 151.

4. Bright, "Blue Mountain Eldorados," 213–14.

5. H.R. Exec. Doc. No. 1, 40th Cong., 2nd Sess. (1867), 71.
6. "The Paiute Princess," *Daily Alta California*, December 24, 1879.
7. *Johnson v. McIntosh*, 21 U.S. 543, 589 (1823).
8. Tanner, "Erminie Wheeler-Voegelin (1903–1988)," 61–62, 64.
9. Steward and Wheeler-Voegelin, *Northern Paiute Indians*, 295. As Paiutes developed a military capability, they did not always use it prudently. According to Superintendent Huntington Paiutes had met with Wasco and Deschutes every summer to socialize, race horses, and gamble, but after the 1855 event two Deschutes families accompanied Paiutes to their territory, where Paiutes robbed and murdered them and sold their children. Years later Weyouwewa is alleged to have killed Chief Poustaminie under a flag of truce. ARCIA 1867, 72, 95–103.
10. Bancroft and Victor, *History of Oregon*, ii, 534.
11. Oregon Commissioners to Commissioner of Indian Affairs, February 8 and April 19, 1851, Office of Indian Affairs, Letters Received, Oregon Superintendency, roll 607, frames 1004–7 and 1011–13.
12. Coan, "The First Stage of the Federal Indian Policy," 82.
13. The six treaties negotiated by the commissioners were for land along the Willamette River south of Portland. The nineteen treaties negotiated by Dart ceded coastal lands extending deeply inland on both sides of the Columbia River; lands near the Clackamas River southeast of Portland; and coastal lands between the Rogue and Coquille Rivers. Coan, "The First Stage of the Federal Indian Policy," 54–62.
14. Prucha, *American Indian Treaties*, 247–48; Coan, "The First Stage of the Federal Indian Policy," 52, 64–65; Hendrickson, *Joe Lane*, 57–58.
15. Annual Report for Oregon Superintendency, October 8, 1853, Office of Indian Affairs, Letters Received, Oregon Superintendency, roll 608, frames 428–29.
16. Teiser, "First Chief Justice of Oregon Territory," 52; Bancroft and Victor, *History of Oregon*, ii, 121.
17. Perry, Chused, and DeLano, "Spousal Letters of Samuel R. Thurston," 46–47.
18. "Notice," *Pioneer and Democrat*, June 29, 1855. The notices were published in many subsequent issues as well.
19. "Treaty and Tribal Reference."
20. H.R. Exec. Doc. No. 1, 40th Cong., 2nd Sess. (1867), 71, 74.
21. For example, the Treaty with the Tribes of Middle Oregon, 1855, 12 Stat, 963.

4. PAIUTE POWER

1. Dictated statement of Robert Thompson, January 15, 1884, Robert Thompson Papers, Bancroft Library, University of California at Berkeley, BANC MSS P-A 117, 10.
2. Macoll, *Money, Merchants and Power*, 87.
3. Thompson to Palmer, March 18, 1856, Oregon Superintendency of Indian Affairs, Letter Books, C:10, National Archives.

4. Thompson to Palmer, March 13, 1856, https://digitalcollections.lib.washington.edu/digital/collection/lctext/id/51/rec/17.

5. Steward and Wheeler-Voegelin, *Northern Paiute Indians*, 23 (see also 4, 9, 305); Kelly, "Ethnography of the Surprise Valley Paiute," 75, 185–86.

6. Steward and Wheeler-Voegelin, *Northern Paiute Indians*, 221, 296–97.

7. Huntington, "J. W. Perit Huntington to Hon. N. S. Taylor," 167–68; Clark and Clark, "William McKay's Journal: Part I," 125–26; Wheeler-Voegelin, "The Northern Paiute of Central Oregon," 260n151.

8. Huntington, "J. W. Perit Huntington to Hon. N. S. Taylor," 167–68; Clark and Clark, "William McKay's Journal: Part I," 125–26; Wheeler-Voegelin, "The Northern Paiute of Central Oregon," 260n151.

9. "The Attack on Warm Springs Agency," *Oregon Statesman*, August 23, 1859; Shane, "Early Explorations," 290–91; Ray et al., "Tribal Distribution," 399.

10. April 12, 2016, interview with Wilson Wewa at Warm Springs.

11. Huntington, "J. W. Perit Huntington to Hon. N. S. Taylor," 167–68.

5. KEEPING UP APPEARANCES

1. Rector, "Autobiographical Sketch," 323–27.

2. Lockley, *History of the Columbia River Valley*, 1078, quoted in O'Donnell, *An Arrow in the Earth*, 71.

3. ARCIA 1861, 155–56. Rector noted that his predecessor had attempted to make contact with the Paiutes, but in a manner that the Paiutes would have seen as hostile.

4. ARCIA 1862, 267.

5. ARCIA 1862, 260.

6. ARCIA 1862, 257–58.

7. Reed, *Report of the Adjutant General of the State of Oregon for the Years 1865–6*, 13.

8. Solomon Richards of the Otter Bar expedition wrote to Buell Woodward's brother that Buell was shot by "Snake Indians." "Arrival of the Julia," *Oregonian*, March 14, 1862. Two days later that paper condemned the "murder of miners on John Day's river by Snake Indians," and called for them to be "speedily punished." *Oregonian*, March 16, 1862.

9. Reed, *Report of the Adjutant General of the State of Oregon for the Years 1865–6*, 13.

6. DARK DAWN

1. Dictated statement of Robert Thompson, January 15, 1884, Robert Thompson Papers, Bancroft Library, University of California at Berkeley, BANC MSS P-A 117, 2.

2. Annual Report of R. R. Thompson, August 14, 1855, Oregon Superintendency of Indian Affairs, Letter Books, C:10.

3. Dictated statement of Robert Thompson, January 15, 1884, Robert Thompson Papers, Bancroft Library, University of California at Berkeley, BANC MSS P-A 117, 36.
4. *An Illustrated History of North Idaho*, 25–26. This book gives three different accounts of the discovery of Florence. The version presented here may have an edge in authenticity. Bancroft presents one of the other two. Bancroft, *Washington, Idaho and Montana*, 244–49.
5. Paul, "After the Gold Rush," 11.
6. *An Illustrated History of North Idaho*, 25–26; Bancroft, *Washington, Idaho and Montana*, 247; Scott, "Pioneer Stimulus of Gold," 155–56.
7. Cornford, "We All Live More like Brutes than Humans," 83.
8. Elliott, "The Dalles-Celilo Portage," 157.
9. Scott, "Pioneer Stimulus of Gold," 166.
10. Wright, *Lewis & Dryden's Marine History of the Pacific Northwest*, 106–7.
11. Johansen, "The Oregon Steam Navigation Company," 181.
12. Scott, "Pioneer Stimulus of Gold," 155.
13. Scott, "Pioneer Stimulus of Gold," 155–56; Bancroft and Victor, *History of Oregon*, 480–82.
14. "A Trip to Celilo," February 20, 1864, 2; "Crowded" and "Another Crowd," March 6, 1864, 2; "The Oneanta" and untitled article on hurdy-gurdy, March 18, 1864, 2; all in *The Daily Mountaineer*.
15. Bancroft and Victor, *History of Oregon*, 493, including note 13; Steward and Wheeler-Voegelin, *Northern Paiute Indians*, 236–37.

7. A MESSENGER TO MY HEART

1. "News from the Crooked River Expedition—A Fight!" *Oregonian*, May 27, 1864.
2. Steward and Wheeler-Voegelin, *Northern Paiute Indians*, 238.
3. This account is based on Knuth and Drake, "Cavalry in the Indian Country," 7–9, 31–37, 39–41; Drake, "The Oregon Cavalry," 396; Kenny, "The Founding of Camp Watson," 6–11.
4. Bancroft and Victor, *History of Oregon*, ii, 500.
5. Historical Note, John Webster Perit Huntington Papers, Archives West, http://archiveswest.orbiscascade.org/ark:/80444/xv94065.
6. ARCIA 1863, 49.
7. ARCIA 1854, 279; California Indian Superintendent Steel to Commissioner of Indian Affairs Dole, March 8, 1864, quoted in *Snake or Piute Indians v. United States*, 112 F Supp. 543, 557 (Fed. Cl. 1953); Granville Owen Haller, undated 1854 dispatch to Captain M. Maloney, University of Washington Special Collections, Accession # 3437-005, Box VF.
8. Madsen, *The Bannock of Idaho*, 100–101, 108.

9. After the 1847 Whitman massacre near Walla Walla, the Cayuse were forced to identify and turn over the perpetrators; those whom the Cayuse produced (probably including some innocents) were then tried and hung. After Coquille Indians killed five explorers near the Oregon coast in 1851, a military command of 130 attacked the camp from opposite directions, killing fifteen Coquilles in a crossfire. The next year Modoc Indians killed about sixty immigrants at Bloody Point on Tule Lake in California, just below the Oregon border. Two months later Ben Wright, a vigilante, walked alone into the Modoc village, pulled out a concealed pistol and began firing, which signaled his men hidden about the camp to open fire. Few Modocs survived. The Shoshone who killed the Ward party in Idaho in 1854 were hunted down the next year and hung. In 1855 settlers wanting Indian lands slaughtered over twenty Rogue River Indians, who responded with a random killing spree. A bloody war ensued, ending with the surviving Rogues forced from their southern Oregon homeland to remote reservations. In 1856 Yakama, Cascade, and other tribes attacked the Cascades community on the Columbia River, killing fourteen settlers. Phillip Sheridan, of Civil War fame, caught a number of Cascade Indians, including nine who had participated in the attack. The nine were tried, convicted, and hung. In each case Indians paid dearly (not necessarily unjustly) for killing noncombatant whites.

   On September 9, 1860, Indians described as "Snakes" attacked the Utter Party of forty-four immigrants in Idaho, not far from the location of the Ward massacre. In a ghastly affair that continued for days, most of the immigrants died. The focus of the military response was rescuing survivors and finding the children, some of whom had been sold to other tribes. As a result of the onset of winter, lack of information to identify and locate the culprits, and the start of the Civil War, no effective effort was made to bring the wrongdoers to justice. Bancroft and Victor, *History of Oregon*, ii, 469–76.

10. In 1857 J. W. Nesmith, superintendent of Indian affairs for the Oregon and Washington Territories, observed that "the Indians within this superintendency have no correct knowledge of the power and extent of the United States" and provided examples of Indians assuming that whites were a tribe just like Nez Perce, Cayuse, and Yakama. ARCIA 1857, 325.

11. Annual Report for Oregon Superintendency, October 8, 1853, Office of Indians Affairs, Letters Received, Oregon Superintendency, roll 608, frames 428–29.

12. Wheeler-Voegelin, "The Northern Paiute of Central Oregon," 245 and note 175.

13. *War of the Rebellion*, v 50, part 2, 1115, 1143–44; William Kelly to John Webster Perit Huntington, November 1, 1864, Oregon Historical Society, Huntington collection; Wheeler-Voegelin, "The Northern Paiute of Central Oregon," 245–46; ARCIA 1865, 103–4; Clark and Clark, "William McKay's Journal, Part I," 127. Huntington's version of this event is that all five Indian men were captured, but

later tried to seize the guns of their captors; four died and one reached Paulina with the news.

14. Wheeler-Voegelin, "The Northern Paiute of Central Oregon," 245–46.
15. ARCIA 1861, 156.
16. Huntington claimed he invited Paulina to meet with Kelly at Fort Klamath. ARCIA 1865, 103.
17. Merriam, "The First Oregon Cavalry," 106.
18. William McKay was the son of Thomas McKay, a Scottish fur trader, and a Chinook from a chief's family, who died when William was an infant. After Thomas's father died his mother married Dr. John McLoughlin, chief factor of the Hudson Bay Company at Fort Vancouver. Young Billy studied medicine in eastern schools and was appointed physician at Warm Springs in 1861. Zenk, "William Cameron McKay."
19. Rinehart, unpublished manuscript 17, Bancroft Library, University of California, Berkeley.
20. "The Snake Indian Treaty—Speeches on Both Sides," *Weekly Oregon Statesman*, September 18, 1865, 1; "The Snake Treaty," *Weekly Oregon Statesman*, September 4, 1865, 2.
21. Merriam, "The First Oregon Cavalry," 106.
22. ARCIA 1865, Appendix, 467.
23. ARCIA 1866, 89. This report casts doubt on claims that the Paiutes were starved out of the Klamath Reservation. Wheeler-Voegelin, "The Northern Paiute of Central Oregon," 246–49; Robinson, *General Crook*, 87.
24. ARCIA 1866, 77–78.
25. Wheeler-Voegelin, "The Northern Paiute of Central Oregon," 250–54.
26. Griffin, "Who Really Killed Chief Paulina?" 16–19; Thompson, *Reminiscences of a Pioneer*, 48–58.
27. "Marauding Indian Recalled," *Oregonian*, May 20, 1928, 78–80.
28. Walker to Edward R. Geary, Superintendent of Indian Affairs, September 9, 1859, Oregon Superintendency of Indians Affairs Records, 1847–73, Letters Received, Letter 166, National Archives Microfilm 2; U.S. Docs., Serial 1324, 71, 74; both quoted in Clark and Clark, "William McKay's Journal, Part I," 122–23.

8. THE SNAKE WAR

1. ARCIA 1867, 95–103 (Statement of Indian Depredations by Superintendent Huntington); ARCIA 1865, 472–74, Appendix No. 1E (List of Depredations by Snake Indians).
2. Governor George L. Woods's September 14, 1868, message to legislative assembly, https://digital.osl.state.or.us/islandora/object/osl%3A16740/datastream/OBJ/view.

3. Bancroft and Victor, *History of Oregon*, ii, 526–27, 530–31.

4. Wilson Wewa, interview with the author, Warm Springs, Oregon, March 2, 2019.

5. *Oregon Argus*, August 8, 1857; "Trail-Making in the Oregon Mountains," *Overland Monthly*, March 1870, 201; Bancroft and Victor, *History of Oregon*, ii, 479n27.

6. W. I. Sanborn, Acting Assistant Adjutant General, to Lieutenant Wm. Barrowe, October 23, 1866, Annual Report of the Oregon Superintendency, http://images .library.wisc.edu/History/EFacs/CommRep/AnnRep67/reference/history.annrep67 .i0007.pdf, 94, accessed May 28, 2019; Carey, *General History of Oregon*, 643; Bancroft and Victor, *History of Oregon*, ii, 531.

7. Woods was not the only advocate of extermination. General Steele issued a written order of extermination (which disappeared without explanation) and noted that "Crooks [*sic*] command takes no prisoners. The scouts dispose of all enemies before the troops get up." Oregon's Indian superintendent Huntington said in his 1866 annual report, "Now, nothing is to be done but fight and exterminate them." In a report a year later he condemned the idea. Report of Steele to Fry, October 15, 1867, National Archives, I.S. Department of the Columbia, cited in Wooster, *The Military and United States Indian Policy*, 127.

8. ARCIA 1867, 70–71.

9. Clark and Clark, "William McKay's Journal, Part II," 328–33.

10. "Gen. Harney's Order," *Weekly Oregon Statesman*, November 23, 1858, 2.

11. Scott, "Indian Diseases as Aids to Pacific Northwest Settlement," 161.

12. *Oregon Statesman*, December 25, 1855, 2–3, and January 1, 1856, 1, 4.

13. Jefferson to François-Jean Chastellux, June 7, 1785, quoted in Prucha, *Great Father*, 137.

14. Jefferson, *Notes on the State of Virginia*, 63.

15. Jefferson to Hawkins, February 18, 1803, quoted in Prucha, *Great Father*, 137–38; Prucha, *Great Father*, 139; Guyatt, "'The Outskirts of Our Happiness,'" 994–95.

16. Not all were affected by the shift. Joel Palmer, Robert Thompson, William Rector, and Lindsay Applegate, for example, did not waver from their respectful treatment of Indians—a treatment that suggests a belief in racial equality.

17. Stern, *Heads and Headlines*, x–xiii.

18. Stern, *Heads and Headlines*, 18–19.

19. Stern, *Heads and Headlines*, 41.

20. Charles White, quoted in Bieder, *Science Encounters the Indian*, 62–63.

21. Fowler and Fowler, *Phrenology Proved*, 30–32.

22. Fowler and Fowler, *Phrenology Proved*, 29–30.

23. Fabian, *Skull Collectors*, 22–26; Bieder, *Science Encounters the Indian*, 55–59, 63–64.

24. Morton, *Crania Americana*, 83, 26.

25. Morton, *Crania Americana*, 5, 7.

26. Morton, *Crania Americana*, 54.

27. Redman, *Bone Rooms*, 25.

28. Morton, *Crania Americana*, 171–73.

29. Prucha, *Great Father*, 185, 189.

30. Horsman, *Race and Manifest Destiny*, 108, 145.

31. Horsman, *Race and Manifest Destiny*, 157.

32. Letter of November 27, 1849, quoted in Gossett, *Race*, 58–59 and note 9.

33. Prucha, *Great Father*, 336–37.

34. Crook, *His Autobiography*, 142–43; "Military Movements," *Boise News*, December 15, 1866, 3; Robinson, *General Crook*, 87–89.

35. Magid, *George Crook*, 21–22.

36. Aleshire, *The Fox and the Whirlwind*, 42.

37. Crook, *His Autobiography*, xxi.

38. Magid, *George Crook*, 102.

39. *Owyhee Avalanche*, December 8, 1866, 3.

40. Meacham, *Wigwam and Warpath*, 214.

41. Wooster, *The Military and United States Indian Policy*, 135.

42. Wooster, *The Military and United States Indian Policy*, 139.

43. Parnell, *Operations against Hostile Indians*, 496.

44. Crook, *His Autobiography*, 144.

45. Wheeler-Voegelin, "The Northern Paiute of Central Oregon," 262n157.

46. Robinson, *General Crook*, 89–90; Magid, *The Gray Fox*, 12.

47. H.R. Exec. Doc. No. 1, 40th Cong., 2nd Sess. (1867), 77.

48. However, according to one account in 1855 Deschutes Indians visiting "Snakes" on the main fork of the John Day River "were treacherously murdered by the Snakes, their horses stolen and their women and children enslaved." Huntington, "Huntington to Taylor," 167. Huntington was, however, a source of mixed reliability. See page 74 herein.

49. Steward and Wheeler-Voegelin, *Northern Paiute Indians*, 52.

50. See endnote 1 to this chapter.

51. Interview with Paiute historian Wilson Wewa.

52. Kelly, "Ethnography of the Surprise Valley Paiute," 167–69; Fowler and Liljeblad, *Northern Paiute*, 450.

53. Bancroft and Victor, *History of Oregon*, ii, 548–49.

54. Howard, *Famous Indian Chiefs*, 260–63. Interview and written communications with Nancy Egan, great-great-great-granddaughter of Chief Egan. General Howard's daughter-in-law adapted this book for young readers. In his late-life writings Howard was often driven more by ambition than accuracy, but was apparently reliable on subjects that had no potential for glorifying or diminishing him personally. See chapter 27. The August 14, 1877, and August 1, 1878,

annual reports of the Malheur Agency show that Egan was raised in the Weiser Valley. See also Steward and Wheeler-Voegelin, *Northern Paiute Indians*, 299.

55. Bancroft and Victor, *History of Oregon*, ii, 550.

56. "Indian Affairs—Military Order," *Oregonian*, July 13, 1868, 3.

57. H.R. Exec. Doc. No. 1, 40th Cong., 3rd Sess. (1868), 71–72; Bancroft and Victor, *History of Oregon*, ii, 549–50; Robinson, *General Crook*, 100–101; "Indian Affairs—Military Order," *Oregonian*, July 13, 1868, 3.

9. A HOME ON THEIR NATIVE SOIL

1. C. S. Hequembourg to Major George Hunt, September 11, 1871, Office of Indian Affairs, Letters Received, Oregon Superintendency, roll 616, frames 1009–13.

2. Huntington, "J. W. Perit Huntington to Hon. N. S. Taylor," 169–72; Steward and Wheeler-Voegelin, *Northern Paiute Indians*, 189.

3. *The Snake or Piute Indians v. United States*, Indian Claims Commission, Docket No. 17, Amended Findings of Fact, December 28, 1956, finding no. 1. The other four chiefs were Ponee, Chowwatnane, Owits, and Tashego.

4. McConnell, "Treaty Rights of the Confederated Tribes of Warm Springs," 195; https://www.findagrave.com/memorial/35362870/mary-wilson, accessed July 5, 2021. Over the next few years Meacham uncovered a series of financial irregularities. At the time he died Huntington was also believed to be in possession of a shipment of gold for the Indian Affairs' payroll, but it was never recovered.

5. *The Snake or Piute Indians v. United States*, Indian Claims Commission, Docket No. 17, Amended Findings of Fact, December 28, 1956, findings nos. 18 and 19. Chief Ochoho and his band moved to Camp Yainax in the fall of 1869 and remained there until the spring of 1873, according to Oliver C. Applegate, son of Lindsay Applegate. Affidavit of Oliver C. Applegate of February 9, 1938, attached to Peter Heuel's Answer to Wilkinson's statement, Additional Statement, on hearing on H.R. 622, Harney County Library.

6. Otis to Assistant Adjutant General, April 15, 1872, Department of Columbia, Office of Indian Affairs, Letters Received, Oregon Superintendency, roll 617, frames 6–10.

7. E. V. Eggleston to E. H. Ludington, February 12, 1872, Office of Indian Affairs, Letters Received, Oregon Superintendency, roll 617, frame 12–13; Parrish to Commissioner, November 25, 1875, Office of Indian Affairs, Letters Received, Oregon Superintendency, roll 622, frames 1065–66. West of Malheur Lake, Harney Lake, in years with sufficient water, was a rich source of tui chub, which Paiutes netted and then preserved by roasting. Malheur National Wildlife Refuge website, https://www.fws.gov/refuge/malheur/about/native_american.html, accessed April 27, 2020.

8. Otis to Adjutant General, Department of the Columbia, June 8, 1871; Otis to Adjutant General, Department of the Columbia, April 15, 1872; E. V. Eggleston to E. H. Ludington, February 12, 1872; Otis to Assistant Adjutant General, April 19, 1872, Office of Indian Affairs, Letters Received, Oregon Superintendency, roll 617, frames 6–24. The Paiutes would have preferred Malheur Lake over the stand of ponderosa pine, but Otis apparently believed that the pine was a critical asset. Couture, Ricks, and Housley, "Foraging Behavior," 151–56.

9. Joel Palmer to George Manypenny, June 23, 1853, reel 11, Oregon Superintendency Records.

10. A TROIKA

1. H.R. Exec. Doc. No. 1, 43d Cong., 1st Sess. (1873).

2. Stern, "Klamath and Modoc," 446–47.

3. Thompson, *Modoc War*; "A Brief History of the Modoc War," National Park Service, Lava Beds National Monument, https://www.nps.gov/labe/planyourvisit/upload/MODOC%20WAR.pdf. The actual names of Boston Charley, Schonchin John, and Black Jim are not known.

4. Linville to Commissioner, January 22, 1874, Office of Indian Affairs, Letters Received, Oregon Superintendency, roll 619, frames 888–90.

5. Otis to Assistant Adjutant General, Department of Columbia, March 15, 1874, Office of Indian Affairs, Letters Received, Oregon Superintendency, roll 620, frames 760–64.

6. Email to author from Wilson Wewa, direct descendant of Weyouwewa, February 4, 2020.

7. Hopkins, *Life among the Paiutes*, 110–11, 129, 163. Sarah described him as "one of the Snake River Piutes, a leading chief."

8. Bancroft interview with Josiah Parrish, June 15, 1878, http://truwe.sohs.org/files/parrish.html; Bancroft and Victor, *History of Oregon*, i, 224.

9. Bancroft interview with Josiah Parrish, June 15, 1878, http://truwe.sohs.org/files/parrish.html.

10. Hopkins, *Life among the Piutes*, 114–15; Otis to Assistant Adjutant General, March 15, 1874, Office of Indian Affairs, Letters Received, Oregon Superintendency, roll 620, frames 760–64.

11. Hopkins, *Life among the Piutes*, 115.

12. Hopkins, *Life among the Piutes*, 106.

13. E. C. Kimble to Commissioner of Indian Affairs, August 18, 1873, Office of Indian Affairs, Letters Received, Oregon Superintendency, roll 618, frames 149–50; 1870 Census, Polk County, Oregon, Buena Vista Post Office; 1880 Census, Polk County, Oregon, Luckimute and Buena Vista Precincts; Pioneer

History, Churches of Christ & Christian Churches in the Pacific Northwest http://ncbible.org/nwh/orhistbc.html, accessed February 9, 2020.

14. Linville to Otis, February 23 and March 7, 1874, Office of Indian Affairs, Letters Received, Oregon Superintendency, roll 620, frames 768–72.

15. July 14, 1874, statement, Office of Indian Affairs, Letters Received, Oregon Superintendency, roll 620, frame 874.

16. Otis to Assistant Adjutant General, March 15, 1874, Department of the Columbia, Office of Indian Affairs, Letters Received, Oregon Superintendency, roll 620, frames 760–65; Parrish to Commissioner of Indian Affairs, August 5, 1874, Office of Indian Affairs, Letters Received, Oregon Superintendency, roll 620, frame 194.

17. Hopkins, *Life among the Piutes*, 127–28.

18. Howard, *Famous Indian Chiefs*, 260–63; ARCIA 1877, 174; ARCIA 1878, 116.

19. Howard, *Famous Indian Chiefs*, 244–45, 253, 258–63; Hopkins, *Life among the Piutes*, 115–16, 144, 146; Steward and Wheeler-Voegelin, *Northern Paiute Indians*, 203. Egan's great-great-great-granddaughter Nancy Egan learned from her grandfather that Chief Egan was Cayuse. Meeting with Ms. Egan, March 2, 2019. In *Indian Chiefs*, 259, General Howard stated that Egan was a Umatilla.

20. Egan's family is taken from a family tree provided by Ms. Nancy Egan.

21. Linville, "Willard Linville's Account of the Malheur Indian Reservation," 3, Harney County, Oregon, Historical Society.

22. Parrish to Commissioner, April 26, 1875, Office of Indian Affairs, Letters Received, Oregon Superintendency, roll 621, frame 590.

23. Hopkins, *Life among the Piutes*, 11–12.

24. Hopkins, *Life among the Piutes*, 8–9, 18–19.

25. Hopkins, *Life among the Piutes*, 5–7, 17–18; Zanjani, *Sarah Winnemucca*, 14–16, 45–48.

26. Hopkins, *Life among the Piutes*, 7, 18.

27. "Indian Agents Denounced," *New York Times*, December 18, 1881, 5.

28. Zanjani, *Sarah Winnemucca*, 17; Hopkins, *Life among the Piutes*, 12.

29. Hopkins, *Life among the Piutes*, 20–21.

30. Hopkins, *Life among the Piutes*, 14–16.

31. Hopkins, *Life among the Piutes*, 21–26.

32. Zanjani, *Sarah Winnemucca*, 45–46 and 311n10 (Zanjani's reason for believing that Elma was the sister with Sarah); Hopkins, *Life among the Piutes*, 58.

33. Hopkins, *Life among the Piutes*, 66–73, 78–80; Zanjani, *Sarah Winnemucca*, 55–67, 77–79.

34. Jackson, *A Century of Dishonor*, Appendix VII; Carpenter and Sorisio, eds., *The Newspaper Warrior*, 93–95; "Sarah Winnemucca," *Harper's Weekly*, May 7, 1870.

35. "Sarah Winnemucca," *Harper's Weekly*, May 7, 1870.

36. Hopkins, *Life among the Piutes*, 107–8.
37. Parrish to Commissioner, April 12, 1875, Office of Indian Affairs, Letters Received, Oregon Superintendency, roll 621, frames 845–50.
38. Parrish to Commissioner, July 3, 1875, Office of Indian Affairs, Letters Received, Oregon Superintendency, roll 621, frames 938–40.
39. Parrish to Howard, April 24, 1876, Office of Indian Affairs, Letters Received, Oregon Superintendency, roll 623, frames 20–26; Hopkins, *Life among the Piutes*, 116–17.
40. Parrish to Commissioner, November 25, 1875, Office of Indian Affairs, Letters Received, Oregon Superintendency, roll 622, frames 1061–72.

11. A NEW AGENT

1. Rinehart, unpublished manuscript 17, Bancroft Library, University of California, Berkeley; Biographical Index Card for William V. Rinehart, Ancestry.com; Hopkins, *Life among the Piutes*, 118.
2. ARCIA 1875, 349.
3. Sarah Winnemucca statement, December 15, 1879, Office of Indian Affairs, Letters Received, Oregon Superintendency, roll 629, frames 319–39; Hopkins, *Life among the Paiutes*, 131–32.
4. ARCIA 1876, 121–22.
5. Reservation land does belong to the government, not to the Indians, unless, as in the case of these Paiutes, the reservation is established on Indian ancestral land that has not been given up by treaty. The Paiutes therefore retained their Indian title to the land on which the Malheur Reservation was located.
6. Hopkins, *Life among the Piutes*, 124, 133–34.
7. Sarah Winnemucca statement, December 15, 1879, Office of Indian Affairs, Letters Received, Oregon Superintendency, roll 629, frames 319–39; Hopkins, *Life among the Piutes*, 128–35.
8. Howard, *Famous Indian Chiefs*, 260, 269; Linville, "Willard Linville's Account of the Malheur Indian Reservation," 2.
9. Hopkins, *Life among the Piutes*, 133.
10. Brimlow, *Harney County*, 81–83.
11. Hopkins, *Life among the Piutes*, 134–35.
12. Rinehart to Howard, December 23, 1876, Office of Indian Affairs, Letters Received, Oregon Superintendency, roll 624, frames 306–7. Rinehart did not dispute that Sarah went to Harney to complain about him. Rinehart to Commissioner, Office of Indian Affairs, Letters Received, Oregon Superintendency, roll 624, frames 301–2.
13. "Pioneer at Baker Recalls Days When Burns Chieftain Was on Warpath—Once Told Egan Where to 'Head In,'" *The Burns News*, July 19, 1929.

14. ARCIA 1877, 175.
15. Hopkins, *Life among the Piutes*, 138–39.
16. Hopkins, *Life among the Piutes*, 137–39, 146–47.

12. THE BANNOCK UPRISING

1. Hailey, *The History of Idaho*, 227–29.
2. Brimlow, *Bannock Indian War*, 61–66; Parsons and Shiach, *An Illustrated History of Umatilla and Morrow Counties*, 211.
3. Madsen, *The Bannock of Idaho*, 176–78.
4. "The Indian Disturbances, a Lack of Government Rations the Cause of the Outbreak," *New York Times*, June 12, 1878, 1.
5. *Idaho Statesman*, June 11, 1878, 3, quoted in Madsen, *The Bannock of Idaho*, 205.
6. Hailey, *The History of Idaho*, 227–29. Variations on this account appear in "The Idaho Indian War!" *Lewiston Daily Teller*, June 7, 1878; *Idaho Semi-Weekly World*, June 4, 1878; Madsen, *The Bannock of Idaho*, 210–11; Brimlow, *Bannock Indian War*, 75–79.
7. Madsen, *The Bannock of Idaho*, 212.
8. Based on photograph and description in Gibson, *Survivors of the Bannock War*, 14, 15.
9. H.R. Exec. Doc. No. 1, 45th Cong., 3rd Sess. (1878), I: 128, 130; Brimlow, *Bannock Indian War*, 75–79.
10. "The Idaho Indian War!" *Lewiston Daily Teller*, June 7, 1878; *Idaho Semi-Weekly World*, June 4, 1878; *Idaho Statesman*, June 8, 1878.
11. Howard, *My Life and Personal Experiences*, 381.
12. Wood, "Bannock Indian Campaign Daily Journal," 1.
13. "Wood Diary," WD Box 29 (4), July 10, 1928, C. E. S. Wood Collection, Huntington Library, San Marino, California, quoted in Venn, "Soldier to Advocate," 38.
14. Hamburger, *Two Rooms*, 1.
15. Venn, "Soldier to Advocate," 36, 38, 39.
16. Russell, *One Hundred and Three Fights and Scrimmages*, 2–7, 10–11, 51–53.
17. "The Bannock War," *Idaho Statesman*, June 8, 1878; "Troops Gone to the Front," *Idaho Statesman*, June 1, 1878; Laufe, *An Army Doctor's Wife*, v.

13. EXODUS

1. Fitzgerald, "Harney County, Its Early Settlement and Development."
2. Sullivan, "Conflict on the Frontier," 175.
3. Fitzgerald, "Harney County, Its Early Settlement and Development"; McArthur, "Early Scenes in Harney County," 125, 127.
4. Annual Report of Malheur Agency, August 1, 1878.

5. Rinehart to Commissioner, June 7, 1878, Office of Indian Affairs, Letters Received, Oregon Superintendency, roll 626, frames 212–16.
6. "'Red' Notes," *Owyhee Avalanche*, July 6, 1878; "The Indian Problem," *Owyhee Avalanche*, July 20, 1878.
7. Lubetkin, *Jay Cooke's Gamble*, 273, 279–82; Lepore, *These Truths*, 335.
8. 1877 and 1878 Annual Reports of Malheur Agency; "Indian Troubles in Idaho," *New York Times*, June 18, 1878, 4.

14. TRUTH MANAGEMENT

1. Rinehart to Commissioner, June 7, 1878, reproduced in Sladen to AAG, June 14, 1878, Office of Indian Affairs, Letters Received, Oregon Superintendency, roll 626, frames 212–16.
2. Steward and Wheeler-Voegelin, *Northern Paiute Indians*, 204; see also 272.
3. Steward and Wheeler-Voegelin, *Northern Paiute Indians*, 193.
4. Zanjani, *Sarah Winnemucca*, 148.
5. Hopkins, *Life among the Piutes*, 138–43. All or nearly all men: "Nevada Takes a Hand in the War," *Morning Oregonian*, June 11, 1878; Madsen, *The Bannock of Idaho*, 212, 216. Rinehart to Commissioner, June 7, 1878, Office of Indian Affairs, Letters Received, Oregon Superintendency, roll 626, frame 212.
6. Hopkins, *Life among the Piutes*, 138–39.
7. ARCIA 1878, 119.
8. "The Bannock War," *Idaho Statesman*, June 8, 1878.
9. Howard to Adjutant General, Division of Pacific, June 2, 1878, in H.R. Exec. Doc. No. 1, 45th Cong., 3rd Sess. (1878), 130.
10. McArthur, *Oregon Geographic Names*, 14.
11. Thompson to AAG, June 9, 1878, in H.R. Exec. Doc. No. 1, 45th Cong., 3rd Sess. (1878), 130.
12. Captain Thompson to Assistant Adjutant General, Division of the Pacific, June 9, 1878, telegram, in H.R. Exec. Doc. No. 1, 45th Cong., 3rd Sess. (1878), 142; Hopkins, *Life among the Paiutes*, 157.
13. Steward and Wheeler-Voegelin, *Northern Paiute Indians*, 168–69, 186, 194–95, 305.
14. Annual Report of Malheur Agency, August 1, 1878.
15. The 1876, 1877, and 1878 annual reports of the Fort Hall Agency show about 660 Bannocks belonging to the agency; Brimlow, *Bannock Indian War*, 160.
16. Donegan, "Historical Sketch," 6. Bannock efforts to recruit Umatilla Indians in advance of the war ran into fierce opposition on at least one occasion. Later, on the morning of the decisive battle of the Umatilla Agency, Umatilla warriors turned out under a white flag, met with Captain Miles, and reassured him that they were friendly. "Notes from Yakima," *Portland Oregonian*, July 16, 1878, 1;

Report of Captain Evan Miles on Bannock War, contained in October 1878 Report of General O. O. Howard on Bannock War, H.R. Exec. Doc. No. 1, 45th Cong., 3rd Sess. (1878), 225; ARCIA 1878, 103. See also "Indians on the War Path," *Silver State*, May 17, 1878 (on Bannock attempt to recruit Paiutes in Idaho).

17. Superintendent Huntington visited the camps of the survivors and counted 1,980. He estimated that twice that number—almost 4,000—died in the war, but provided no explanation or support for the estimate. Huntington, "J. W. Perit Huntington to Hon. N. S. Taylor," 169, 171. Huntington also overstated the number of women and children killed pursuant to Governor Woods's order in the Snake War. Clark and Clark, "William McKay's Journal, Part II," 328–33. There are additional reasons to doubt the reliability of Huntington's numbers. McConnell, "Treaty Rights of the Confederated Tribes of Warm Springs," 195.

18. Faust, *Republic of Suffering*, 8.

19. 1878 Annual Report of Malheur Agency, 119; Rinehart to Commissioner, April 16, 1878, Office of Indian Affairs, Letters Received, Oregon Superintendency, roll 626.

20. *Snake or Piute Indians v. United States*, 112 F. Supp 543, 557 (Ct. Cl. 1953).

21. Rinehart to Commissioner, June 4, 1878, Office of Indian Affairs, Letters Received, Oregon Superintendency, roll 626, frame 189.

22. Rinehart to Commissioner, June 7, 1878, Office of Indian Affairs, Letters Received, Oregon Superintendency, roll 626, frames 212–16.

23. Fourteen months after the war ended, Sarah wrote to Secretary Schurz that she was told the Paiutes left the reservation "because they were starved by Agent Rinehart, who told Jerry Long that no appropriations had been made since he had been there as agent." Sarah Winnemucca to Carl Schurz, December 15, 1879, Office of Indian Affairs, Letters Received, Oregon Superintendency, roll 629, frame 335. Meager rations had clearly eroded the bond between Paiutes and Malheur by the time of the group departure. However, Sarah's sources on the reason for the mass departure would have been Jerry Long and possibly Egan and Bannock Jack. None of the three had been at the reservation when the exodus began. Jerry Long was picking up the mail and Bannock Jack and Egan were at the fish traps. When Jerry reached Rinehart that evening he was stunned to learn that Indians had left the reservation. He had also noted Bannocks at the reservation and told Sarah, "A great many of the Bannocks are here with us now, and I don't know what they are going to do here." Hopkins, *Life among the Piutes*, 141. Sarah may not have known of the small party of Bannocks that in all probability arrived at Malheur on the afternoon of June 4 and on the next day confiscated Paiute arms and threatened the Paiutes.

24. Weatherford, *Bannack-Piute War*, 17.

25. Report of Brigadier-General O. O. Howard to Secretary of War, October 1878, H.R. Exec. Doc. No. 1, 45th Cong., 3rd Sess. (1878), 214.

26. "Indian War News," June 14, 1878, *Idaho Semi-weekly World*.

27. Greene, *The Heart of the Matter*, quoted in Bartlett, *Bartlett's Familiar Quotations*, 738.

28. Rinehart to Commissioner, June 14, 1878, Office of Indian Affairs, Letters Received, Oregon Superintendency, roll 626, frame 187.

29. "The Idaho Indian War!" *Morning Oregonian*, June 17, 1878, 1; "The Idaho Indian War!" *Morning Oregonian*, June 15, 1878, 1.

30. Brimlow, *Harney County*, 105; Rinehart to Commissioner, August 14, 1878, ARCIA 1878, 120; Rinehart to Commissioner, March 23, 1878, National Archives M 574, Roll 74, Special File No. 268, Office of Indian Affairs.

31. J. W. Scott affidavit, June 21, 1879, Office of Indian Affairs, Letters Received, Oregon Superintendency, roll 628, frame 214.

32. "The Indian Uprising," *Canyon City Times*, July 1, 1878, 2, from *Silver State*, July 2, 1878.

33. Rinehart to Commissioner, August 14, 1878, ARCIA 1878, 120.

34. C. S. Hequembourg to George G. Hunt, September 11, 1871, Office of Indian Affairs, Letters Received, Oregon Superintendency, roll 616, frames 1009–13.

35. Report, Sergeant John Grim to Assistant Adjutant General, December 20, 1876, Department of the Columbia, National Archives, M 574, roll 74, special file 268, Office of Indian Affairs.

36. Parsons and Shiach, *An Illustrated History of Umatilla and Morrow Counties*, 213.

37. "The Idaho Indian War!" *Morning Oregonian*, June 17, 1878; "The Indian Revolt!" *Morning Oregonian*, June 20, 1878, 1; "Indian News from Grant County," *Morning Oregonian*, June 22, 1878, 1; "Murderous Miscreants," *Oregonian*, July 20, 1878, 1; "The Hostiles," *Silver State*, June 21, 1878; "Indian News from Grant County," *Morning Oregonian*, June 22, 1878, 1.

38. A written statement by a Mrs. Johnson, wife of the Malheur blacksmith employed by Rinehart, sought to incriminate Egan. Rinehart's account of Oits that day matches the person whom Mrs. Johnson thought was Egan. According to Rinehart, "Oits and seven of his men came early"—similar to Mrs. Johnson's statement that "Egan and all his warriors rode up." In Rinehart's account, Oits "said they were going hunting." According to Mrs. Johnson, Egan "said they were going hunting." Rinehart's account implied that Egan came alone, which does not match up with the person that Mrs. Johnson thought was Egan, because that person arrived "with all his warriors." Mrs. Johnson's statement sought to attest to distant events that she could have known about only from a third party whose identity she kept secret.

A year and a half later, Rinehart sought to discredit Sarah Winnemucca using the same tactic that he had used against Egan. He collected affidavits defaming

Sarah from people over whom he had leverage, including the Malheur blacksmith, Mr. Johnson, who was just as cooperative in his affidavit against Sarah as Mrs. Johnson was in hers against Egan. Rinehart's successes with this tactic against Egan and Sarah were such that he would use it a third time and, probably, a fourth. Brimlow, *Harney County*, 104–5; Rinehart to Commissioner, June 7, 1878, Office of Indian Affairs, Letters Received, Oregon Superintendency, roll 626, frame 214; Rinehart to Commissioner Hayt, January 15, 1880; letter from Citizens to Hon. T. H. Brents, January 14, 1880, and attached affidavits of William Currey, Thomas O'Keefe, W. W. Johnson, National Archives, M 574, special file 268, Office of Indian Affairs; Zanjani, *Sarah Winnemucca*, 207–8 and 332n14.

15. BARREN VALLEY IMBROGLIO

1. "Naches and Winnemucca," *Silver State*, June 1, 1878, 3; Assistant Adjutant General to C. O., Camp McDermitt, June 3, 1878; C. O. Thompson to AAG, June 4, 1878, H.R. Exec. Doc. No. 1, 45th Cong., 3rd Sess. (1878), I: 132.

2. "Papers Received," *Silver State*, November 27, 1876, 3; "What Chief Naches Says," *Silver State*, May 4, 1878; "Naches and Winnemucca," *Silver State*, June 1, 1878, 3; Zanjani, *Sarah Winnemucca*, 145. Rinehart to Commissioner, June 7, 1878, Office of Indian Affairs, Letters Received, Oregon Superintendency, roll 626, frame 212.

3. Knack and Stewart, *As Long as the River Shall Run*, 75; Zanjani, *Sarah Winnemucca*, 87; Steward and Wheeler-Voegelin, *Northern Paiute Indians*, 214, 218; Rinehart to Commissioner of Indian Affairs, April 14, 1877, National Archives, M 574, roll 74, special file 268, Office of Indian Affairs.

4. Rinehart to Commissioner of Indian Affairs, April 14, 1877, National Archives, M 574, roll 74, special file 268, Office of Indian Affairs; Rinehart to Commissioner, April 16, 1878, Office of Indian Affairs, Letters Received, Oregon Superintendency, roll 626, frame 113.

5. McDowell to Adjutant General, October 21, 1878, Office of Indian Affairs, "Case of Sarah Winnemucca."

6. Steward and Wheeler-Voegelin, *Northern Paiute Indians*, 4, 299–300.

7. "The Piute Chiefs," *Silver State*, June 8, 1878.

8. Winnemucca had been to San Francisco. Zanjani, *Sarah Winnemucca*, 76. The account of the Bannocks' shush and Winnemucca's tears is from J. W. Scott affidavit, Office of Indian Affairs, Letters Received, Oregon Superintendency, roll 628, frame 215.

9. Knack and Stewart, *As Long as the River Shall Run*, 27; Steward and Wheeler-Voegelin, *Northern Paiute Indians*, 4, 9, 23, 54, 305.

10. Knack and Stewart, *As Long as the River Shall Run*, 27; "More Depredations and Murders," *Morning Oregonian*, June 26, 1878, 1.

11. Wood, "Private Journal," 21.
12. "Letter from Camp Harney," *Morning Oregonian*, June 28, 1878, 1.
13. "The Indian Uprising," *Canyon City Times*, July 1, 1878, 2 (from *Silver State*, July 2, 1878).

16. RESCUE

1. Hopkins, *Life among the Piutes*, 141.
2. Hopkins, *Life among the Piutes*, 141–47.
3. Bancroft and Victor, *History of Oregon*, ii, 548–49; "Indian News," *Oregonian*, June 24, 1868, 1; Howard, *Famous Indian Chiefs*, 244–45, 253, 258–63; Hopkins, *Life among the Piutes*, 115–16, 144, 146; Steward and Wheeler-Voegelin, *Northern Paiute Indians*, 203; Linville, "Willard Linville's Account of the Malheur Indian Reservation," 3; Linville to Otis, February 23 and March 7, 1874, Office of Indian Affairs, Letters Received, Oregon Superintendency, roll 620, frames 768–72.
4. Hopkins, *Life among the Piutes*, 112–13, 118, 124–26, 133–35.
5. Report, Sergeant John Grim to AAG, December 20, 1876, Department of the Columbia, National Archives, M 574, roll 74, special file 268, Office of Indian Affairs; Hopkins, *Life among the Piutes*, 146; "The Indian Uprising," *Canyon County Times*, July 6, 1878, from *Silver State*, July 2, 1878.
6. Howard, *My Life and Personal Experiences*, 384–87; Brimlow, *Bannock Indian War*, 91–92.
7. Howard, *My Life and Personal Experiences*, 388. Bernard had left the stone house for Sheep's Ranch, which had telegraph service. Sarah soon joined him there and learned of Howard's approval of her mission.
8. Howard, *My Life and Personal Experiences*, 377, 388; Laufe, *Army Doctor's Wife*, 335–36; Hopkins, *Life among the Piutes*, 151, 153–54; Howard to AAG, Division of the Pacific, June 14, 1878, H.R. Exec. Doc. No. 1, 45th Cong., 3rd Sess. (1878).
9. Hopkins, *Life among the Piutes*, 155–59.
10. On June 15, 1878, one day past full, the moon rose at 8:55 p.m. (www.timeanddate.com).
11. Hopkins, *Life among the Piutes*, 159–63; "Indian War Notes," *Owyhee Avalanche*, June 22, 1878.
12. Wood, "Private Journal," 15.
13. Howard, *My Life and Personal Experiences*, 391; "Indian War Notes," *Owyhee Avalanche*, June 22, 1878; Laufe, *An Army Doctor's Wife*, 335–36.
14. Hopkins, *Life among the Piutes*, 164–65.

17. STEENS MOUNTAIN

1. Steward and Wheeler-Voegelin, *Northern Paiute*, 272; Beal and Wells, *History of Idaho*, 470; Parsons, *History of Umatilla County*, 212; Weatherford, *Bannock-Piute*

War, 19; Trenholm and Carley, *The Shoshonis*, 262; Gregg, *Pioneer Days in Malheur County*, 135.

2. Rinehart to Commissioner, July 24, 1877, Office of Indian Affairs, Letters Received, Oregon Superintendency, roll 624, frames 154–60. These names are from the 1877 census. Some may not have been to the 1878 camp on Steens Mountain.

3. Howard Report on Bannock War, H.R. Exec. Doc. No. 1, 45th Cong., 3rd Sess. (1878), 213.

4. "The Idaho Indian War!" *Oregonian*, June 12, 1878, 1; "Indian War News," *Owyhee Avalanche*, June 22, 1878; "The Idaho Indian War!" *Lewiston Daily Teller*, June 7, 1878; "The Idaho Indian War!" *Morning Oregonian*, June 17, 1878, 1; "The Idaho Indian War!" *Morning Oregonian*, June 12, 1878, 1; Howard, *My Life and Personal Experiences*, 388.

5. "A Brave Squaw," *The New York Times*, June 17, 1878, 1; Wood "Private Journal," 17.

6. *The New York Times*, June 17, 1878, 1; McCoy, *Chief Joseph, Yellow Wolf, and the Creation of Nez Perce History*, 108, 216n16.

7. "Indian War News," *Owyhee Avalanche*, June 22, 1878.

8. "The Idaho Indian War!" *Oregonian*, June 19, 1878, 1; "Indian War Notes," *Owyhee Avalanche*, June 22, 1878; "An Indian Massacre Feared," *New York Times*, June 19, 1878, 1.

.9. "The Idaho Indian War!" *Oregonian*, June 19, 1878; McDowell to Sherman, July 12, 1878, H.R. Exec. Doc. No. 1, 45th Cong., 3rd Sess. (1878). A Paiute eyewitness, Charley Wewa, testified in 1931: "I seen where they guarded our chiefs to make them take part in the war. I know that Chief Egan tried his best not to see the Piutes go into war. He went to Chief Oytes to persuade them to stay [out] of war and told all the people to get away from there. I know also that Winnemucca tried to get them away from the Bannocks." Affidavit of Charley Wewa, January 19, 1931, N.A. Record Group 75: Records of the Office of Indian Affairs, Entry 1210A: Central Classified Files, 1907–1939, Warm Springs Agency, File # 8686-1921-735, Part 3 of 5 (Folder 2 of 2), Location: 11E3, 8/24/3, Box 95 (Tabbed).

10. Parrish to Commissioner, April 26, 1875, Office of Indian Affairs, Letters Received, Oregon Superintendency, roll 621, frames 589–90.

11. Linville to Otis, March 7, 1874, Office of Indian Affairs, Letters Received, Oregon Superintendency, roll 620, frames 768–70.

12. Linville to Commissioner, March 1, 1874, Office of Indian Affairs, Letters Received, Oregon Superintendency, roll 619, frames 929–30; Linville to Commissioner, July 13, 1874, Office of Indian Affairs, Letters Received, Oregon Superintendency, roll 620, frames 876–78; Statement to Commissioner, July 14, 1874, Office of Indian Affairs, Letters Received, Oregon Superintendency, roll 620, frame 874.

13. Hopkins, *Life among the Piutes*, 110–11.
14. ARCIA 1877, 116.
15. Steward and Wheeler-Voegelin, *Northern Paiute Indians*, 3–4.
16. Steward and Wheeler-Voegelin, *Northern Paiute Indians*, 4, 299–300.
17. Fitzgerald, "Harney County, Its Early Settlement and Development," 14–15.
18. Rinehart to Commissioner, June 7, 1878, Office of Indian Affairs, Letters Received, Oregon Superintendency, roll 626, frames 212–16; Salden to Adjutant General, Pacific Division, June 14, 1878, quoting Rinehart's June 7 telegram, and June 4, 1878, telegram Thompson to Assistant Adjutant General, Department of California, in H.R. Exec. Doc. No. 1, 45th Cong., 3rd Sess. (1878); "The Indian Uprising," *Canyon County Times*, July 6, 1878, from *Silver State*, July 2, 1878.
19. "Indian War News," *Owyhee Avalanche*, June 22, 1878.

18. SILVER CREEK

1. Howard's account does not give the date of the attack. Weatherford, *Bannock-Piute War*, 24, dates it June 16. The *Owyhee Avalanche* reported that "Old Winnemucca brought in the report on Monday [June 17] that the hostiles had left Stein's Mountain the previous day." *Owyhee Avalanche*, June 22, 1878.
2. Brimlow, *Harney County*, 111–15; *Owyhee Avalanche*, July 5, 1878.
3. "Letter from Camp Harney," *Oregonian*, June 28, 1878, 1.
4. Harney County Library, Oral History No. 300; Fitzgerald, "Harney County, Its Early Settlement and Development"; Brimlow, *Harney County*, 111–12. Later two friendly Indians, Tabby and Squaw Fish Charlie, related to Darius that they heard that his father and brother killed or wounded thirty-five Indians that night.
5. "A Change of Base," *Silver State*, July 8, 1878, 2; "Indian War Notes," *Owyhee Avalanche*, June 22, 1878.
6. Hailey, *History of Idaho*, 235–37.
7. Hailey, *History of Idaho*, 235–37.
8. Meacham, *Wigwam and Warpath*, 210.
9. Hailey, *History of Idaho*, 234–37, 242–43; "Murderous Miscreants," *Oregonian*, July 20, 1878, 1.
10. Captain H. C. Hasbrouck to Assistant Adjutant General, Division of Pacific, July 9, 1878, H.R. Exec. Doc. No. 1, 45th Cong., 3rd Sess. (1878).
11. "What Piutes Say about Egan," *Silver State*, July 13, 1878, 3.
12. "What Piutes Say about Egan," *Silver State*, July 13, 1878, 3. This newspaper report of the incident is likely from a separate source from the account in military reports. Although both clearly refer to the same incident, the telling differs markedly.
13. Hopkins, *Life among the Paiutes*, 170; Brimlow, *Harney County*, 120; Wood, "Private Journal," 22.

19. A GREAT CIRCLE

1. Howard to Assistant Adjutant General, June 19, 1878; Howard to Adjutant General, San Francisco, July 2, 1878; Howard to Assistant Adjutant General, July 9, 1878; all in H.R. Exec. Doc. No. 1, 45th Cong., 3rd Sess. (1878).
2. Hopkins, *Life among the Piutes*, 174–76.
3. Brimlow, *Bannock Indian War*, 214.
4. Laufe, *Army Doctor's Wife*, 341.
5. H.R. Exec. Doc. No. 1, 45th Cong., 3rd Sess. (1878), I: 223.
6. Howard, *My Life and Personal Experiences*, 407; Carpenter, *Sword and Olive Branch*, 267.
7. *Owyhee Avalanche*, July 20, 1878; H.R. Exec. Doc. No. 1, 45th Cong., 3rd Sess. (1878), I: 224; Gilbert, *Historic Sketches*, 482.
8. "The Grand Review," *New York Times*, May 23, 1865, 1; "The Grand Review," *Washington Daily National Intelligencer*, May 25, 1865, 3.
9. Howard, *Autobiography*, i, 207.
10. Carpenter, *Sword and Olive Branch*, 16–17, 86.
11. Carpenter, *Sword and Olive Branch*, 83.
12. Howard, *Autobiography*, ii, 209–10.
13. Carpenter, *Sword and Olive Branch*, 172–76, 205–8, 229–35, 242–43; Cox and Cox, "General O.O. Howard and the 'Misrepresented Bureau,'" 427–36.
14. Howard, *Autobiography*, ii, 461–62; Utley, "The Frontier and the American Military Tradition," 305–6.
15. OOHP: Geo. W. Dyer to Howard, September 5, 1876, Box 13, Folder 48, Series 4.
16. "The Hostile Savages," *New York Times*, September 22, 1876, 5.
17. Joseph, "An Indian's View of Indian Affairs," 421.
18. Howard, "The True Story of the Wallowa Campaign," 61.
19. Joseph, "An Indian's View of Indian Affairs," 423–25.
20. Hines, "Indian Agent's Letter-Book," 9.
21. Venn, "Soldier to Advocate," 34–38.
22. Bingham, *Charles Erskine Scott Wood*, 14. Plume hunting prompted President Theodore Roosevelt to create the Malheur Wildlife Refuge in 1908 to protect waterfowl.
23. Venn, "Soldier to Advocate," 50–51.
24. Carpenter, *Sword and Olive Branch*, 261; Sharfstein, *Thunder in the Mountains*, 1–7, 396–400, 427–28, 434–44.
25. Wood "Private Journal," 29.
26. Wood "Private Journal," 29–31.

20. CRANIA ABSENTIA

1. *Owyhee Avalanche*, August 3, 1878, from *East Oregonian*. Howard's overall campaign in the Bannock War, however, drew praise from Utley, "The Frontier and the American Military Tradition," 329.

2. Weatherford, *Bannock-Piute War*, 49. Military historian Robert M. Utley credited Howard with a well-run campaign, "but Howard almost alone deserves praise for the manipulation of many commands over a large and rugged expanse of territory in such a manner as to box the quarry and leave no alternative but to fight or scatter." Utley, "The Frontier and the American Military Tradition," 329.

3. Evan Miles should not be confused with Nelson Miles, who fought in the Nez Perce War.

4. Weatherford, *Bannock-Piute War*, 60.

5. Weatherford, *Bannock-Piute War*, 66–68; author's interview on March 2, 2019, in Boise, Idaho with Nancy Egan, great-great-great-granddaughter of Chief Egan.

6. Howard, *My Life and Personal Experiences*, 410; Howard, *Indian Chiefs*, 276–77; Brimlow, *Bannock Indian War*, 150–54; Parsons and Shiach, *An Illustrated History of Umatilla and Morrow Counties*, 217–18; Santee, "Egan of the Piutes," 20–22; Utley, "The Frontier and the American Military Tradition," 327; Hailey, *History of Idaho*, 242–43.

7. Hailey, *History of Idaho*, 242.

8. Laufe, *Army Doctor's Wife*, 346.

9. Hailey, *History of Idaho*, 67.

10. "Princess Sallie Winnemucca," *Silver State*, August 1, 1878, 3, col. 2, reproduced in Carpenter and Sorisio, *Newspaper Warrior*, 161–62.

11. Hopkins, *Life among the Piutes*, 182.

12. Memorandum from V. B. Hubbard to Surgeon-General, November 8, 1878, provided to author by Nancy Egan, descendant of Chief Egan.

13. Photo Lot 6A 09721600, National Anthropological Archives, Smithsonian Institution.

14. Juzda, "Skulls, Science, and the Spoils of War," 163.

15. Bieder, "The Representations of Indian Bodies," 174.

16. R. B. Hitz to J. K. Barnes, September 3, 1868, National Archives reel 1, quoted in Fabian, *Skull Collectors*, 183.

17. Kober, *Reminiscences of George Martin Kober*, 268.

18. Fabian, *Skull Collectors*, 186–88, citing George Hachenberg to J. K. Barnes, Fort Randall, D. T., January 18, 1869, NAA reel 2, 481–506.

19. Fabian, *Skull Collectors*, 177, 183–85; Redman, *Bone Rooms*, 26.

20. Bieder, "The Representations of Indian Bodies," 174.

21. In *Great Father* Francis Paul Prucha wrote that Morton's theories were "replaced by the evolutionary theories of Charles Darwin, whose *Origin of Species* was published in 1859." Morton and those of similar belief "turned out to be scientific oddities . . . The dominance of evangelical Protestant views in Indian policy

after the Civil War was, if anything, stronger than it had been before." Prucha, *Great Father*, 338. Juzda makes much the same point. Juzda, "Skulls, Science, and the Spoils of War," 159. While Morton's impact on Indian policy may have been negligible, his theories continued to hold sway at the AMM despite the publication of *Origin of Species*. Indeed it was the end of Civil War hostilities that led the surgeon general to reinvigorate the museum by asking medical officers to collect Native American skulls, motivated by "the Mortonian and other magnificent craniological cabinets." The vigorous postwar pursuit of Morton's theories, discredited though they were, led to the desecration of hundreds of Native American corpses, Egan's among them.

Of incidental interest is that tit-for-tat scalping and skull-taking reached extremes in the Second Seminole War. Strang, "Violence, Ethnicity, and Human Remains."

22. Lamb, "A History of the United States Army Medical Museum, 1862 to 1917," 56A. From his study Dr. Otis concluded that "judging from the capacity of the cranium, the American Indian must be assigned a lower position in the human scale than has been believed heretofore." He provided no further explanation in this document.

23. Redman, *Bone Rooms*, 30.

24. Juzda, "Skulls, Science, and the Spoils of War," 162.

25. Lamb, "A History of the United States Army Medical Museum, 1862 to 1917," 56A.

26. Juzda, "Skulls, Science, and the Spoils of War," 157.

27. Juzda, "Skulls, Science, and the Spoils of War," 158, 165.

28. Redman, *Bone Rooms*, 34. Later Holmes arranged for the skulls to be moved to the Smithsonian.

29. Since 1864 Oregon criminal laws provided, "If any person shall willfully and wrongfully . . . remove or convey away any human body, or the remains thereof, such person . . . shall be punished by imprisonment . . . not less than three months nor more than one year." Hill's Annotated Laws of Oregon 1887, section 1875.

30. S. Exec. Doc. No. 1, 33rd Cong., 2nd Sess. (1854), 462–67, quoted in Clark, "Military History of Oregon, 1849–59," 28–29.

31. H.R. Exec. Doc. No. 1, 40th Cong., 2nd Sess. (1867), 71, 74, quoted in Clark and Clark, "William McKay's Journal, Part I," 12.

21. PLACING THE PAIUTES

1. General McDowell to Army Adjutant General, January 20, 1882, ARSW 1882/1883, 122.

2. "War Notes and Opinions," *Owyhee Avalanche*, July 13, 1878.

3. "'Red' Notes," *Owyhee Avalanche*, August 3, 1878.

4. *Idaho Statesman*, August 15, 1878.

5. "The Punishment of the Indians," *Idaho Statesman*, August 15, 1878.
6. Howard to Assistant Adjutant General, August 10, 1878, H.R. Exec. Doc. No. 1, 45th Cong., 3rd Sess. (1878), I: 185.
7. Edward Longacre, "Irvin McDowell (1818–1885)," *Encyclopedia Virginia*, Virginia Humanities.
8. Assistant Adjutant General, Pacific Division, to Howard, August 10, 1878; and Howard to Assistant Adjutant General, Pacific Division, August 13 and August 15, 1878; both in H.R. Exec. Doc. No. 1, 45th Cong., 3rd Sess. (1878), I: 185–86.
9. Howard to Adjutant General, Pacific Division, August 20, 1878; and Assistant Adjutant General, Division of the Pacific, to Howard, August 21, 1878; and Howard to Adjutant General, Pacific Division, August 23, 1878; all three in H.R. Exec. Doc. No. 1, 45th Cong., 3rd Sess. (1878), I: 187.
10. Howard to General McDowell, August 23, 1878, H.R. Exec. Doc. No. 1, 45th Cong., 3rd Sess. (1878), I: 187.
11. General McDowell to Howard, August 23, 1878, H.R. Exec. Doc. No. 1, 45th Cong., 3rd Sess. (1878), I: 187.
12. Carpenter, *Sword and Olive Branch*, 257.
13. Edward C. Mason, Scrapbooks, 1877–78, cited in Sharfstein, *Thunder in the Mountains*, 341.
14. Wilkins to Adjutant General, Division of Pacific, September 28, 1878, Office of Indian Affairs, Letters Received, Oregon Superintendency, roll 626, frames 1185–86 (Howard's telegram to Wilkins is quoted in Wilkins' telegram to Adjutant General).
15. Assistant Adjutant General, Division of Pacific, to Howard, September 12, 1878, H.R. Exec. Doc. No. 1, 45th Cong., 3rd Sess. (1878), I: 191; Assistant Adjutant General, Division of Pacific, to Wilkins, September 13, 1878, Office of Indian Affairs, Letters Received, Oregon Superintendency, roll 626, frames 1181–82; Brimlow, "Two Cavalrymen's Diaries," 248–52; Zanjani, *Sarah Winnemucca*, 226.
16. McDowell to Adjutant General, Division of Pacific, October 21, 1878, Office of Indian Affairs, Letters Received, Oregon Superintendency, roll 626, frames 1194–99; McDowell to Adjutant General of the Army, January 20, 1882, National Archives, M 574, roll 74, special file 268, Bureau of Indian Affairs.
17. Hopkins, *Life among the Piutes*, 200–201, 206.
18. Wood to Nanny Moale Smith, September 7, 1878, C. E. S. Wood Collection, Watzek Library, Lewis and Clark College, Portland, Oregon; OOHP: Wood to Howard, October 10, 1878, Series 4, Box 14, Folder 37.
19. "Joseph; Details of the Surrender of the Nez-Perces," *Chicago Daily Tribune*, October 19, 1877; Hamburger, *Two Rooms*, 54–55.
20. Howard, "The True Story of the Wallowa Campaign," 53–54. Howard's and Wood's efforts included an elaborate report of the Nez Perce War: Report of

Brigadier General O. O. Howard, H.R. Exec. Doc. No. 1, 45th Cong., 2nd Sess. (1877), 585–641; Sharfstein, *Thunder in the Mountains*, 416–17.

21. OOHP: Wood to Howard, October 19, 1878, Box 14, folder 38, series 4.

22. Wood, "Private Journal," 31.

23. McDowell understood the proposal to mean that the Malheur Reservation would be abolished, allowing Fort Harney to be closed permanently. OOHP: Wood to Howard, October 19, 1878, Box 14, folder 38, series 4.

24. OOHP: Wood to Howard, October 19, 1878, Box 14, folder 38, series 4; Wood, "Private Journal," 17.

25. OOHP: Wood to Howard, October 19, 1878, and circa November 5, 1878, Box 14, folders 38 and 40, series 4. In his later summary of this decision McDowell was explicit that it was not only Fort Harney that would be closed, but that the Malheur Reservation would be broken up as well. McDowell to Adjutant General, Washington DC, October 21, 1878, National Archives Special File 268.

26. Venn, "Soldier to Advocate," 72–73.

27. Ficken, "After the Treaties," 450; ARCIA 1879, 156; ARCIA 1880, 165–66.

28. OOHP: Wood to Howard, November 24, 1878, Box 14, Folder 42, Series 4.

29. Report of Brig. Gen. O. O. Howard to the Secretary of War, September 1879, "Removal of the Bannock and Piute Prisoners from Fort Harney," H.R. Exec. Doc. No. 1, 46th Cong., 2nd Sess. (1879), 149.

30. Chief Joseph, Lincoln Hall Speech, January 14, 1879, https://www.24-7pressrelease .com/attachments/035/press_release_distribution_0359771_70177.pdf.

31. Fort Harney log, January 2, 1879, Harney County Library, Burns, Oregon.

32. ARCIA 1879, 129.

33. Hopkins, *Life among the Piutes*, 206–7.

34. The names are from the January 1877 census of the Malheur Reservation, except for one, Becky, who was close to the end of her pregnancy. Becky represents a real person whose name is unknown. Hopkins, *Life among the Piutes*, 208–9.

35. Rinehart to Commissioner, February 6, 1879, National Archives M 574, roll 74, special file 268, Bureau of Indian Affairs; McDowell to Adjutant General, January 26, 1879, Office of Indian Affairs, Letters Received, Oregon Superintendency, roll 628, frames 1000–1001.

36. Hopkins, *Life among the Piutes*, 205–6.

37. Fort Harney log, January 6–14, 1879, Harney County Library.

38. Gibson, *Survivors of the Bannock War*, 39; Hopkins, *Life among the Piutes*, 208; Fort Harney log, January 14, 1879, Harney County Library.

39. Hopkins, *Life among the Piutes*, 208–9.

22. A BIG TALK

1. Wilbur to Hayt, January 30, 1879, Office of Indian Affairs, Letters Received, Oregon Superintendency, roll 919, frames 158–60.

2. Wilbur to Hayt, February 3, 1879, Office of Indian Affairs, Letters Received, Oregon Superintendency, roll 919, frames 128–29.

3. Wilbur to Hayt, March 24, 1879, Office of Indian Affairs, Letters Received, Oregon Superintendency, roll 919, frames 358–59.

4. Hopkins, *Life among the Piutes*, 209–10.

5. Wilbur to Hayt, February 6, 1879, Office of Indian Affairs, Letters Received, Oregon Superintendency, roll 919, frames 222–23.

6. Whitner, "Grant's Indian Peace Policy," 137; Keller, *American Protestantism*, 56, 159–60, 178. Keller's balanced study of Wilbur is based entirely on his treatment of the Yakamas. Paiutes are not mentioned.

7. Coe, "An Indian Agent's Experience," 66–67.

8. *Portland Oregonian*, quoted in Helland, *There Were Giants*, 184.

9. Helland, *There Were Giants*, 179.

10. Seymour, *Indian Agents*, 47.

11. ARCIA 1871, 283.

12. Wilbur to Hayt, July 9, 1879, Office of Indian Affairs, Letters Received, Oregon Superintendency, roll 919, frames 573–74. Sarah continued to describe herself as a Methodist after her relationship with Wilbur ended. "The Piute Princess," *Daily Alta California*, December 24, 1879.

13. Wilbur to Hayt, July 9, 1879, Office of Indian Affairs, Letters Received, Oregon Superintendency, roll 919, frames 573–74.

14. Hopkins, *Life among the Piutes*, 211.

15. Hopkins, *Life among the Piutes*, 209–14; Major Sanford to AAG, Division of the Pacific, August 9, 1881, in 1880 Annual Report of Secretary of War, Report of General Irvin McDowell (containing Lee Winnemucca's claim that the Yakamas took all their horses.)

16. Hopkins, *Life among the Piutes*, 208, 212.

17. Turner to Rinehart, November 21, 1877, National Archives, M 574, roll 74, special file 268, Bureau of Indian Affairs.

18. Rinehart to Commissioner of Indian Affairs, December 17, 1877, and March 23, 1878, National Archives M 574, roll 74, special file 268, Bureau of Indian Affairs.

19. Captain E. F. Thompson to AAG, February 11, 1878, Division of the Pacific; General McDowell to Adjutant General, U.S. Army, March 25, 1878; and Captain E. F. Thompson to AAG, Division of Pacific, May 16, 1878; all in Office of Indian

Affairs, Letters Received, Oregon Superintendency, roll 626, frames 900–903, 960–63, and 969.

20. Rinehart to Commissioner, describing commissioner's telegram, April 22, 1879, Office of Indian Affairs, Letters Received, Oregon Superintendency, roll 628, frames 130–33.

21. Rinehart to Commissioner, April 30, 1879, Office of Indian Affairs, Letters Received, Oregon Superintendency, roll 628, frames 136–39.

22. Rinehart to Commissioner, May 12, 1879, National Archives M 574, roll 74, special file 268, Bureau of Indian Affairs.

23. Petition to commanding general of Pacific Division, September 4, 1879, Office of Indian Affairs, Letters Received, Oregon Superintendency, roll 628, frames 1133–35.

24. Corliss to Pacific Division, October 15, 1879, Office of Indian Affairs, Letters Received, Oregon Superintendency, roll 628, frames 1136–40.

25. The letter is described in ARCIA 1880, 140, first paragraph.

26. Fitzgerald, "Harney County, Its Early Settlement and Development."

27. Rinehart to Commissioner, May 18, 1878; Rinehart to Scott, May 18, 1878; Rinehart to Commissioner, May 20, 1878, Office of Indian Affairs, Letters Received, Oregon Superintendency, roll 626, frames 163–65, 168, 170–73.

28. Carlson, "Nevada Place Names," 374–76. The town may have been named after a nearby mountain, spring, or mining district, all of which took the Winnemucca name before the town did.

29. "An Indian Pow-wow," *Silver State*, November 6, 1879, 3; Scott report to Rinehart, November 6, 1879, Office of Indian Affairs, Letters Received, Oregon Superintendency, roll 628, frames 810–14.

30. "An Indian Pow-wow," *Silver State*, November 6, 1879, 3.

31. The *Morning Oregonian* had erroneously blamed Egan for lifting Scott by the hair. "More Depredations and Murders," *Morning Oregonian*, June 26, 1878, 1.

32. "An Indian Pow-wow," *Silver State*, November 6, 1879, 3; Hopkins, *Life among the Piutes*, 220. Natchez later explained: "My horse fell down and died. I cried out to Jack Scott, and he let me jump up behind him, but he left me and rode on." Hopkins, *Life among the Piutes*, 220.

23. DOING RIGHT BY THE PAIUTES

1. *New York Times*, June 17, 1878.

2. Carpenter and Sorisio, *Newspaper Warrior*, 61.

3. "The Princess Sarah," *Morning Call*, February 22, 1885, 1, reproduced in Carpenter and Sorisio, *Newspaper Warrior*, 429.

4. "The Piute Princess," *Silver State*, November 28, 1879.

5. "Princess Sarah," *Daily Alta California*, November 26, 1879.

6. *Daily Alta California*, November 26 and 28 and December 4 and 24, 1879; "The Piute Princess," *Silver State*, November 28, 1879. The final speech on December 24 was on a bitterly cold night and probably for that reason was lightly attended.

7. Petition of Winnemucca and others, December 3, 1879, Office of Indian Affairs, Letters Received, Oregon Superintendency, roll 629, frames 342–44; Sarah Winnemucca statement, December 15, 1879, Office of Indian Affairs, Letters Received, Oregon Superintendency, roll 629, frames 319–41; "What the Piutes Want," *New York Times*, December 16, 1879, 1.

8. "Piutes Gone to Washington," *Silver State*, January 14, 1880; "The Piutes in Washington," *Silver State*, January 31, 1880; Hopkins, *Life among the Piutes*, 217–19.

9. Hopkins, *Life among the Piutes*, 219.

10. Trefousse, *Carl Schurz: A Biography*, 14–36.

11. Trefousse, "Carl Schurz and the Indians," 109–13.

12. "Hayt's Alleged Frauds," *New York Times*, January 15, 1880, 2; Meyer, "Ezra A. Hayt," 156, 160–61.

13. "Hayt's Alleged Frauds," *New York Times*, January 15, 1880, 2.

14. Hopkins, *Life among the Piutes*, chapter 8.

15. This letter is reproduced in Hopkins, *Life among the Piutes*, 263–64.

16. "Reform in the Indian Bureau," *New York Times*, January 30, 1880, 4; Meyer, "Ezra A. Hayt," 160–61.

17. Priest, *Uncle Sam's Stepchildren*, 70–71.

24. BACKLASH

1. This letter is reproduced in Hopkins, *Life among the Piutes*, 263.

2. *New York Times*, January 25, 1880, 2.

3. Hopkins, *Life among the Piutes*, 234.

4. Hopkins, *Life among the Piutes*, 234–37.

5. Hopkins, *Life among the Piutes*, 238.

6. Wilbur to Commissioner of Indian Affairs, July 21, 1879, M 574, roll 74, special file 268, Bureau of Indian Affairs, National Archives; Wilbur to Commissioner of Indian Affairs, May 22, 1880, H.R. Exec. Doc. No. 1, 46th Cong., 3rd Sess. (1880).

7. Wilbur to Commissioner of Indian Affairs, May 31, 1880, M 574, roll 74, special file 268, Bureau of Indian Affairs, National Archives.

8. Oliphant, *On the Cattle Ranges of the Oregon Country*, 292, 296.

9. Oliphant, *On the Cattle Ranges of the Oregon Country*, 296, 301n29.

10. ARSW 1882, Sanford to AAG, Division of Pacific, August 9, 1881, 135–37.

11. Bernard to AAG, Department of the Pacific, 1882/1883 ARSW, 137, emphasis added.

12. Wilbur to Price, October 17, 1881, arsw 1882/1883, 131.

13. Wilbur to Price, October 27, 1881, arsw 1882/1883, 125–26.

14. Wilbur to Price, November 1, 1881, arsw 1882/1883, 123–24.

15. Miles to aag, Department of Columbia, November 15, 1881, arsw 1882/1883, 127.

16. James H. Wilbur to Commissioner of Indian Affairs, June 29, 1880, Office of Indian Affairs, Letters Received, Oregon Superintendency, roll 920, frames 1067–70.

17. arcia 1884, 175.

18. Hopkins, *Life among the Piutes*, 188–89, 237. Paddy Caps was a subchief who led his followers to the Duck Valley Reservation on the Idaho-Nevada border from Yakama. Clemmer, "Differential Leadership Patterns," 44.

19. Whitner, "The Methodist Episcopal Church and Grant's Peace Policy," 281, quoted in Prucha, *Great Father*, 523n48.

20. Tucker, "James H. Wilbur (1811–1887)."

21. Coe, "An Indian Agent's Experience," 67.

22. Before the end of the Bannock War Howard wrote on August 10, 1878, that he had six hundred prisoners; that the leaders should be turned over to civil authorities; and that the rest should be sent away to where they could never return (Howard to Adjutant General, Division of the Pacific, August 10, 1878, H.R. Exec. Doc. No. 1, 45th Cong., 3rd Sess. [1878], I: 185). Bannock War leaders who were turned over to civil authorities in Umatilla County, Oregon, were tried and hanged (Report of Brig. Gen. O. O. Howard, H.R. Exec. Doc. No.1, 46th Cong., 2nd Sess. [1879], 150). Whether these convictions were justified is uncertain, but in general Indians rarely received fair treatment in civil courts. In his October 1878 report to the secretary of war Howard repeated this recommendation (Report of General Howard to Secretary of War, October 1878, 235, H.R. Exec. Doc. No. 1, 45th Cong., 3rd Sess. [1878]). In January 1879 he told a reporter that "the Malheur Reservation must and shall be broken up" (*The Snake or Piute Indians v. United States, Indian Claims Commission*, No. 17, Amended Findings of Fact, December 28, 1956, Finding No. 31), prompting cattlemen and ranchers to rush to stake out claims of reservation land (arcia 1879, 130). He recommended to the interior secretary that Paiute leaders be sent to Alcatraz Island Military Prison (Secretary of Interior Schurz to Secretary of War, July 23, 1879, reproduced in Gibson, *Survivors of the Bannock War*, 50. Howard's recommendation was not adopted). He protested to the secretary of war that returning the Paiutes to Malheur would lead to the war being "fought over again" (September 1879 Report of General Howard to Secretary of War, 160). He wrote to the army adjutant general that returning Leggins to Malheur would have "inevitably resulted in war" (Howard to Adjutant General, December

16, 1882, National Archives M 574, roll 74, special file 268, Bureau of Indian Affairs).

23. Leggins's band "took no part in the Bannock outbreak" and "were not hostile," according to Major General Irving McDowell. McDowell to Adjutant General of the Army, January 20, 1882, M 574, roll 74, special file 268, Bureau of Indian Affairs, National Archives.

24. John Muldrick and others to T. H. Brents, January 14, 1880, and Rinehart to Hayt, January 15, 1880, National Archives M 574, roll 74, special file 268, Bureau of Indian Affairs.

25. Zanjani, *Sarah Winnemucca*, 207. William and Edwin Hall signed Rinehart's letter. Rinehart's 1880 annual report includes the "Hall Bros." among those penalized for grazing cattle on the reservation. ARCIA 1880, 141.

26. Rinehart to Howard, December 23, 1876, Office of Indian Affairs, Letters Received, Oregon Superintendency, roll 624, frames 305–8; nine citizens to Representative T. H. Brents, January 14, 1880, National Archives M 574, roll 74, special file 268, Bureau of Indian Affairs. A military officer who knew Sarah scorned Rinehart's "false affidavits" by "paid tools." Kober, *Reminiscences of George Martin Kober*, 262.

27. Goldman, "Rowland E. Trowbridge (1880–1881)," 167–71.

28. Deacon, "On the Road with Rutherford B. Hayes," 184–85.

25. UNTETHERED FROM TRUTH

1. As Sarah wrote, "we did not come on of ourselves, we were sent for." Hopkins, *Life among the Piutes*, 221; "The Wrongs of the Red Men," *Silver State*, December 30, 1879, 3.

2. Sarah wrote, "Neither my father or brother made any agreement to go to Malheur until those who belonged there could come back from Yakima, and till Reinhard [*sic*] should be sent away." Hopkins, *Life among the Piutes*, 221. Long before January 24 Ochoho had told Indian Affairs, "I will never return there [the Malheur Reservation]." William M. Turner to Rinehart, November 21, 1877, National Archives M 574, roll 74, special file 268, Bureau of Indian Affairs. McDowell cited detailed evidence of Ochoho's unshakeable opposition to moving to Malheur (General McDowell to Adjutant General, March 25, 1878, U.S. Army, Office of Indian Affairs, Letters Received, Oregon Superintendency, roll 626, frames 900–903). In his August 15, 1879, report to the commissioner, Rinehart stated that "on account of the removal of Leggins in company with the hostiles to Yakama, [Winnemucca and his people] now refuse to return to this agency."

3. Rinehart to Hayt, June 18, 1879, Office of Indian Affairs, Letters Received, Oregon Superintendency, roll 628, frames 175–76.

4. *The Snake or Piute Indians of the Former Malheur Reservation in Oregon v. United States*, Indian Claims Commission Docket No. 17, Amended Findings of Fact, December 28, 1956, finding no. 2.

5. *Snake or Piute Indians v. United States*, 112 F. Supp. 543, 560 (Ct. Cl. 1953). See also *The Snake or Piute Indians of the Former Malheur Reservation in Oregon v. United States*, Indian Claims Commission Docket No. 17, Amended Findings of Fact, December 28, 1956, finding no. 32; ARCIA 1879, 131.

6. McDowell to Adjutant General, Washington DC, January 26, 1879, Office of Indian Affairs, Letters Received, Oregon Superintendency, roll 628, frames 1000–1001. See also Brooks to Sarah Winnemucca, March 29, 1880, reproduced in Hopkins, *Life among the Piutes*, 263. Soon after Schurz's January 24, 1880, letter, Indian Affairs urged Sarah that the Paiutes at Yakama should come to Malheur promptly because the supplies were waiting for them. Then Indian Affairs forbade the Paiutes to come to Malheur for their supplies and blamed the Winnemuccas for wasting the supplies that Indian Affairs would not allow the Paiutes to access.

7. An Act to Establish the Territorial Government of Oregon, ch. 177, 9 Stat. 323–31 (1848). The act provided that "nothing in this Act shall be construed to impair the rights of person or property now pertaining to the Indians in said Territory, so long as such rights shall remain unextinguished by treaty between the United States and such Indians."

8. The first of the six is Act of July 22, 1790, Pub. L. No. 1–33, § 4, 1 Stat. 137, 138.

9. *The Snake or Piute Indians of the Former Malheur Reservation in Oregon v. United States*, Indian Claims Commission Docket No. 17, December 28, 1856, Amended Findings of Fact no. 40.

10. Oregon House Joint Memorial No. 6, October 7, 1880.

11. ARCIA 1881, 66.

26. GOLD AND CATTLE

1. Oliphant, "Cattle Herds and Ranches of the Oregon Country," 219–20, citing U.S. General Land Office, Report of the Commissioner, 1872, 176, on white sage.

2. Oliphant, "Cattle Herds and Ranches of the Oregon Country," 220; see also Simpson, *Community of Cattlemen*, 4–5.

3. Oliphant, "Cattle Herds and Ranches of the Oregon Country," 227.

4. Oliphant, *On the Cattle Ranges of the Oregon Country*, 296, 301n29.

5. Igler, *Industrial Cowboys*, 13–18, 147–51, 226n13.

6. Simpson, *Community of Cattlemen*, 33.

7. Oliphant, *On the Cattle Ranges of the Oregon Country*, 300.

8. ARCIA 1882, 72. The following year Commissioner Price complained about the persistent refusal of Congress to appropriate funds to survey the boundaries of Indian reservations. He wrote: "The wonder is that the conflicts between Indians and settlers are not more frequent than they are, when it is considered that in very many instances it is impossible to determine which party is right. . . . The settlers, miners, or herders, as the case may be, approaching from all directions, and gradually circumscribing the Indians to the vicinity of their agencies, are finally confronted by the Indians or their agent with the warning that they are encroaching on the reservation. This, in all likelihood, is disputed, and in the absence of proper marks indicating the boundaries of the reservation the dispute continues, engendering the bitterest feeling which too often ends in unfortunate strife." ARCIA 1883, 17.

9. *Snake or Piute Indians v. United States*, December 28, 1856, Amended Finding of Fact by Indian Claims Commission, findings 36 and 37.

27. ACCORDING TO HOWARD

1. "'Red' Notes," *Owyhee Avalanche*, August 3, 1878, quoting *East Oregonian*.
2. Rinehart to Commissioner, September 18, 1878, Office of Indian Affairs, Letters Received, Oregon Superintendency, roll 626, frames 414–17.
3. Howard, *My Life and Personal Experiences*, 398.
4. Howard, *Indian Chiefs*, 276.
5. Brimlow, *Bannock Indian War*, 210 and 49, quoting Howard, *Indian Chiefs*, 277.
6. Santee, "Egan of the Piutes," 19.
7. Beal and Wells, *History of Idaho*, 470.
8. Utley, "The Frontier and the American Military Tradition," 324–25.
9. Steward and Wheeler-Voegelin, *Northern Paiute Indians*, 193, 272.
10. Zanjani, *Sarah Winnemucca*, 165.
11. Madsen, *The Bannock of Idaho*, 218.
12. Hamburger, *Two Rooms*, 65.
13. Parsons and Shiach, *An Illustrated History of Umatilla and Morrow Counties*, 213.
14. Trenholm and Carley, *The Shoshonis*, 263.
15. According to Hailey the "three main fighting chiefs [of the hostiles were] Buffalo Horn, Bear Skin and Egan." Hailey, *History of Idaho*, 243.
16. Howard to Assistant Adjutant General, December 20, 1878, Division of the Pacific, reproduced in Gibson, *Survivors of the Bannock War*, 47.
17. Hopkins, *Life among the Piutes*, 170.
18. Hopkins, *Life among the Piutes*, 158.
19. Steward and Wheeler-Voegelin, *Northern Paiute Indians*, 195.
20. Rinehart to Commissioner of Indian Affairs, April 16, 1878, Office of Indian Affairs, Letters Received, Oregon Superintendency, roll 626, frame 116.

21. Howard probably wrote *Indian Chiefs* and *My Life and Personal Experiences* contemporaneously. Although *Indian Chiefs* was published in 1908 and *My Life and Personal Experiences* in 1907, the copyright for *Indian Chiefs* is 1907 and 1908. Howard's daughter-in-law's adaptation of *Indian Chiefs* for young readers may explain the second copyright.

22. Howard, *My Life and Personal Experiences*, 419.

23. Howard, *Indian Chiefs*, 272–73.

24. Annual report of Malheur Reservation, August 15, 1879.

25. James H. Wilbur to Commissioner, March 24, 1879, Office of Indian Affairs, Letters Received, Oregon Superintendency, roll 919, frames 358–59.

26. Howard to Adjutant General, Washington DC, January 26, 1879, Office of Indian Affairs, Letters Received, Oregon Superintendency, roll 628, frames 1000–1001.

27. Wilbur to Howard, November 24, 1879, reel 627.

28. Howard, *My Life and Personal Experiences*, 419.

29. H.R. Exec. Doc. No. 1, 45th Cong., 3rd Sess. (1878), 217.

30. ARCIA 1879, 128–29.

31. *The Snake or Piute Indians of the Former Malheur Reservation in Oregon v. United States*, Indian Claims Commission Docket No. 17, December 28, 1856, Amended Findings of Fact, Finding no. 41.

32. Howard, *My Life and Personal Experiences*, 420.

33. C. H. Hall, "The Anglo-American Race," *Weekly Oregon Statesman*, February 13, 1875, 1.

34. Howard's claim that Egan led the Bannock-Paiute forces also contradicts Sarah-Winnemucca, who said that Egan "persistently refused to join the hostiles; that he was kept a close prisoner by them and compelled to remain with them against his will." "Sarah Winnemucca," *Idaho Statesman*, August 31, 1878, 3. Howard claimed that Egan "commanded in several battles," but military records contain no report of Egan in command. There are multiple accounts of Bannocks holding Paiute prisoners. Surely Egan was not in command of forces that were holding his own people prisoner for resisting the Bannocks just as Egan had. A war chief had to be with his warriors in dangerous and demanding situations. With a bullet wound to his groin in addition to his broken wrist strapped around his waist to press his upper arm over the bullet wound in his chest, Egan was an unlikely candidate for a war chief. Dr. Fitzgerald examined his body shortly after his death and concluded that he would not have lived more than a few days longer. Hailey, *The History of Idaho*, 243. There is no indication that Howard even knew of Egan's injuries. Why would the Bannocks choose as a war chief one who told them, "Go away . . . We are at peace. Why do you bring the soldiers upon my people? I will not fight"? One who attempted to escape from them? One whom they distrusted so thoroughly that they disarmed him, took his horse, and held him a "close prisoner"?

28. A YALE HO-CHUNK

1. Schurz to Winnemuccas, January 24, 1880, Office of Indian Affairs, Letters Received, Oregon Superintendency, roll 629, frames 398–400.

2. Steward and Wheeler-Voegelin, *Northern Paiute Indians*, 307.

3. L. P. Towle, Acting Area Director, to the Commissioner, Bureau of Indian Affairs, June 24, 1954, Portland Area Office, Jurisdiction files of area, Realty Office, 1935–1961, Box 216, file 003, General Correspondences, Burns Paiute, 1949–1956, quoted in SSDS: 268–69, 337.

4. "Government Thrift Wave Submerges Paiutes' Plans," *Sunday Oregonian*, July 13, 1947.

5. Donegan, "Historical Sketch," 5.

6. Donegan, "Historical Sketch," 8–9.

7. E. B. Meritt, Assistant Commissioner to Charles W. Rastall, Superintendent, Warm Springs Agency, November 9, 1922. CCF 8686-21-Warm Springs-735, Pt. 1, RG 75, NA, quoted in SSDS 270.

8. Johnny Capp to Joseph Chez, January 17, 1930, Central Classified Files, 8686-21-Warm Springs-735, Pt 2, RG 75, National Archives, quoted in SSDS 268.

9. Donegan, "Historical Sketch," 8–9.

10. Stone, *The Cross in the Middle of Nowhere*, 71, 88–89, 114–16.

11. Prucha, *The Great Father*, 808–9.

12. A. F. Loeser to Roe Cloud, August 19, 1932, RG 75, Bureau of Indian Affairs, Entry 121-A, Central Classified Files, 1907–1939, Warm Springs Agency #8686-1921-735, Part 3 of 5 (Folder 2 of 2) National Archives, Seattle, Washington.

13. F. E. Perkins to Commissioner, December 2, 1931, RG 75, Bureau of Indian Affairs, Entry 121-A, Central Classified Files, 1907–1939, Warm Springs Agency #8686-1921-735, Part 3 of 5 (Folder 2 of 2) National Archives, Seattle, Washington.

14. Henry Roe Cloud to Commissioner of Indian Affairs, September 20, 1932, RG 75, Bureau of Indian Affairs, Entry 121-A, Central Classified Files, 1907–1939, Warm Springs Agency #8686-1921-735, Part 3 of 5 (Folder 2 of 2) National Archives, Seattle, Washington.

29. WHITE WHIM, PAIUTE PENURY

1. Fowler and Liljeblad, "Northern Paiute," 450.

2. Steward and Wheeler-Voegelin, *Northern Paiute Indians*, 296–97.

3. Hopkins, *Life among the Piutes*, 107–8, 110–11, 113; Otis to Assistant Adjutant General, March 15, 1874, Office of Indian Affairs, Letters Received, Oregon Superintendency, roll 620, frames 760–64; Linville to Otis, February 23 and March 7, 1874, Office of Indian Affairs, Letters Received, Oregon Superintendency, roll 620, frames 768–72.

4. Hopkins, *Life among the Piutes*, 110, 113.

5. Hopkins, *Life among the Piutes*, 115, 117–18, 120, 123, 124, 127.

6. Howard to Assistant Adjutant General, Division of the Pacific, December 20, 1878, reproduced in Gibson, *Survivors of the Bannock War*, 47.

7. Hopkins, *Life among the Paiutes*, 237.

8. Hopkins, *Life among the Paiutes*, 237.

9. Wilkerson, *Caste*, 212.

10. Schmeckebier, *The Office of Indian Affairs*, 10.

11. Hoopes, *Indian Affairs and Their Administration*, 29.

12. Gallaher, "The Indian Agent," 14.

13. Wilbur to Commissioner Trowbridge, May 22, 1880, H.R. Exec. Doc. No. 1, 47th Cong., 2nd Sess. (1882), 131–33.

14. H.R. Exec. Doc. No. 1, 46th Cong., 3rd Sess. (1880), 4.

15. *The Snake or Piute Indians of the Former Malheur Reservation in Oregon v. United States*, Indian Claims Commission Docket No. 17, Amended Findings of Fact, December 28, 1956, 602.

16. Helland, *There Were Giants*, 150.

17. ARCIA 1882, 170.

18. ARCIA 1871, 283.

19. Wilbur's statements: Wilbur to Commissioner Trowbridge, May 22, 1880, H.R. Exec. Doc. No. 1, 46th Cong., 3rd Sess. (1880), 131–33; Wilbur to Trowbridge, May 31, 1880, M 574, roll 74, special file 268, Bureau of Indian Affairs, National Archives; ARCIA 1880, 168. Milroy's statements: Milroy to Price, August 11, 1883, Office of Indian Affairs special file No. 268; ARCIA 1883, 152; ARCIA 1884, 175; *The Snake or Piute Indians of the Former Malheur Reservation in Oregon v. United States*, Indian Claims Commission Docket No. 17, Amended Findings of Fact, December 28, 1956, 602.

20. Wilbur to Commissioner, March 20, 1880, Office of Indian Affairs, Letters Received, Oregon Superintendency, roll 920, frame 907; Wilbur to Commissioner, April 28, 1880, Office of Indian Affairs, Letters Received, Oregon Superintendency, roll 920, frame 975; Wilbur to Commissioner, May 22, 1880, H.R. Exec. Doc. No. 1, 46th Cong., 3rd Sess. (1880), 131; Wilbur to Commissioner, May 31, 1880, National Archives, M 574, roll 74, special file 268, Bureau of Indian Affairs; Wilbur to Commissioner, June 29, 1880, Office of Indian Affairs, Letters Received, Oregon Superintendency, roll 920, frames 1067; Wilbur to Commissioner, August 2, 1880, Office of Indian Affairs, Letters Received, Oregon Superintendency, roll 920, frame 1161.

21. NobelPrize.org. Nobel Media AB 2020. Wed. July 22, 2020, https://www.nobelprize.org/prizes/peace/1964/king/acceptance-speech/.

22. Brimlow, *Bannock Indian War*, 190–91.
23. Jackson, *A Century of Dishonor*, appendix 7; Carpenter and Sorisio, *Newspaper Warrior*, 93–95.
24. Helland, *There Were Giants*, 5.
25. *Snake or Piute Indians v. United States*, 112 F. Supp. 543, 569 (Ct. Cl. 1953).

CONCLUSION

1. ARCIA 1884, 175. Oits's band of ninety represented about fifteen percent of the 543 Paiutes brought to Yakama.
2. Brimlow, *Bannock Indian War*, 214.
3. Santayana, *The Life of Reason*, quoted in Knowles, *Oxford Dictionary of Quotations*, 667.

EPILOGUE

1. "Government Thrift Wave Submerges Paiutes' Plans," *Sunday Oregonian*, July 13, 1947, 65.
2. For example, "S. L. Harryman to Take Charge of Indian School," *Burns Times-Herald*, November 9, 1945; "Deer Hides Asked for Piute Class in Leather Work," *Burns Times-Herald*, November 16, 1945; "Piutes Stage Tribal Dinner," *Burns Times-Herald*, December 28, 1945; "Piutes Seek Community Building," *Burns Times-Herald*, December 28, 1945; "Supt. to Present Indian Projects to Department," *Burns Times-Herald*, January 25, 1946; "Fine Workmanship Shown in Indian Handicraft," *Burns Times-Herald*, February 1, 1946; "Berry Plants for Indian Village," *Burns Times-Herald*, May 10, 1946; "Pageant to Depict History of Piutes on Pioneer Day," *Burns Times-Herald*, May 24, 1946.
3. *Snake or Piute Indians v. United States*, Indian Claims Commission docket number 17, December 28, 1956, Opinion of the Commission, 625.
4. Venn, "Soldier to Advocate," 70; Bingham, *Charles Erskine Scott Wood*, 9, 26; Barnes, "C. E. S. Wood (1852–1944)," *Oregon Encyclopedia*, https://www.oregonencyclopedia.org/articles/c_e_s_wood/#.X6WRMi9h1TY.
5. Stone, *The Cross in the Middle of Nowhere*, 117.
6. Father A. F. Loeser statement, August 19, 1932, RG 75, Bureau of Indian Affairs, Entry 121-A, Central Classified Files, 1907–1939, Warm Springs Agency #8686-1921-735, Part 3 of 5 (Folder 2 of 2) National Archives, Seattle, Washington.
7. H.R. Rep. No. 101–877, at 9 (1990).
8. "Solemn Ceremony Celebrates Return of Paiute Chief's Remains," *Burns Times-Herald*, May 5, 1999.
9. March 2, 2019, interview with Nancy Egan in Boise, Idaho.

BIBLIOGRAPHY

ABBREVIATIONS

ARCIA   Annual Report of the Commissioner of Indian Affairs
ARSW   Annual Report of the Secretary of War
OOHP   Oliver Otis Howard Papers
SSDS   Susan Stowell dissertation

ARCHIVES AND MANUSCRIPT MATERIALS

Dorsey, Griffin. "Who Really Killed Chief Paulina?" Multnomah County Library, Portland OR, call number 979.504 G851W.

Haller, Granville Owen. Papers. Collection Number 3437. Special Collections. University of Washington Libraries.

Howard, Oliver Otis. Papers. M091, Special Collections & Archives. Hawthorne-Longfellow Library, Bowdoin College, Brunswick ME.

Huntington, John Webster Perit. Papers. 1855–69. MSS 759. Oregon Historical Society.

Rinehart, William V. Unpublished manuscript 17. Bancroft Library, University of California, Berkeley.

Thompson, Robert. Papers. BANC MSS P-A 87. Bancroft Library, University of California, Berkeley.

Wood, C. E. S. "Bannock Indian Campaign Daily Journal, June 7–September 10, 1878." C. E. S. Wood Collection, WD Box 26, items 3 and 4. Huntington Library, San Marino CA.

Wood, C. E. S. Collection. Watzek Library, Lewis and Clark College, Portland OR.

PUBLISHED WORKS

Aleshire, Peter. *The Fox and the Whirlwind: General George Crook and Geronimo, a Paired Biography*. New York: John Wiley & Sons, 2000.

ARCIA 1853: *Report of the Commissioner of Indian Affairs, Transmitted with the Message of the President at the Opening of the First Session of the Thirty-Third Congress, 1853* (Washington: Robert Armstrong, Printer, 1853).

ARCIA 1854: *Report of the Commissioner of Indian Affairs Transmitted with the Message of the President at the Opening of the Second Session of the Thirty-Third Congress, 1854* (Washington: A. O. P. Nicholson, 1855).

ARCIA 1857: *Report of the Commissioner of Indian Affairs, Accompanying the Annual Report of the Secretary of the Interior for the Year 1857* (Washington: William A. Harris, 1858).

ARCIA 1861: *Report of the Commissioner of Indian Affairs Accompanying the Annual Report of the Secretary of the Interior for the Year 1861* (Washington: Government Printing Office, 1861).

ARCIA 1862: *Report of the Commissioner of Indian Affairs for the Year 1862* (Washington: Government Printing Office, 1863).

ARCIA 1863: *Report of the Commissioner of Indian Affairs for the Year 1863* (Washington: Government Printing Office, 1864).

ARCIA 1865: *Report of the Commissioner of Indian Affairs for the Year 1865* (Washington: Government Printing Office, 1866).

ARCIA 1866: *Report of the Commissioner of Indian Affairs for the Year 1866* (Washington: Government Printing Office, 1866).

ARCIA 1867: *Report on Indian Affairs by the Acting Commissioner for the Year 1867* (Washington: Government Printing Office, 1868).

ARCIA 1875: *Report of the Commissioner of Indian Affairs to the Secretary of the Interior for the Year 1875* (Washington: Government Printing Office, 1875).

ARCIA 1876: *Report of the Commissioner of Indian Affairs to the Secretary of the Interior for the Year 1876* (Washington: Government Printing Office, 1876).

ARCIA 1877: *Report of the Commissioner of Indian Affairs to the Secretary of the Interior for the Year 1877* (Washington: Government Printing Office, 1877).

ARCIA 1878: *Report of the Commissioner of Indian Affairs to the Secretary of the Interior for the Year 1878* (Washington: Government Printing Office, 1878).

Bancroft, Hubert Howe. *History of Washington, Idaho, and Montana, 1845–1889 (1890)*. San Francisco: The History Company, 1890. Reprint, Whitefish MT: Kessinger Legacy, 2008.

Bancroft, Hubert Howe, and Auretta Fuller Barrett Victor. *History of Oregon 1848–1888*. San Francisco: The History Company, 1888.

Barnes, Tim. "C. E. S. Wood (1852–1944)." *Oregon Encyclopedia*. https://www.oregonencyclopedia.org/articles/c_e_s_wood/#.X6WRMi9h1TY.

Bartlett, John. *Bartlett's Familiar Quotations.* 18th ed. New York: Little, Brown, 2012.

Beal, Merrill D., and Merle W. Wells. *History of Idaho.* New York: Lewis Historical Publishing, 1959.

Bieder, Robert E. "The Representations of Indian Bodies in Nineteenth-Century American Anthropology." *American Indian Quarterly* 20, no. 2 (Spring 1996): 165–79.

————. *Science Encounters the Indian, 1820–1880: The Early Years of American Ethnology.* Norman: University of Oklahoma Press, 1986.

Bingham, Edward R. *Charles Erskine Scott Wood.* Boise: Boise State University, 1990.

Bright, Verne. "Blue Mountain Eldorados: Auburn, 1861." *Oregon Historical Quarterly* 62, no. 3 (September 1961): 213–36.

Brimlow, George Francis. *The Bannock Indian War of 1878.* Caldwell ID: Caxton Printers, 1938.

————. *Harney County Oregon and Its Range Land.* Burns OR: Harney County Historical Society, 1980.

————. "Two Cavalrymen's Diaries of the Bannock War, 1878: I. Lt. William Carey Brown, Co. L. 1st U.S. Cavalry." *Oregon Historical Quarterly* 68, no. 4 (December 1967): 293–316.

Caldbick, John. "Rains, Heavy Snow, and Unprecedented Cold Hit Washington Territory during the Winter of 1861–1862." HistoryLink.org Essay 164. February 20, 2012. https://www.historylink.org/File/164.

Carey, Charles H., *General History of Oregon.* Portland OR: Binfords & Mort, 1971.

Carlson, Helen S. "Nevada Place Names: Origin and Meaning." https://digitalrepository.unm.edu/engl_etds/239.

Carpenter, Cari M., and Carolyn Sorisio, eds. *The Newspaper Warrior: Sarah Winnemucca Hopkins's Campaign for American Indian Rights, 1864–1891.* Lincoln: University of Nebraska Press, 2015.

Carpenter, John A. *Sword and Olive Branch: Oliver Otis Howard.* New York: Fordham University Press, 1999.

Clark, Carlton. "Military History of Oregon, 1849–59." *Oregon Historical Quarterly* 36, no. 1 (March 1935): 14–59.

Clark, Donna, and Keith Clark. "William McKay's Journal: 1866–1867: Indian Scouts, Part I." *Oregon Historical Quarterly* 79, no. 2 (Summer 1978): 121–71.

Clark, Keith, and Donna Clark. "William McKay's Journal, 1866–67: Indian Scouts, Part II." *Oregon Historical Quarterly* 79, no. 3 (Fall 1978): 268–333.

Clemmer, Richard O. "Differential Leadership Patterns in Early Twentieth-Century Great Basin Societies." *Journal of California and Great Basin Anthropology* 11 (1989): 35–49.

Coan, C. F. "The First Stage of the Federal Indian Policy in the Pacific Northwest, 1849–1852." *Quarterly of the Oregon Historical Society* 22, no. 1 (1921): 46–89.

Coe, Henry C. "An Indian Agent's Experience in the War of 1886." *Quarterly of the Oregon Historical Society* 14, no. 1 (1913): 65–67.

Cornford, Daniel. "We All Live More like Brutes than Humans: Labor and Capital in the Gold Rush." *California History* 77, no. 4 (Winter 1998/1999): 83.

Couture, Marilyn D., Mary F. Ricks, and Lucile Housley. "Foraging Behavior of a Contemporary Northern Great Basin Population." *Journal of California and Great Basin Anthropology* 8, no. 2 (1986): 150–60.

Cox, John, and LaWanda Cox. "General O. O. Howard and the 'Misrepresented Bureau.'" *Journal of Southern History* 19, no. 2 (November 1953): 427–56.

Crook, General George. *His Autobiography*. Norman: University of Oklahoma Press, 1946.

Deacon, Kristine. "On the Road with Rutherford B. Hayes: Oregon's First Presidential Visit, 1880." *Oregon Historical Quarterly* 112, no. 2 (Summer 2011): 170–94.

Donegan, J. J. "Historical Sketch of Harney County, Oregon, a Presentation given to the Kiwanis Club, March 19, 1936." Harney County Library.

Drake, John M. "The Oregon Cavalry." *Oregon Historical Quarterly* 65, no. 4 (1964): 392–400.

Edwards, G. Thomas. "Oregon Regiments in the Civil War Years: Duty and the Indian Frontier." Master's thesis, University of Oregon, 1960.

Elliott, T. C. "The Dalles-Celilo Portage; Its History and Influence." *Oregon Historical Quarterly* 16, no. 2 (June 1915): 133–74.

———. "Peter Skene Ogden, Fur Trader." *Oregon Historical Quarterly* 11, no. 3 (September 1910): 229–78.

Fabian, Ann. *The Skull Collectors*. Chicago: University of Chicago Press, 2010.

Faust, Drew Gilpin. *This Republic of Suffering Death and the American Civil War*. New York: Knopf, 2008.

Ficken, Robert E. "After the Treaties: Administering Pacific Northwest Indian Reservations." *Oregon Historical Quarterly* 106, no. 3 (Fall 2005): 442–61.

Fitzgerald, Maurice. "Harney County, Its Early Settlement and Development." 1940. Harney County Library.

Fowler, Catherine S., and Sven Liljeblad. "Northern Paiute." In *Handbook of North American Indians*, ed. Warren L. d'Azevedo, 11. Washington DC: Smithsonian Institution, 1986.

Fowler, Orson S., and Lorenzo N. Fowler. *Phrenology Proved, Illustrated and Applied*. New York, 1846.

French, Giles. *The Golden Land*. Portland: Oregon Historical Society Press, 1958.

Gallaher, Ruth A. "The Indian Agent in the United States before 1850." *Iowa Journal of History and Politics* 14 (January 1916): 3–55.

Gibson, Benson, *Survivors of the Bannock War*. Box 27, Duck Valley Indian Reservation, Owyhee NV.

Gilbert, Frank T. *Historic Sketches*. Portland OR: A. G. Walling, 1882.

Goldman, Michael A. "Rowland E. Trowbridge (1880–1881)." In *The Commissioners of Indian Affairs, 1824–1977*, ed. Robert M. Kvasnicka and Herman J. Viola, 167–72. Lincoln: University of Nebraska Press, 1979.

Gossett, Thomas F. *Race: The History of an Idea in America*. New York: Oxford University Press, 1963.

Greene, Graham. *The Heart of the Matter*. New York: Penguin, 1948. Reprint, 2004.

Guyatt, Nicholas. "'The Outskirts of Our Happiness': Race and the Lure of Colonization in the Early Republic." *Journal of American History* 95, no. 4 (March 2009): 986–1011.

Hailey, John. *The History of Idaho*. Boise: Syms-York, 1910.

Hallowell, A. Irving. "The Impact of the American Indian on American Culture." *American Anthropologist* 59, no. 2 (April 1957): 201–17. https://anthrosource .onlinelibrary.wiley.com/doi/abs/10.1525/aa.1957.59.2.02a00020.

Hamburger, Robert. *Two Rooms*. Lincoln: University of Nebraska Press, 1998.

Helland, Maurice. *There Were Giants: The Life of James H. Wilbur*. Yakima WA: Shields Bag and Printing, 1980.

Hendrickson, James E. *Joe Lane of Oregon*. New Haven: Yale University Press, 1967.

Hines, Clarence. "Indian Agent's Letter-Book: I. The Piute-Bannock Raid of July, 1878." *Oregon Historical Quarterly* 39, no. 1 (March 1938): 8–15.

Hines, H. K. *An Illustrated History of the State of Oregon*. Chicago: Lewis Publishing, 1893.

Hoopes, Alban W. *Indian Affairs and Their Administration: With Special Reference to the Far West, 1849–1860*. Philadelphia: University of Pennsylvania Press, 1932.

Hopkins, Sarah Winnemucca. *Life among the Piutes*. New York: G. P. Putnam's and Sons, 1883. Reprint, Reno: University of Nevada Press, 1994.

Horsman, Reginald. *Race and Manifest Destiny: The Origins of American Racial Anglo-Saxonism*. Cambridge MA: Harvard University Press, 1981.

Howard, Oliver Otis. *Autobiography of Gen. O. O. Howard*. New York: Baker & Taylor, 1907.

———. *Famous Indian Chiefs I Have Known*. New York: The Century Co., 1908.

———. *My Life and Personal Experiences among Our Hostile Indians*. Hartford CT: A. D. Worthington, 1907.

———. "The True Story of the Wallowa Campaign." *North American Review* 129 (July 1879): 53–64.

Hunn, Eugene S. *Nch'i-Wana, "The Big River."* Seattle: University of Washington Press, 1990.

Huntington, J. W. Perit. "J. W. Perit Huntington to Hon. N. S. Taylor, Umatilla Reservation, December 22, 1868." *Ethnohistory* 3, no. 2 (1956): 167–68.

Igler, David. *Industrial Cowboys: Miller and Lux and the Transformation of the Far West, 1850–1920*. Berkeley: University of California Press, 2001.

An Illustrated History of North Idaho: Embracing Nez Perces, Idaho, Latah, Kootenai and Shoshone Counties, State of Idaho. N.p.: Western Historical , 1903. https://archive .org/details/illustratedhisto00slwerich/page/n12/mode/2up.

"The Isaac I. Stevens and Joel Palmer Treaties, 1855–2005. *Oregon Historical Quarterly* 106, no. 3 (2005).

Jackson, Helen. *A Century of Dishonor*. Boston: Roberts Brothers, 1889.

Jefferson, Thomas. *Notes on the State of Virginia*. Chapel Hill: University of North Carolina Press, 1996.

Jennings, Francis. "A Growing Partnership: Historians, Anthropologists and American Indian History." *Ethnohistory* 29 (1982): 21–34.

Jewell, James Robbins. "'Doing Nothing with a Vengeance': The Diary of David Hobart Taylor, First Oregon Cavalry, January 1 through May 30, 1862." *Oregon Historical Quarterly* 110, no. 4 (Winter 2009): 603–16.

Johansen, Dorothy O. "The Oregon Steam Navigation Company: An Example of Capitalism on the Frontier." *Pacific Historical Review* 10 (1941): 179–88.

Johnson, Overton, and William H. Winter. "Route Across the Rocky Mountains with a Description of Oregon and California, etc., 1843." *Oregon Historical Quarterly* 7, no. 2 (June 1906): 163–210.

Johnson, Stephen R. "Staging and Wintering Areas of Snow Geese Nesting on Howe Island, Alaska." *Arctic* 49, no. 1 (March 1996): 86.

Johnson, Theodore T., and Samuel M. Thurston. *California and Oregon, or Sights in the Gold Region and Scenes by the Way*. Philadelphia: Grigg, Elliot. Reprinted by Book on Demand, 2015.

Joseph, Young. "An Indian's View of Indian Affairs." *North American Review* 128 (April 1879): 412–33.

Juzda, Elise. "Skulls, Science, and the Spoils of War: Craniological Studies at the United States Army Medical Museum, 1868–1900." *Studies in History and Philosophy of Biological and Biomedical Sciences* 40 (2009): 156–67.

Keller, Robert H., Jr. *American Protestantism and United States Indian Policy, 1869–82*. Lincoln: University of Nebraska Press, 1983.

Kelly, Isabel T. "Ethnography of the Surprise Valley Paiute." In *University of California Publications in American Archaeology and Ethnology*, edited by A. L. Kroeber and Robert H. Lowie, 31: 67–195. New York: Kraus Reprint Corporation, 1965.

Kenny, Judith Keyes. "The Founding of Camp Watson." *Oregon Historical Quarterly* 58, no. 1 (March 1957): 4–16.

Knack, Martha C., and Omer C. Stewart. *As Long as the River Shall Run: An Ethnohistory of Pyramid Lake Indian Reservation*. Berkeley: University of California Press, 1984.

Knowles, Elizabeth, ed. *The Oxford Dictionary of Quotations*. 8th ed. Oxford: Oxford University Press, 2014.

Knuth, Priscilla, and John M. Drake. "Cavalry in the Indian Country, 1864." *Oregon Historical Quarterly* 65, no. 1 (March 1964): 4–118.

Kober, George M. *Reminiscences of George Martin Kober, M.D.L.L.D., Emeritus Dean and Professor of Hygiene of the School of Medicine, and Member of the Board of Regents, Georgetown University, Washington D.C.* Washington DC: Kober Foundation, 1930.

Lamb, D. S. "A History of the United States Army Medical Museum, 1862 to 1917, Compiled from the Official Records by Dr. D. S. Lamb." https://collections.nlm.nih.gov/ext/kirtasbse/12710920R/PDF/12710920R.pdf.

Lamb, Sydney M. "Linguistic Prehistory in the Great Basin." *International Journal of American Linguistics* 24, no. 2 (1958): 95–100.

Laufe, Abe, ed. *An Army Doctor's Wife on the Frontier.* Pittsburgh: University of Pittsburgh Press, 1962.

Lepore, Jill. *These Truths, a History of the United States.* New York: W. W. Norton, 2018.

Limerick, Patricia Nelson. *Something in the Soil: Legacies and Reckonings in the New West.* New York: W. W. Norton, 2000.

Linville, Willard. "Willard Linville's Account of the Malheur Indian Reservation." Harney County, Oregon, Historical Society.

Lockley, Fred. *History of the Columbia River Valley from The Dalles to the Sea.* Chicago: S. J. Clarke Publishing, 1928.

Lockley, Fred, and T. Neilson Barry. "Autobiography of William Henry Rector." *Oregon Historical Quarterly* 30, no. 1 (March 1929): 63–69.

Lubetkin, M. John. *Jay Cooke's Gamble: The Northern Pacific Railroad, the Sioux, and the Panic of 1873.* Norman: University of Oklahoma Press, 2006.

Ludlow, Fitz Hugh. *The Heart of the Continent: A Record of Travel across the Plains and in Oregon.* New York: Hurd and Houghton, 1870.

Macoll, E. Kimball. *Money, Merchants and Power.* Athens GA: Georgian Press, 1988.

Madsen, Brigham D. *The Bannock of Idaho.* Moscow: University of Idaho Press, 1996.

Madsen, David B. "Dating Paiute-Shoshoni Expansion in the Great Basin." *American Antiquity* 40, no. 1 (January 1975): 82–86.

Magid, Paul. *George Crook: From the Redwoods to Appomattox.* Norman: University of Oklahoma Press, 2011.

———. *The Gray Fox: George Crook and the Indian Wars.* Norman: University of Oklahoma Press, 2015.

Mass, Cliff. *The Weather of the Pacific Northwest.* Seattle: University of Washington Press, 2008.

McArthur, Lewis A. "Early Scenes in Harney County." *Oregon Historical Quarterly* 32, no. 2 (June 1931): 125–29.

———. *Oregon Geographic Names.* 5th ed. Portland: Press of the Oregon Historical Society, 1982.

McConnell, Les. "The Treaty Rights of the Confederated Tribes of Warm Springs." *Pacific Northwest Quarterly* 97, no. 4 (Fall 2006): 190–201.

McCoy, Robert R. *Chief Joseph, Yellow Wolf, and the Creation of Nez Perce History in the Pacific Northwest*. New York: Routledge, 2004.

Meacham, Alfred Benjamin. *Wigwam and Warpath*. Boston: J. P. Dale, 1875.

Merriam, L. C., Jr. "The First Oregon Cavalry and the Oregon Central Military Road Survey of 1865." *Oregon Historical Quarterly* 60, no. 1 (March 1959): 89–124.

Meyer, Roy M. "Ezra A. Hayt (1877–80)." In *The Commissioners of Indian Affairs, 1824–1977*, ed. Robert M. Kvasnicka and Herman J. Viola, 155–66. Lincoln: University of Nebraska Press, 1979.

Miller, George R. "The Great Willamette River Flood of 1861." *Oregon Historical Quarterly* 100, no. 2 (summer 1999): 182–207.

Morton, Samuel George. *Crania Americana*. Philadelphia: J. Dobson, 1839.

O'Donnell, Terrence. *An Arrow in the Earth: General Joel Palmer and the Indians of Oregon*. Portland: Oregon Historical Society Press: 1991.

Ogden, Peter Skene, and T. C. Elliott "The Peter Skene Ogden Journals." *Oregon Historical Quarterly* 10, no. 4 (December 1909): 331–65.

Oliphant, J. Orin. "The Cattle Herds and Ranches of the Oregon Country, 1860–1890." *Agricultural History* 21, no. 4 (October 1947): 217–38.

———. *On the Cattle Ranges of the Oregon Country*. Seattle: University of Washington Press, 1968.

Parnell, W. R. *Operations against Hostile Indians with General George Crook, 1867–1868*. N.p.: United Service, 1889.

Parsons, William, and W. S. Shiach. *An Illustrated History of Umatilla and Morrow Counties*. Spokane WA: W. H. Lever, 1902.

Paul, Rodman W. "After the Gold Rush: San Francisco and Portland." *Pacific Historical Review* 51, no. 1 (February 1982): 1–21.

Perry, James R., Richard H. Chused, and Mary DeLano. "The Spousal Letters of Samuel R. Thurston, Oregon's First Territorial Delegate to Congress: 1849–1851." *Oregon Historical Quarterly* 96, no. 1 (Spring 1995): 4–79.

Priest, Loring Benson. *Uncle Sam's Stepchildren: The Reformation of United States Indian Policy, 1865–1887*. New York: Octagon Books, 1969.

Prucha, Francis Paul. *American Indian Treaties: The History of a Political Anomaly*. Berkeley: University of California Press, 1994.

———. *The Great Father*. Lincoln: University of Nebraska Press, 1984.

Ramsey, Jarold ed. *Coyote Was Going There: Indian Literature of the Oregon Country*. Seattle: University of Washington Press, 1977.

Ray, Verne F., George Peter Murdock, Beatrice Blyth, Omer C. Stewart, Jack Harris, E. Adamson Hoebel, and D. B. Shimkin. "Tribal Distribution in Eastern Oregon and Adjacent Regions." *American Anthropologist* 40, no. 3 (July–September 1938): 384–415.

Rector, William Henry. "Autobiographical Sketch of William Henry Rector." *Oregon Historical Quarterly* 29, no. 4 (December 1928): 323–36.

Redman, Samuel J. *Bone Rooms: From Scientific Racism to Human Prehistory in Museums.* Cambridge MA: Harvard University Press, 2016.

Reed, C. A. *Report of the Adjutant General of the State of Oregon for the Years 1865–6.* Portland OR: Henry L. Pittock, 1966.

Rinehart, William Vance. "War in the Great Northwest." *Washington Historical Quarterly* 22, no. 2 (April 1931): 83–98.

Robinson, Charles M., III. *General Crook and the Western Frontier.* Norman: University of Oklahoma Press, 2001.

Ruby, Robert H., et al. *A Guide to the Indian Tribes of the Pacific Northwest.* Norman: University of Oklahoma Press, 2013.

Russell, Don. *One Hundred and Three Fights and Scrimmages: The Story of General Reuben F. Bernard.* Mechanicsburg PA: Stackpole Books, 1936.

Santee, J. F. "Egan of the Piutes." *Washington Historical Quarterly* 26, no. 1 (January 1935): 16–25.

Schmeckebier, Laurence F. *The Office of Indian Affairs: Its History, Activities and Organization.* Baltimore: Johns Hopkins Press, 1927.

Scott, Lalla, *Karnee: A Paiute Narrative.* Reno: University of Nevada Press, 1966.

Scott, Leslie M. "Indian Diseases as Aids to Pacific Northwest Settlement." *Oregon Historical Quarterly* 29, no. 2 (June 1928).

———. "Pioneer Stimulus of Gold." *Oregon Historical Quarterly* 18, no. 3 (September 1917): 147–66.

Seymour, Flora Warren. *Indian Agents of the Old Frontier.* New York: D. Appleton-Century, 1941.

Shane, Ralph M. "Early Explorations through Warm Springs Reservation Area." *Oregon Historical Quarterly* 51, no. 4 (December 1950): 273–309.

Sharfstein, Daniel J. *Thunder in the Mountains, Chief Joseph, Oliver Otis Howard, and the Nez Perce War.* New York: W. W. Norton, 2017.

Shaver, Frederic Ambrose, ed. *An Illustrated History of Central Oregon.* Spokane WA: Western Historical, 1905.

Simpson, Peter K. *The Community of Cattlemen:A Social History of the Cattle Country of Southeastern Oregon 1869–1912.* Moscow: University of Idaho Press, 1987.

Soucie, Minerva T. "Burns Paiute Tribe." In *The First Oregonians,* ed. Laura Berg, 45–59. Portland: Oregon Council for the Humanities, 1991.

Stern, Madeleine B. *Heads and Headlines: The Phrenological Fowlers.* Norman: University of Oklahoma Press, 1971.

Stern, Theodore. "Cayuse, Umatilla, and Walla Walla." In *Handbook of North American Indians.* Vol. 12, *Plateau,* ed. Deward E. Walker Jr., 395–419. Washington: Smithsonian Institution, 1998.

———. "Klamath and Modoc." In Handbook of North American Indians. Vol. 12, Plateau, ed. Deward E. Walker Jr., 446–66. Washington: Smithsonian Institution, 1998.

Steward, Julian H., and Erminie Wheeler-Voegelin. The Northern Paiute Indians. New York: Garland Publishing, 1974.

Stewart, Omer C. "The Northern Paiute Bands." In University of California Publications in Anthropological Records, ed. A. L. Kroeber, R. H. Lowie, R. L. Olson, and E. W. Gifford, 127–49. Berkeley: University of California Press, 1939.

Stone, William S. The Cross in the Middle of Nowhere. Bend OR: Maverick Publications, 1993.

Stowell, Susan. "The Wadatika of the Former Malheur Indian Reservation." PhD diss., University of California, Davis, 2008.

Strang, Cameron B. "Violence, Ethnicity, and Human Remains during the Second Seminole War." Journal of American History 100, no. 4 (March 2014): 973–94.

Sullivan, Margaret L. "Conflict on the Frontier: The Case of Harney County, Oregon, 1870–1900." Pacific Northwest Quarterly 66, no. 4 (October 1975): 174–81.

Sutton, Mark Q. "Warfare and Expansion: An Ethnohistoric Perspective on the Numic Spread." Journal of California and Great Basin Anthropology 8, no. 1 (1986): 65–82.

Tanner, Helen Hornbeck. "Erminie Wheeler-Voegelin (1903–1988), Founder of the American Society for Ethnohistory." Ethnohistory 38, no. 1 (Winter 1991): 58–72.

Teiser, Sidney. "The First Chief Justice of Oregon Territory: William P. Bryant." Oregon Historical Quarterly 48 (1947): 45–54.

Thompson, Colonel William. Reminiscences of a Pioneer. San Francisco: Plaindealer, 1912.

Thompson, Erwin N. Modoc War: Its Military History & Topography. Sacramento: Argus Books, 1971.

"Treaty and Tribal Reference." Oregon Historical Quarterly 106, no. 3 (Fall 2005): 352–55. http://www.jstor.org/stable/20615554.

Trefousse, Hans L. Carl Schurz: A Biography. Knoxville: University of Tennessee Press, 1982.

———. "Carl Schurz and the Indians." Great Plains Quarterly 4, no. 2 (Spring 1984): 109–20.

Trenholm, Virginia Cole, and Maurine Carley. The Shoshonis: Sentinels of the Rockies. Norman: University of Oklahoma Press, 1964.

Tucker, Kathy. "James H. Wilbur (1811–1887)." Oregon Encyclopedia. https://www.oregonencyclopedia.org/articles/wilbur_james_h_1811_1887_/.

United States. The War of the Rebellion: A Compilation of the Official Records of the Union and Confederate Armies. Washington: General Printing Office, 1880.

Utley, "Frontier and the American Military Tradition." In American Military on the Frontier, ed. James P. Tate. Honolulu: University Press of the Pacific, 2002.

Venn, George. "Soldier to Advocate: C. E. S. Wood's 1877 Diary of Alaska and the Nez Perce Conflict." *Oregon Historical Quarterly* 106, no. 1 (Spring 2005): 34–75.

Victor, Frances Fuller. "The First Oregon Cavalry." *Oregon Historical Quarterly* 3, no. 2 (December 1902): 123–63.

Weatherford, Mark V. *Bannack-Piute War: The Campaign and Battles*. Corvallis OR: Lehnert Printing, 1957.

Wells, Edward Lansing. "Notes on the Winter of 1861–1862 in the Pacific Northwest." *Northwest Science* 21, (1947).

Wheat, Margaret M. *Survival Arts of the Primitive Paiutes*. Reno: University of Nevada Press, 1967.

Wheeler-Voegelin, Erminie. "The Northern Paiute of Central Oregon: A Chapter in Treaty-Making, Part 2." *Ethnohistory* 2 (1955): 241–72.

Whitner, Robert Lee. "Grant's Indian Peace Policy on the Yakima Reservation, 1870–82." *Pacific Northwest Quarterly*, 50 (October 1959): 135–42.

———. "The Methodist Episcopal Church and Grant's Peace Policy: A Study of the Methodist Agencies, 1870–1882." PhD diss., University of Minnesota, 1959.

Wiart, Pierre, and Clive Oppenheimer. "Largest Known Historical Eruption in Africa: Dubbi Volcano, Eritrea, 1861." *Geology* 28, no. 4 (2000): 291–94.

Wilkerson, Isabel. *Caste: The Origins of Our Discontents*. New York: Random House, 2020.

Wilson, Robert M. *Seeking Refuge: Birds and Landscapes of the Pacific Flyway*. Seattle: University of Washington Press, 2010.

Wood, C. E. S. "Private Journal, 1878." *Oregon Historical Quarterly* 70, no. 1 (March 1969): 4–38.

Woodward, Walter Carlton. *The Rise and Early History of Political Parties in Oregon, 1843–1868*. Portland OR: J. K. Gill, 1913.

Wooster, Robert. *The Military and United States Indian Policy, 1865–1903*. Lincoln: University of Nebraska Press, 1988.

Wright, E. W. *Lewis & Dryden's Marine History of the Pacific Northwest*. Portland OR: Lewis & Dryden Printing, 1895.

Zanjani, Sally. *Sarah Winnemucca*. Lincoln: University of Nebraska Press, 2001.

Zenk, Henry. "William Cameron McKay (1824–1893)." *Oregon Encyclopedia*. https://oregonencyclopedia.org/articles/mckay_william_c/#.XahxHOdKhTY.

INDEX

Italicized page numbers refer to illustrations.

Fabian, Ann, 158
Failing, William, 6, 7, 9, 14, 239n2,
240n22
"Failing's Hotel," 6
family units, 18–19, 20, 214, 215;
autonomy for, 33, 216
Ferry, governor of Washington Terri-
tory, 142
fish traps, Malheur River, 91, 103, 104,
105, 111, 118, 126, 131, 132, 162,
256n23
Fitch, Thomas L., 33, 34
Fitzgerald, John, 97–98, 141, 148, 155,
236, 274n34; Egan and, 156; Sarah
Winnemucca and, 156; skull collect-
ing by, 156, 158
Five Crows, 155
Florence mines, 8, 41, 245n4; gold
rush to, 42
Ford's Theater, 157
Fort Bidwell, 150, 179
Fort Boise. *See* Camp Boise
Fort Colville, 24
Fort Dalles, 33, 35, 37
Fort Hall, 55, 95, 101, 103, 104, 106,
107; Bannocks at, 91, 92, 94
Fort Hall Reservation, 116
Fort Harney, 74, 80, 90, 109, 161, 164,
169, 170, 172, 180, 215, 266n23,
266n25; Sarah Winnemucca at, 81
Fort Klamath, 47, 49, 73, 74, 247n16;
executions at, 77; Paulina at, 50
Fort Lemhi, 47, 95
Fort McDermitt, 106, 121, 132, 161,
166, 178, 179; prisoner confusion,
163–65; Sarah Winnemucca at, 81
Fort Vancouver, 5, 78, 96, 150, 247n18
Fort Warner, 74, 215
Fowler, Charlotte, 61

Fowler, Lorenzo, 61
Fowler, Orson, 61
Fowler lectures, advertisement for, *62*
Frazier, Lynn, 212
Freedmen's Bureau, 145, 146, 203
Fremont, John C., 82
French, Pete, 13, 134, 198–99

Gall, Franz Joseph, 60, 61
George (accompanied Sarah
Winnemucca), 14, 121–22, 124
Glenn, Hugh, 198, 199
Glenns Ferry, 95, 105, 120, 128, 133
gold rush, 24, 42, 46, 57, 198, 199
Grand Ronde River, 140, 141, 142,
144, 148, 149, 161
Grant, Ulysses S., 67, 75, 144; Peace
Policy of, 76, 79, 178, 192
graves, 151, 157, 159, 166, 172–73,
229, 230, 232, 233, 236, 237, 242n1;
desecration of, 158
Great Basin, 12, 15, 17, 21, 93, 218;
subsistence living in, 19; tribes of, *20*
Great Father (Prucha), 263n21
Great Reinforcement, 78
Gregg, Jacob Ray, 126
Grim, John, 110

Hachenberg, George P., 157
Hailey, John, 155
Hall Bros., 271n25
Halleck, H. W., 24, 29, 55, 57, 71; on
injustice to Indians, 160
Haller, Granville, 47
Hamburger, Robert, 204
Handley, Dan, 14
Happy Valley, 100, 131, 134, 135
Harney, William S., 33
Harney Lake, 34, 75, 134, 228, 250n7,
253n12

Harney Valley, 99, 100, 105, 180, 198, 209, 223
Harper's Weekly, 84
Harryman, S. L., 227
Hatch, 204
Haworth, J. M., 184, 185, 186, 195
Hayden Island, 96
Hayes, Rutherford B., 186, 194–95
Hayt, Ezra, 112, 113, 168, 169, 174, 177, 186, 187, 194; corrupt acquisition of silver mine, 186–87; discharge, 187; order to move Paiutes, 179
Healy, John, 41
Heuel, Peter, 25, 227, 229–30, 231, 232; character of, 211–12; Father Loeser and, 213
Hightower (Otter Bar miner), 10, 13
Hines, Edward, 209, 212
Hines Lumber Company, 209, 212
"History of the United States Army Medical Museum, 1862–1917," 159
Holmes, Oliver Wendell, 65
Holmes, William Henry, 159
Holy Family Parish, 211
Homily, Chief, 155
Hopkins, Lewis, 164
Horsman, Reginald, 65
House Report of the Repatriation Act, 236
Howard, Bessie, 96
Howard, Grace, 96
Howard, Guy, 96
Howard, Lizzie, 145, 146
Howard, Oliver Otis, 22, 77, 85, 90, 95–96, 98, 108, 124, 142, *143*, 144, 147, 167, 190, 202, 228; accusations against, 161–62; appointment to head Freedman's Bureau, 145–46;

Bannocks and, 126; Bannock War and, 152, 262n1, 270n22; Bernard and, 120; children of, 96; Cornoyer and, 149; Egan and, 203, 205, 207, 274n34; errors of, 206–7; first meeting with Wood, 96; great circle of, 142, *142*, 151, 154; McDowell and, 162–63, 165, 166; Nez Perce and, 96, 148; notified of Bannock outbreak, 95–96; on Oits, 204; prisoners/punishment and, 161; Sarah Winnemucca and, 120–21, 124, 125, 140; Sherman and, 145; at Silver Creek, 137–38, 139; at Steens Mountain, 134; Toohoolhoolzote and, 147–48, 170; Umatilla Reservation and, 141; vulnerability of, 154; and Wilkins, prisoner issues, 164; Wood and, 96–97, 150, 151, 152, 153, 165, 166, 168, 169; writing of, 203–4, 274n21
Howluck, Chief, 44, 52, 130–31
Hubbard, V. B., 156, 236
Hudson Bay Company, 5, 247n18
Humboldt River, 83, 112, 181
hunting, 19, 20, 21, 26, 108, 109
Huntington, Ben, 73
Huntington, John Webster Perit, 46, 53, 73, 74, 106, 196, 243n9, 246n13, 247n16, 248n7, 249n48; appointment of, 47; death, 250n4; Paiute survivors and, 256n17; Paulina and, 48, 49, 50; removal, 74; treaty and, 52, 74–75, 210; Warm Springs Indians and, 49; Woods and, 58
Huntington, Mary, 73
Huntington, Perit, 73, 74

Idaho Statesman, 94, 105, 162
immigrants, 23, 24–25, 43